FROM
8,000 MILES

A True Story of Internet Danger
and How Our Daughter Was Saved

DESTINY DAWN

DISCLAIMER

The following is a true story about traumatic events that our family experienced in 2018. My intention in writing this book is to be as transparent and truthful as possible. I've attempted to recount my experience to the best of my knowledge and memory.

I believe this is a story of public interest; however, in an effort to protect the privacy of certain individuals involved, certain names, likenesses, occupations, and places of interest have been changed.

ISBN: 9798338494714

Published by www.TriumphPress.com

I've loved writing since I was a little girl,
but I never thought my first book would be this one.

Contents

Part I
Finding Out

Monday, September 17, 2018

Tuesday, September 18, 2018

Wednesday, September 19, 2018

Thursday, September 20, 2018

Friday, September 21, 2018

Saturday, September 22, 2018

Sunday, September 23, 2018

Part II
India

Monday, September 24, 2018 Us
Tuesday, September 25, 2018 In

Wednesday, September 26, 2018

Part III
The Aftermath

October - November 2018

December 2018- June 2019

October 2022- March 2024

DEDICATION

For My Beloved Daughter

"You shall know the truth and the truth shall set you free."

I didn't want to write this book until you came back into our lives so we could write the ending together. However, time is short and now my prayer is that this book may bring about that good ending.

I write to share my experience with you and I invite you to write your own book. To tell your story. To share what you experienced. We never got the chance to talk about what happened. You're a good writer and I know you can do a beautiful job of telling things from your perspective. Your experience and your feelings are completely valid because they are yours and you have the right to them.

Writing this book has been extremely healing for me and I know it will be for you, too.

Others, such as Princess Diana, have written the truth about their own lives, as painful as it was, because sharing is also freeing. It is like opening your private journal for all to see in the hopes that someone can relate or understand. Some will understand, some won't. Either way, it's your story and you get to tell it.

I named you *Victoria* in this book because I believe you are going to be victorious!

TO GIVE THE WHOLE STORY

I write this for those who have poured out their hearts to us, in our family, as well as friends and complete strangers, who have shared in our shock, horror, and pain, but who have only heard bits and pieces. You haven't learned the whole story. So here, I give it to you in its entirety.

FOR OTHERS WHO HAVE SUFFERED

I write this for those who have experienced your own tragedies, so that you may feel solace and comfort in knowing that someone else can relate and that you are not alone in your pain.

Pain is the human experience.

FOR THOSE WHO HAVE NOT

I write this for those who have not experienced anything like this, so that they may never have to.

There are others who, no matter what I say or how I say it, will still accuse my efforts because they only want to believe as they choose, and that's okay, that is their right. I just want you to remember, that if it ever happens to you, I will not accuse you. There is no perfect parent, especially when faced with the unimaginable.

TELL YOUR STORY

I encourage you, dear reader, to tell your story, because it can bring healing to both you and others. Even God Himself wrote about what happened to Him, letting us know that He can relate to our pain. He was mocked, despised, and rejected; a man of sorrows, acquainted with grief. As life plays out, He is now letting us all decide, letting us be the judges in the court of public opinion, between Himself and the Accuser of the Brethren.

ACKNOWLEDGMENTS

United States

Ms. Doris Stewart – For telling me to keep all documentation because I would want to write a story. Thank you for having the foresight.

William Davis (Mr. Bill) – You stood in my office for two hours after hearing the news and stressed to me that I needed to write this book *yesterday*. I was overwhelmed and in no position at that point to start writing, but you continued to drill into me the importance of it, that it *had* to be done, now! Here it is Mr. Bill, finally.

Eddie Upchurch (deceased) – To my father figure who has now passed from this life. From the time I was in diapers, you believed in me. I was hoping you would be here to see this book and its ending. You were a fighter with me in this story, cheering me on.

Pastor Leite – You played an instrumental role in this story. I knew from the first time I spoke with you, that you were going to be special in helping us. If it weren't for you, I know I wouldn't have survived. I thank God every day for you being there for us in our greatest time of need. May God bless you. I believe the turkey is almost done!

Sergeant Cotner with the Child Advocacy Center - Thank you for your investigation, for doing your job well, helping us see the emergency we were facing, and for caring for us and our situation. You truly cared as if our daughter was your own daughter.

Michelle Jordahl – Your connections to Homeland Security were invaluable. Thank you for caring for us so much.

Lynette Struntz – Thank you for helping us. Your connections made it all possible, and without it, we wouldn't have the story we have.

Brynn Herring with Eye Heart World Human Trafficking Agency – Thank you so much for all you did to help us, for your investigations, and for being a friend.

Richard Rajarathinam – What you did that night in the airport when our daughter landed in India will be written in the books in Heaven. Your tact and your skill, with the aid of the Holy Spirit, helped her make the choice she did. It will be forever remembered for all eternity. You helped save our daughter's life. We can never thank you enough.

Victor Singh –As Richard's assistant, you helped guide us and navigate the logistics through this terrible tragedy and you were a great friend! Your care and concern for Mom and me meant the world to us.

Amanda Rodriguez – Your coordination between the church conference, the pastors, and the family in India got us the help we needed, without which I truly believe our daughter wouldn't be alive today. You did so much behind the scenes that I wasn't even aware of. Your expertise came at just the right time to help our family. We are forever grateful.

U.S. Homeland Security – You helped save our daughter's life by, I believe, thwarting a plan that is very real and is happening in this world. Thank you for acting so quickly, for being where and when you needed to be, and for caring for a family you did not know. Thank you for calling even when you didn't have any new information, "just to see how I was doing."

U.S. Congressman Bradley Byrne and Office Staff – If it wasn't for your office getting the U.S. Marshals to surround my daughter in the airport, she could have been gone forever. I believe you helped thwart a plan that day and my daughter is still alive because of you. Then you went one step further, thinking ahead, to expedite our passports so we could go get our daughter and bring her home. We are truly grateful to you and can never thank you enough for helping save our daughter's life.

Jimmy Stewart – For being family, for being our spokesperson, for encouraging us that this is all part of God's plan and He will use it for good, as we give Him glory. Thank you for all the prayers and scripture, and for being there for us when we needed you. You truly made us feel like you were feeling what we were feeling. Thank you for caring so much. You are like a brother.

Carrie Stewart – Our dear friend, you were there with us through this very trying time. I will never forget your encouraging words in our group while we were in India. Thank you for your prayers, gentleness, and encouragement, and for saying, "God did not bring you this far to leave you." Thank you for being family.

Matt Meyers – Thank you for talking me through preparing for India. You made me feel more equipped for the journey, and the information you gave helped us understand how serious this was. Thank you for caring.

Dusty Meyers – Thank you for offering to go with me to India and for talking with me on the phone. Thank you for caring for us so much.

Becky and Duane Carr – Thank you for being our friends and coming to check on us right in the middle of the chaos. Becky, thank you for sending me screenshots of your devotionals several times a week, for over a year almost without fail, to encourage me. We love you both.

Nicole Milano Fierro with NBC local news channel – Thank you so much for caring about us and wanting to help get our story out to help others be aware this is real and happening. Thank you for praying for us. Thank you for allowing us to tell our story. You made us feel heard.

Ray Morgan – For being willing to go with us to India, and for your unique insight and care.

Sally, Airline worker – For messaging Mom and giving her the itinerary. You helped save our daughter's life.

Dr. Richard Atwell – Thank you for calling to check on us years after our daughter left, and for having the faith to tell me, "I want to see both of you sitting in front of me when she comes back to tell her story."

Ashley Varnadore Tippens – My dear friend of over thirty years, thank you for listening to me as I sat in your chair ever so often, getting my hair done. You asked for the latest news on our story. Thank you for caring so much and for being so eager to know, for not letting me hide or stay tucked into my shell, but making me talk about it, and just asking and being interested. It was healing for me. Stylists are therapists, and so are friends! You are both and you helped me get through this!

Andrea Peck – For reaching out to me so unexpectedly and meeting with me consistently from out of town to listen to me and ask how things were going. For caring so much and giving me that shoulder.

GoFundMe Donors – Thank you to all who donated to help us with the expenses getting to our daughter. I know your kind acts will be remembered in Heaven for helping save a young woman's life.

Prayer Warriors – For all those who prayed for us and sent us Scripture. Especially Judy Jackson Krause and Belinda McCaskill with Mom's prayer group who specifically prayed that night. Everything you said came true. Your prayers helped make it all possible to get her on that plane home.

Uncle Jimmy and Aunt Jeanette – For loving us, coming to our home with food, and especially being the prayer warriors that you are!

BB – Thank you for being such a dear friend and for wanting to fight for us! Your words were truly comforting to me in those early hours and I'm so thankful for your love and care for our family. Thank you for allowing Brad to go with us. It was such a blessing.

The Adventist Church in Mobile, Alabama – Thank you for all your prayers, encouragement, donations, and hugs!

Our Customers at The Right Touch, Inc. – Thank you for your patience, for caring, praying, and continuing to support us during this trial!

My Beta Readers – Thank you all so much for taking time to read this book before it was ready to go out into the world; for your love, support, and encouragement in making this book all it needed to be.

Melanie Davis with Triumph Press – My editor and new best friend. You are like a dream! God truly sent you to me. It has been an honor to work with you on this project. You are so patient and go the extra mile. Instead of being ready to be finished, you are always wanting to make it "even better." I will always cherish our time together, especially in that first week of our connecting. I look forward to what else God has in store!

To Uncle Billy – When I was a little girl you made a point to tell me I would be a writer one day. Thank you for encouraging what you saw in me: my love for writing. I've never forgotten.

My Mother-in-law (deceased- name omitted to protect the privacy of family) – Who has passed from this life. We met when I was 15 and you were 43. We spent over 30 years together and you were the perfect example of a homemaker. I will surely miss you.

Patricia Lombard – Thank you for being there by Dad's side through all of this and for being there for us! Your support, encouragement, and ideas will never be forgotten.

Dad - You were there for me from the moment I gave you the news, and were willing to go with me if need be. You diligently watched our plane on the app, there and back. You repeatedly told me how much you loved me, how much you needed me to be strong, and to make it back. You told me I was a lady and a good mother. Thank you for your guidance and for being there with me through all of this. I know you will continue to be. You are the best dad. I love you always and forever.

Mom – You were there through it all with me, and still are!!! You stood by my side and you hurt like I hurt. You were another part of me, feeling what I was feeling, but even more because, like a Russian doll, this was your daughter from your daughter, double the pain. I can't wait to see what's in store. It was an honor to be working with you on something as special as this. You are special and I will never forget you being there for me. I love you!

Brandon – I love you so much. There was a purpose for you staying in America. Thank you for being the good son to me that you are and for staying so close to me. You are such a blessing in my life and have helped me so much. If it weren't for you and Brad, I don't think I would have survived. I love you!

Brad – Baby, I love you so much. Thank you for going to India with us. You took time off from your new job to be there for your sister and for us. You don't know how much you helped. You are such a blessing to us. If you hadn't been there and continued to be the son that you are, I don't think I would have survived. You mean the world to me and I love you!

Brent - My dear husband, if it weren't for you providing for our household, providing for me, I wouldn't have had the freedom to write this book. I thank God every day for you. You truly are a provider and the best there ever was. You've been there for me when I didn't deserve it. You've stuck it out through the toughest of times. I look forward to all God has in store for us. You are a great father, my best friend, and my business and life partner. I can't imagine being with anyone but you. We've been through so much together from such a young age. Seeing how we made it through all the things before this, helped me know we would make it through this, too, with God as our helper. I love you!

My Creator and Heavenly Father, The Redeemer Christ His Son, and The Comforter the Holy Spirit who dwells in us – I would not be alive today without Your help. My daughter would not be alive. You sent all these people to help me. They were Your hands and feet, some knowingly, some unknowingly. Then there were the times I was all alone with You. You came so close to me in my pain. You never left my side. I owe you the rest of my life as I said when I prayed that dangerous prayer: Please use me for whatever You want, as long as You want. I still mean that. I trust You will continue to be by my side through whatever comes. As I said, I would rather walk through the valley of the shadow of death holding Your hand than walk anywhere without You. Thank You for dying for me and for saving me. I love you.

India

Dr. Parkash Masih Family - For getting out of your comfortable beds at 3:00 a.m. to help an American family, for providing your home as a safe haven for our daughter until we could reach her. You truly helped save her life. May God continue to bless you for the rest of yours.

Vikesh Masih- God used you in a special way. He allowed you to visit your parents at just the right time and to stay for just as long as we needed you. If you hadn't been there we would have had no one to help us communicate. God knew what he was doing when He sent you. You were sweet and loving to us. You cared and made it bearable.

You helped us coordinate, were our main guide, and watched over our daughter like a big brother, taking care of her before we could reach there. I know you didn't expect your visit home to end up like it did. Thank you for all you endured, because of us. We are forever grateful to you. You are our family on the other side of the world, and we love you.

Pastor Samson – For your sweet and gentle demeanor. For your humbleness and selflessness. For getting out of your bed at 3:00 a.m. to accompany Dr. Parkash and meet our daughter in the airport. For praying with us and over our daughter. For just everything.

Johnson Massey– For your love and charisma, your passion to help us, your warmth, charm, and for giving us the medicine of laughter. Thank you for getting out of bed at 3:00 a.m. to help an American family. For being our friend. Without you, we wouldn't have survived. We'll never forget you.

Brian Samuel – For being our friend and helping us with our flights; just having you there and knowing you cared enough to tell me the truth that, "If you make her come home with you, she may never speak to you again." You were right. But I stood by what I said, and I'm glad she was able to return safely to her own country. Time will tell how this all will end. We will never forget you.

Minister of State Dr. Raj Kumar Verka V.C.- For taking time out of your news press to listen to us. For giving me the most precious gift – allowing me and making it possible to take my daughter home, telling us it was only your duty. We are forever grateful to you.

Vikas Dutt news reporter in India – For making the media press public, allowing us to be heard, and for checking to make sure we had returned home safely.

Church Boys and their Social Ministry - Thank you for being there for us, for praying for us, and helping us bring our daughter home. You helped make it all possible in those very last moments. You're such a sweet group of young men. I pray God will bless each one of you and your ministry abundantly as you continue to serve Him.

Church Boy's uncle, the politician - Thank you for taking us to the Minister of State's office. Thank you for walking by the church that fateful evening at twilight, for using your connections and acting on our behalf, for making it possible to bring our daughter home. Thank you, thank you, thank you. From the bottom of our hearts.

Minister of State's Military Guards – Thank you for getting our daughter and bringing her to us. You helped save her life. Thank you for your kindness and for making us feel more at home.

The Adventist Church in India - Thank you for all your prayers and encouragement, and for the sermon that was preached that Sabbath morning.

FOREWORD

Destiny's family and my family raised our children hundreds of miles apart. We share a strong Christian faith, a deep love for our children and family, and a trusting relationship with our spouses. We both have two sons and one daughter. We both love our children deeply and are fiercely protective of them. I live in Dallas-Fort Worth; Destiny's family is in coastal Alabama. We would have never met, except our daughters fell victim to the same type of online attack from distant countries. Behind both attacks lurked predators whose goal was to traffic our daughters—or at the very least, manipulate them for their own selfish ambitions to gain U.S. citizenship. Both of our daughters made plans to secretly leave the United States to rendezvous with their secret connection in a foreign country. And that is where our stories diverge. In my case, I had 25 days' notice that my daughter was secretly planning to leave the country. In Destiny's case, she learned of her daughter's plan only after she had left.

From 8,000 Miles is an unfiltered account of what transpired in a head-spinning web of actions to rescue Destiny's daughter. Destiny expertly details, blow-by-blow, the myriads of challenges she faced and how she tackled each one with the maternal ferocity and intensity you would expect from a mother completely focused on saving her baby girl from harm. Along the way, she encounters incredible acts of kindness and generosity; but also, breath-taking acts of betrayal, even cruelty, from people she once considered to be friends and family. Overlaying it all is a mother and father who leaned heavily on their Christian faith for guidance, wisdom, and comfort.

This book is equally an unflinching memoir and cautionary tale for families who read it. The online predators who targeted our daughters are different people from different countries, but the tactics they used were almost identical: take it slow, build trust, separate them from their families, separate them from their friends, separate them from their faith; then convince them to come join them. Read this book to see how those tactics unfold so you can take steps to ensure your daughter doesn't fall prey to the same kind of attack. It can and does happen. In 2023, over 50% of children under 15 years old were contacted by a stranger online. My daughter and Destiny's mistook that contact for being someone who loved them, and it put them in very dangerous territory. Destiny's description of what happened hit me, as a parent, in a deeply personal way. I could feel her fear and steadfast determination to save her daughter. I could feel her pain and shock when people you thought were friends turned out to be something far different. I could understand how her family could only lean on their faith in Christ, and Christ followers, to sustain them with hope, love, and support.

Read *From 8,000 Miles* to see how one family fought to get their daughter back. To see how real friends love and support each other. To understand the two-edged sword of social media. To feel the sting and hurt of duplicity. To gain insights into red flags of predatory behavior so you can prevent this from happening to your family. Most of all, to experience the strength that Jesus Christ gave to a mother in the midst of the fight of her life.

John Baldwin
Author of *Almost Gone*

A MOTHER'S STORY

I had to tell this story, to help save girls and those who may get caught in a similar trap. Predators are real, and human trafficking, marriage fraud, and other crimes are very much happening in our world. Even in our own hometowns. I wrote this book to bring awareness by telling our story in the hopes that it prevents this from happening to someone else. I encourage parents to get inside their children's heads to know them and what they're thinking. We can't eliminate evils, but we can be aware of and prevent them. *Education not condemnation.*

Predators have always been around, but now with the invention of the internet, our loved ones are accessible from anywhere in the world, at any time. Deception abounds and the first part of our story involves the dangers of the internet.

The second part of our story involves the danger of interference from others who cause alienation of affection from our loved ones, sometimes endangering their lives. This causes estrangement in families which is a current epidemic in our world.

Furthermore, I hope you take away from this book that spiritual warfare is real. There is a real enemy, and the battle is for the minds of men. The war is raging and escalating, so I admonish you to protect your and your family's mind at all costs.

There are many characters in this story and it's sometimes hard to keep track of everyone. For this reason, I've included a helpful key listing the main characters in the APPENDIX.

PART I

FINDING OUT

MONDAY, SEPTEMBER 17, 2018

CHAPTER 1

GONE

Sitting at the desk behind my open laptop in front of the freshly painted, sunny, pastel walls, the sound of a pressure washer hummed outside and the smell of new leather drifted in from the garage bay adjacent to me. It was September 17, 2018, around 10 a.m. on a Monday. I was taking a short break from training our very first manager, Norman, who was ten years or so my senior. I spent a few hours helping him become acquainted with our business, and his new role as he was just getting started. Running a company had been a lot of work for my husband and me. Twenty years earlier, we started an auto detailing business, doing everything from washing, waxing, polishing, and steam cleaning to window tinting, graphics, and leather repair. We were so good at "details" that we ended up with clients who had us work on their boats, RVs, and even airplanes! Finally, two decades of determination and good decisions later, we were stepping up in a new direction and taking some of the burden of management off our shoulders.

As I gave Norman time to practice what he'd been taught, I opened my computer to do a routine check of our bank accounts. I scanned over the list of transactions and everything looked good. I would reconcile it all later, but for now, this quick glance sufficed. Nothing out of the ordinary, we were in the black; always a good thing. Next, I did a spot check of the other accounts we shared with each of our three adult children. All of them (ages 24, 21, and 20) were still living with us, even though the two boys were currently away from home, and all of their bank accounts still had my name on them. Preston, our oldest child, was studying at a health and wellness center in north Alabama, five hours away, while Luke, our youngest, had just taken a new job in California after a long internship specializing in musculoskeletal health.

I randomly clicked one of the children's bank accounts to do a quick inspection and make sure everything looked good. We had recently been victims of fraud, with a major purchase being made from my account by someone transferring money from my son's account to mine, since they were all linked. Another time, fraudulent charges were made on my daughter Victoria's account, so I was vigilant in watching for anything suspicious.

Scanning my daughter's account, I immediately saw something strange. The dollar amounts were small and there were three, but what it was for, had me questioning. I grabbed my cell and called her, knowing she would be going to work soon, if she hadn't left already. No answer. She would often ignore my calls, which frustrated me, but she barely responded to anything I'd say in person, much less over the line, so I texted her:

> *Victoria, I think there may be more fraudulent charges on your account. You need to check on it!*

I had been advised by the bank that criminals always try small charges first to see if they will go through (and are likely something you won't notice), then they hit you with the big ones, as had been the case with the fraudulent activity on my account.

The three charges that had me questioning were from Uber. Victoria wouldn't have any reason to take an Uber anywhere. She has a car, unless it was broken down. But why not just ask us to help with it, or to drive her to work?

I waited. No answer. I looked at my watch. She should be leaving for work any minute. Victoria was a fitness trainer at our local gym where we all had memberships just minutes from our home. I was sure she was supposed to be there at 10:30 a.m. It only takes four minutes to get to her job from here. *Here*, at our business. It was also our home. We had the good fortune to work from home. It wasn't what I had planned or dreamed of, but neither were other parts of my life. Things don't always turn out how you've planned, but I was grateful that we had a business that allowed us the ability to raise our family where we could provide a good living for them, as well as keep a close eye on them, where we could be there for them when they needed us.

Myself, I was a latchkey kid, where I came home to an empty house, and took care of myself and my younger brother until my mom came home from work. That was not unlike most kids whose parents were divorced. My stepfather abandoned us and left my mother to raise our family all on her own, performing the role of both mother and father. So, she had to abandon being the stay-at-home mom that she was for the first thirteen years of my life. It was all she ever wanted to be, and it had to be given up for our survival.

So, I was grateful my kids didn't have to do that. They had not one, but both parents at home, when they came in from school, every single day of their lives. Fortunate and rare. That was one of the pros, and there were cons, like living at work and not being able to truly separate from it. Not having a "normal" home in a neighborhood where the kids could play and make friends down the street. But it came with the territory, and you can't have it all. Victoria certainly had made it known that she disapproved. "It's so embarrassing," she commented one day. "When I get off the bus in front of the house and people are like, 'You live at a business?'" "Well, it has given you nice things. And we're able to be home with you when you get home from school."

I responded. "That's important." And it was a nice home with a four-car garage that we ran the business from. Our kids also had built-in jobs when they got older. When they were little, we paid them for every tire they shined and when they became teenagers, they worked with us in the shop to pay for their first cars, us matching each dollar they put towards the purchase. We taught them a strong work ethic and all enjoyed working together.

With still no answer, I decided to just walk inside the house and tell her. I got up from my desk and walked out of the garage passing by her "It's Green O'clock" colored Ford Mustang. She wanted a Mustang since she was nine years old because it had the "horsey" on the front. Victoria had a thing for horses, and all animals, growing up. Recently, she had her car painted that color and won first place in a car show competition. Since her father was a car guy, and we own a car business, we had one of our business partners do the paint job, which she paid for. It was her idea to go to the show to celebrate her twenty-first birthday, as she and her dad enjoyed going to them together.

She's still here, I thought, as I walked past the car, and past my husband, quickly telling him what I had learned as I made my way up the steps to the front of the house. I went inside to her room, calling her name. She wasn't there. I went through the house and outside into the backyard. Victoria was nowhere. It was 10:30 a.m.... time for her to be at work.

I walked back out to the front of the house where her dad had started her car. "It's working fine," he said as he pulled it over to the other side of the house. Her car was here, but she wasn't. Why would she take an Uber when her car was working fine? And why wouldn't she have asked us if she needed help? Again, the questions were running through my head, trying to make sense of it. Our daughter didn't go anywhere but to work and back home. She didn't socialize much and wasn't the outgoing type. She was a homebody like me. She mostly stayed in her room all the time. It had been that way all growing up. Even now after high school, she was quiet and reserved and stayed to herself.

"She's not here. Why would she take an Uber to work if her car is here and working?" I asked my husband. I was really confused now. "Where would she take an Uber? I'm going to her work to see if she's there," I told him. "Where else could she be? I'll let you know what I find out," I said walking to my car.

He nodded, also puzzled and concerned.

I drove a short distance to the traffic light and took a right. Being a personal trainer was Victoria's dream job. Both she and her younger brother, Luke, worked there together. He had gotten the job first and when he left for his internship, she became the trainer and used her knowledge of nutrition to help the people she trained.

We were proud of her. Victoria loved this job. She loved fitness and nutrition. Here she was able to do both, and she was making a difference in people's lives. Best of all, it was also helping her. She was overcoming being shy and introverted and really seemed to enjoy it even though talking to people was hard for her. Victoria was growing as a person, and it was good. Very good. She had been there for almost a year now, and we often told her how positive it was for her.

As I turned into the parking lot of the gym, I began to calm myself. I mean, she was at work. Why was I worried? Why was I so worked up? She would be there. Maybe she just made a friend, and they wanted to ride to work together. That would be wonderful! She didn't have any close friends. I knew I would be relieved once I saw her inside, I just had to find out why she had not driven her working car there. I opened the door and walked inside.

CHAPTER 2

THE NIGHTMARE BEGINS

Once inside, I walked up to the desk where a young girl stood smiling. She was about my daughter's age with long, curly, blonde hair. Before she could speak, I nervously asked, "May I see Victoria, please?" I looked beyond her to the purple and yellow machines where she would have been training someone.

"Oh, Victoria doesn't work here anymore," the girl responded with a smile.

My face started to drop into what I suspected was a look of dread and confusion.

"*What?*" I asked, hardly able to speak.

She probably thought I was a client, so I proceeded to clarify, "What do you mean she doesn't work here anymore?! I'm her mother!"

The girl began to look worried and said in a softer voice, "Yes, she went to India to see a friend. She gave a six-week notice and has been training her replacement for the past two weeks."

India? My head started whirling. I vaguely remembered her mentioning India quite a while back as a fleeting thing; she was curious about it, like a fantasy, but not as in actually going there, not as something real that she would ever actually do, and certainly not without telling us! And she had given a six weeks' notice? She had been planning this out? I couldn't believe what I was hearing.

"India?" I felt woozy. "Six weeks! I know nothing about this. Is Rachel here? The manager! I need to talk to her!"

The girl nodded and quickly went to get the manager. Rachel was a young woman in her mid-thirties and a mother herself. She was friendly and I liked her from the first time I met her, when she took right to both of my children, and hired them, telling me what good kids they were.

Rachel had been speaking with another person when she came around to the front of the desk and very nonchalantly said, "Yeah, Victoria put in her notice. She went to India. I'm sorry you didn't know about it."

A young girl tells you she's going to India, a third world country, where poverty and crime abounds, on the other side of the globe *alone* and you don't question it? You don't tell anybody? You don't mention it? That's like someone telling you they're going to commit suicide, and you brush it off as if it were nothing!

Didn't these young people know anything? What kind of place did they think India was? A vacation getaway? Not a place for a young girl alone. No place was. But certainly not India. The country is well known for sex trafficking and other heinous atrocities. In 2018, India was named the most dangerous country for women in terms of human trafficking and sexual violence with New Delhi, the nation's capital, being home to the country's largest red-light district.

I was beginning to feel anger. Angry at the ignorance of these young women. But then again, they live in this world with no borders, because the internet has made it seem like everyone is your friendly next-door neighbor. You think you know them, but you can't possibly know someone behind a computer screen and believe what they say. They can be anybody they want to be.

"Here is the notice she gave," Rachel pulled out a piece of paper and my eyes darted back and forth across the page as I read it.

"She told you she went to India and you didn't think anything of it? That it is dangerous?" I asked, still in shock over what was happening and obviously distraught.

"She said she was going to meet a friend she went to school with, who used to live here, but went back home there," Rachel said.

None of this made sense to me. She had lied to them. That's why they weren't as alarmed, but she was still going *alone* to a very dangerous area! We would later learn that two kids from church had also known about her leaving for India, but supposed it was for a mission trip and thought we knew, so they said nothing.

"Did she say when she was coming back?" I asked breathlessly, starting to feel my legs weaken.

"In two months. I told her I would hold her job that long."

"Oh God, I can't believe this! I can't believe this is happening!" I said, starting to shake and tremble, and fall to pieces as they both stood there with blank stares, their mouths open, as I turned, and walked out the door and down the steps.

ㅅ　　ㅅ　　ㅅ

I wasn't crying. I couldn't cry. Not yet. I had work to do. I had to get to the airport and see if she might still be there waiting on a plane, or if someone at the airline could tell me if there had been any flights to India that day, and what time they left. Anything. I had to get information. I had to pinpoint where she might be right now and when she would arrive there. I had to try.

We lived close to everything and the airport was just a mile away. I called my husband on the way. "Brent, she's gone! Victoria's gone! They told me she went to India!" I moaned, holding it somewhat together.

There was silence on the other end.

"I'm on my way to the airport to see if they can give me any information on times or flights to India today."

"Okay," he replied. "Be careful. I love you."

"I will," I said. "I love you, too."

Once inside the airport, I quickly walked up the stairs to the security check-in line to see if she might still be waiting in the lobby. No one was there. I walked back downstairs to the airline check-in desk. There was no line. It was a small airport and it wasn't busy. I stood behind the sign at the counter and looked expectantly at the two men behind it.

"May I help you?" one of them finally asked.

"Yes! I need to find out if there have been any flights to India today and what the schedule might be."

"Oh, we can't give out that information."

"You mean you can't tell me about your flights that have already gone out today?"

"No, we can't."

"What if I came in here to buy a ticket and needed that information?"

"We don't give that information at the desk. You must make your purchase online. We only check in your bags here."

"My daughter got on a plane today to go to India and I need to know what time! Please help me!"

"I'm sorry ma'am. There's nothing I can do." He really did seem like he wanted to help.

"Okay, thank you." Exasperated, I walked away.

On the way back to the car, I called my husband and explained that the airport was no help, but he had the information I was looking for.

"I searched her room. She left a letter. She wrote her itinerary down."

"Oh, thank God!" I cried. "I'll be there in a minute."

As I arrived back home, my husband handed me the letter.

"I found it laying on her desk with the words '<u>OPEN</u>' written on it," he said as he handed it to me, having already read it.

I took the letter. It was tri-folded with the words as he described on the outside. Victoria wanted us to see it.

"She left her Bible, too," he said, glancing at the book with the turquoise cover laying on the desk with her name engraved in silver. The look on my husband, Brent's face was one of sadness, confusion, and disbelief, but he had to return to work. He worked with his hands and was a good provider. He could fix anything, but he couldn't fix this. The best thing he could do right now was finish the customer vehicles, so he would be available later to do whatever he needed.

As he returned outside, I held the letter in my hand, staggered towards the dining table near the kitchen, and sat down. As I began to read, it was all a blur. I could hardly think.

The letter was typed out. Victoria wrote how she was very sorry, and didn't want us to be mad at her, and how she couldn't tell us even though she wanted to, but that she knew we wouldn't let her go if she did. She talked about how in love she was with this guy she had met online and had been talking to him for two years.

There were pictures of him with his family and his dog as well as a penciled sketch he had drawn of Victoria. She talked about how they had a lot in common. How he grew up watching the same movies she had, and how he liked working out at the gym as much as she did, and how he told his dad he wanted to be a vegetarian like her.

Victoria said his sister was an actress and had included beautiful pictures of her. "And look, Mom, she's reading the same book you have!" In one of the photos, his sister was holding a book entitled, *How to Win Friends and Influence People.* Victoria assured me that even though she knew this would sound extremely crazy and unsafe for her to do, that she was perfectly fine and one hundred percent safe with this family. She said she has taken a lot of time and thought it through, that she has good discernment, and that she believes she is making the right decision.

His name was Ranjit. Victoria had met all his family and friends online. They thanked her for coming into his life and told her how much he had changed since he met her. They told Victoria how he used to never smile before, but now he smiles all the time, and that he is so happy. They love her and call her family.

She said she wanted to tell me about everything she had been hiding from us, that she knows not many people experience what she has, and that it's special.

> "*When you get so close to someone it's hard not to meet them. It becomes very difficult to go on in life without meeting the people who make you cry and laugh every day,*"

Victoria wrote.

She talked about how they had celebrated her birthday with her, by buying a birthday cake, and lit the candles so she could "blow" them out through the computer screen, as they blew them out for her.

14

"I want to finally meet the people who have been so good to me. I want to meet them face to face at least once before the waiting becomes too unbearable."

She said his parents had paid for her plane ticket to come to their country in the amount of $1,000. There was no mention of a return ticket, and she didn't state when she was coming back. There was no address to the place she would be staying, no phone numbers of any of the family, and no last name mentioned, only first names. At the bottom of the page was her itinerary. It read:

Mobile>>>>Dallas>>>>Hong Kong>>>>New Delhi>>>>Amritsar

It was typed just above her name. There was no signature, just her name typed out:

"Love, Victoria" and "Happy Birthday, Dad"

The next day was my husband's birthday. We had just gone out to his favorite Italian restaurant where Victoria and I had shared a slice of cheesecake not even twenty-four hours ago.

Yeah, Happy Birthday. What a day it would be. A day we will never forget.

I remembered how I had hugged her goodnight before going to bed just last night. Embracing me, she leaned into me warmly, not the robotic, rigid way of old. It was the new way. The new Victoria. The one that I believed had been set free and cured by a miracle of God from something that had a hold on her, her entire life. Anxiety. Depression. Lack of expression and affection.

I felt relieved. Yes, it was her. The new Victoria was still there. Even though in the last several weeks there had been a looming ice-cold friction in the house that I could barely stand, and didn't know where it was coming from. Maybe I hadn't wanted to see that she may have been sliding back into the old ways. But I was satisfied that this hug *was real.*

It was still there.

We were safe.

I said goodnight and went to bed.

Then I remembered how I had gotten up at 4:30 a.m. to use the bathroom and as I walked back to bed, the fact that I was wide awake caught my attention. I had looked out our bedroom door, across the kitchen, to where her bedroom door was closed.

The moment struck me as odd that I would pause and look at her door as if someone was trying to tell me something.

Unbeknownst to me, my little girl was not there.

She was already gone.

CHAPTER 3

SUSPICIOUS ACTIVITY

With the letter in my hand, I sat bewildered. *India*, I thought. *She's as good as dead. I'll never see her again.* I cannot begin to describe the way I felt at that moment. Unless you are a parent who has walked in those shoes, you cannot understand or imagine it. I felt so helpless. She was not dead, she was alive. But for how long? And how would I even know?

There was no way I could possibly catch up to her. Nobody could. Even if I got on a plane right at that moment, I couldn't reach her before she landed. It was hopeless. I had heard how horrible a place it is. We had just seen a movie about it, that *she* suggested we watch about the sex trafficking that goes on there.

I immediately got out my phone and sent her a desperate text:

Victoria,

We love you very much and wish you would come back. You have no idea what you are doing to us. We are afraid for your life. India is not a good place for you to go. They prostitute girls to make a living. Even the females, like you saw in the movie, help get girls for the men. I know you think you know, but you don't know what you're getting yourself into.

I wish you would have talked to us first so we could counsel you. You didn't give us a chance. I could have at least gone with you, but you didn't give me a chance. You just left. He could have come here instead. It would have been safer, but you didn't ask.

You can stay right where you are, and I'll come get you. Please don't leave! Unless God protects you, I believe you are as good as dead. I'm afraid of what might happen to you. Please let me come with you to meet them, so I know you are okay.

She might be in the air and not able to get my text, or her phone may be dead and there may not be a way to charge it. I could only hope she would text back.

I had almost forgotten about my trainee. I walked back outside and found him in the garage talking with another employee. I walked up to him and shouted over the noise of the equipment,

"I'm sorry, but we have a family emergency. I must leave work. I don't know when I'll be back, or *if* I'll be back."

Completely unfazed, and without questions he simply replied, "Okay."

I went back inside, and sat alone in the kitchen for about an hour, dumbfounded and in shock. I couldn't think. I was just numb.

My worst fear as a child was being kidnapped or separated from my parents and my worst fear as a parent was having my child taken from me by a stranger. I had raised them, they were grown adults, and we were past that. Or so I thought.

Finally, I decided I might as well make a report about it. I should call the police. I knew there was nothing they could do, but someone needed to document it. Then I thought about calling the news. If the police can't help, you call the news.

So, I called the police and as I waited for the officer to arrive, I called our local TV station, but couldn't get through. There was only an outgoing message and their e-mail address. I couldn't think to put words in an email, so I let go of the idea.

When the officer arrived, I showed him the letter and gave him the information I had, answering all his questions. He said he couldn't label it as a missing person's report because she had left the letter so she wasn't missing, but that he would report it as "Suspicious Activity."

That's right. It was suspicious alright.

The officer left.

It had been three hours since I found out the news at the gym.

I then reluctantly made the call I knew I had to make but was dreading.

"Mom," I said, "what are you doing?"

"I'm at the office making copies of a contract," she replied sounding a little worried. "What's wrong?"

My mom, Priscilla Reinhardt, was a real estate agent and landlord, and was working in the office finishing up on a sale. She must have immediately picked up on the sound of my voice and knew something was desperately wrong.

"Are you sitting down?" I asked.

"I'm coming over there. I'll be there in a minute."

She hung up the phone without giving me a chance to tell her anything. It was just as well.

She would later explain to me that she knew if I told her over the phone, whatever it was, she wouldn't have been able to drive and she wanted to get to me without getting in a wreck. She didn't know if someone had died or what, but she knew it wasn't good.

Her office wasn't far and she was there within about ten minutes. She walked through the front door with a look of concern so great it appeared she was about to cry. She grabbed both my hands.

"What is it?" she asked, her brown eyes searching mine, full of questions. Her long eyelashes reached her eyebrows. Her short, brown hair flipped up on her shoulders. She was dressed in black leggings, booties, and a colorful poncho.

"Nobody has died," I just wanted to get that out of the way and give her some immediate relief for what was about to come. We had our trials before, but this was a whole new kind of nightmare.

"It's Victoria," I said, "she got on a plane and went to India." I showed her the letter. "To see some guy she's been talking to online!"

My mother braced herself, putting both hands on the dining room table. Her head went back as she looked straight up at the ceiling, her mouth opened wide, and she began to wail,

"NOOOOOOOO!!!!!! VIC-TOR-IAAAAAA!!!!!!!! NOOOOOOOO!!!!!"

Tears immediately began streaming from the corners of her eyes and down the sides of her face as she held the letter in her hand.

Seeing my mom like that, I finally let it go.

I had not cried yet.

I had still been trying to wrap my mind around what was happening.

Trying to figure out what to do next.

I tried to console my mom as I cried with her and rubbed her back. We hugged and she just kept crying, "OH GOD, NOOOOO! VICTORIA! NOOOO!"

CHAPTER 4

SCRAMBLING

When my mom could finally calm down, we tried to put our heads together. She called my brother, Sebastion, or Seb as we called him, and told him the news, sobbing, then sent him the letter Victoria left. She wanted to make another trip to the airport. I told her I had tried, but she insisted on going anyway. Again, they were no help.

As we walked out of the airport, she was again talking to my brother and then handed the phone to me. I took it reluctantly. My brother and I hadn't been on the best of terms. It had been three months since we last spoke and it wasn't pretty. Not pretty at all.

Sebastion was a likable guy. Even when people knew he could con his way into anything, and anyone could be the target, they still liked him. He used to be lovable and funny, never-ending a phone call with Mom or me without saying, "I love you." As a kid, he always made us laugh with his physical comedy. I missed those days. He wasn't funny anymore. He wasn't even happy.

"Hey," I said, putting the phone to my ear as I walked in the parking lot towards the car. My brother lived across the country with his fiancé, Sophie, a 20-hour drive from us. He was almost eight years my junior and we had different dads.

"I'm checking the airport in Dallas," he replied, "to see if I can get any information on thè flights. If Victoria is on any of them, maybe we can get them to stop her."

The conversation was short and a blur.

"Thank you, I appreciate your help," I said handing the phone back to Mom as I pulled the car through the exit to pay the parking fee.

There really wasn't much for me to say and I'm sure he didn't want to talk to me any more than I wanted to talk to him. My world was currently in a state of chaos, and I was trying to figure out what to do next, but Mom had just handed me the phone saying, "Here, tell your sister."

She figured maybe this could somehow bridge the divide. Tragedy has a way of doing that. It brings everyone together to work on something when it devastates the whole family.

Sebastion and I had gotten on bad terms when I defended Mom against his fiancé, Sophie. She was dirty mouthing our mother and they weren't even married yet. Sophie had been sending Mom text messages for a year, complaining about Sebastion's "bad childhood" and how unsupportive she was of him, but was always there for me. Sebastion had been saying the same things ever since he met Sophie, where he had never said those things before. He and I had a good childhood, despite his father abandoning us. I'd say Sebastion was spoiled, but Mom laughed and said Sebastion couldn't be, because he always wanted more and nothing was ever enough. I, on the other hand, didn't want things; I wanted to be independent and grown up.

I had been patient with Sophie, but then she crossed a line. She went too far when she told my mom, "You were dealt a sh**ty life because your mother was disabled," and "You're the common denominator in your failed marriages." Sophie had cut deep, going places she never should have, speaking of things she knew nothing about, events that happened before she was born.

My mom worked so hard, even from childhood, because her mother needed help. Then when Sebastion's dad left us, my mom again had to work hard to support our family, so she got used to it, and now that's all she did. Work, work, work. She had recently been diagnosed with melanoma, a dangerous and fast-spreading disease and was going through a third divorce. Mom was extremely stressed as many of her rental properties were empty and in need of repair. All while needing to keep her real estate license active. Any one of those things would be enough to kill a person!

Sebastion and Sophie were expecting Mom to help with their bills while not controlling their spending. They were going to roll her right into her grave. I called Sophie, telling her not to contact my mother again. I was genuinely worried about the risk to Mom's health from the attacks Sophie was making and so I was very blunt when I told her, "No more!" I then called Sebastion and laid into him, telling him he shouldn't be allowing Sophie to treat our mother badly; he wasn't standing up for her and shouldn't be asking our mother for money, especially while Mom was going through so much. I concluded by warning him he shouldn't marry that girl because, "If your mother and wife can't get along, you won't be a happy man."

I'm sure that's something I didn't need to leave unsaid and have regrets later. There was definitely a problem there, and I didn't want to see the whole family living in turmoil.

From childhood, Sebastion struggled with ADHD, and to this day he can't find his wallet or keys when he needs them. He has severe anxiety for which he takes medication and marijuana to calm his nerves; he even moved out West so he could grow his own. Sebastion felt we thought of him as a drug dealer, which was not the case.

23

Soon, Mom was on the phone again, this time with Claudia, our previous pastor's wife. Mom had recently listed their home for sale as they moved across the country to another church, so she had been in close touch.

"Thank you for your help," Mom said, as she ended the call.

"Claudia is going to help. She's getting us in touch with the church's Conference leadership in Washington D.C., a man named Richard who used to be the head of the Conference in India. He knows people over there who might assist us in some way."

This was all so heavy and unbelievable.

I still had to call my dad, my mother-in-law, and Victoria's brothers. When we arrived back home, I called Dad first.

"Dad?" He was home, having recently retired as a software engineer at a shipyard. I was glad he had retired. If this had happened while he was working, his job already being so stressful, it would've been too much for him.

He had been remarried to a nice lady named, Isabel. I was glad he was in a relationship again. It was good for him and I was happy he was not alone.

"What are you doing?"

"Oh, just......."

I didn't even hear what he said, I was ready to get this over with and tell him the news.

"I have some bad news, Dad," I started to whimper.

"What?" he asked with concern in his voice.

"Victoria got on a plane in the middle of the night and went to India to see some guy she met online. She left us a note."

He immediately started thinking hard about what to do and asking questions. Then he just said, "Hmm Hmm Hmm. I'll continue to think and figure out what we can do. Call me if you find out anything else. I'll be over later."

Next, I called my mother-in-law. "What's wrong?" I hardly ever called, so she knew something was up.

I didn't want her to have to anticipate too long so I immediately said, "No one has died."

She started to cry and it seemed like a long time before I finally was able to say, "It's Victoria. She got on a plane last night and went to India without telling us."

"India?" she cried. "Oh, God!"

I told her about the letter she left, filing the police report, and going to her work and the airport. She said she and Brent's dad would come over soon.

My youngest son, Luke, was spending his last night in Australia. He had been doing a week-long seminar with the vice president of the company he started working for just two weeks prior. I knew it was the middle of the night there, so I needed to wait until it was morning for him. He certainly didn't need to hear this news before getting on a fourteen-hour flight the next day. So, I called my oldest son, Preston, who was three years older than Victoria.

Preston was studying at a health and wellness center, the one Victoria recently left because, after years of wanting to go there, she realized she didn't like it. I went on to tell him the news. Preston was sad to hear it and really wanted to be there with me. I told him there was nothing he could do, that he had his studies, and I would keep him informed as he told me everyone at the center would be praying.

Mom was on the phone again. I could hear her in the other room. She had called my aunt and uncle and some friends of hers who were prayer warriors.

"Sebastion texted me an article reporting that New Delhi is the human trafficking capital of the world, and that's where she is flying into," she told someone.

I was surprised and a little disappointed that she had sent Victoria's letter to Sebastion. It was so precious and private, but I knew we needed as much help as possible, as fast as possible. "He may know somebody who can glean something from it," she told me.

"I called my friend, Fern, in real estate. She volunteers with *Eye Heart World*, a human trafficking agency. She's going to do some digging."

I nodded. Good. Maybe we were getting somewhere; getting some people on board.

A text came through on my phone:

> *We didn't want to bug you while you're busy trying to get information, but I'm happy to help do some internet detective work. If you want to send the pictures she left, names, addresses, or anything you have, I can run it through some search programs and see what I can track down.*

Who is this? I texted back, not recognizing the number.

Kelli.

It was my sister-in-law, my husband's youngest brother, Grant's, wife. Grant and Kelli lived out of state about seven hours north of us, and Grant was about nine years Brent's junior.

I was surprised to receive Kelli's text. It was unusual that she was contacting me. She never texted or called me before! We'd never had much of a relationship. There had been a twelve-year rift between her and Grant and Brent and me. We were still civil, but there was definitely a distance between us. Though it was unusual for her to contact me, the whole situation was unusual, and with such a horrific event taking place, I was comforted and glad they were offering to help.

Can you confirm the flight information she gave you? I have people that can intersect her at the airport.

There was a knock at the door.

I'll have to get back with you on that, I texted.

I opened the front door to find a person standing there that I saw once in a blue moon.

It was my brother Sebastion's dad. My ex-stepfather, my mom's second husband. The one who abandoned us when I was thirteen.

He must know about what's going on, I thought. When I opened the door, he had a shocked look on his face. He must have seen the grief on mine. I asked him to come in. He stood inside the door and hesitantly told me his father just had a heart attack and he wanted me to know. It was extremely odd that he even cared to tell me.

Brent and my mom came from the dining room and stood inside the doorway, hearing the news.

"We're sorry to hear that," I said. "Our daughter left in the middle of the night, without telling us, to go to India. We're trying to figure out what to do," I said, explaining the look on my face while holding back tears.

"Well I better go, you have your own problems to deal with."

Then he said something that shocked me.

"Whatever you do, don't get Sebastion involved. He's mentally unstable right now."

I couldn't believe my ears. He never said anything out of the way about his son, and he said it in front of all three of us. The two of them must not have been getting along. Something was going on.

"We'll be praying for your situation," I told him. He thanked me and left.

I sat on the edge of the brown leather recliner in the living room and texted our previous pastor, Pastor Mark. He was Claudia's husband who mom had just been in touch with. He and Claudia were both children of evangelists and had grown up traveling with their parents from a young age. They had been on every continent except Antarctica and Australia and had been to India several times, even recently. I texted him what was going on and asked for advice as to what to do. I figured he may have some special insight for me.

I then made a group text with our immediate family who were helping us so we could communicate and keep everyone on the same page. I included my dad and Isabel, his wife, Brent's parents, my sister-in-law Kelli, and Grant, her husband.

We're still trying to figure out what to do, I texted the group, *I'll keep everyone updated through this group chat.* There was some texting among the group and some talk about us going over there to get her, to which I made no response.

Before going back to work, Brent asked if we had heard anything else, and I filled him in on who we had contacted and informed him that our family would be coming over soon. Mom had taken a call from someone wanting to buy a house and had stepped outside.

CHAPTER 5

BROTHER'S KEEPER

I was left alone for a moment. I walked through my bedroom and into the master bathroom. I paced back and forth and tried to think.

She has gotten herself into this mess, maybe she needs to get herself out, I thought.

You can't just go around fixing your kid's problems, they must learn some things the hard way. At least that's what I had learned growing up and that's what I believed.

What if we did have to go over there? There was no telling how much that would cost. I couldn't make rash decisions. I was a businessperson, I was calculated and thought things through. *No, we could not go. It was insane to even think about. We had the business. We had employees, it was not responsible. She was going to have to figure this out on her own.*

I marched outside, down the front porch steps, to the garage to talk to Brent. I needed to hash this out with him. In case it came down to it, I needed to know where we stood.

"What if we have to go over there and get her?" I asked him, my arms crossed, my brow furrowed, standing next to him in one of the garage bays. He was applying window tint to the glass on one of the doors of a red firebird.

"We *are not* going to India!" he said emphatically, smoothing the tint onto the glass. "That's ridiculous. I have a business to run and do you know how much that would cost? Even if we did go, it might not even help!"

"I know," I said. "I just wanted to double-check with you. I'm going to text the family group that we are not going!"

I went back to the bathroom.

We are not going to India, I texted the group, to which no one responded.

I started having second thoughts. *What if we didn't go and something bad happened to her? What if I never saw or heard from her again? I would have no way of contacting her, or knowing if she needed help. What if she ended up being tortured? Everything may be okay as she says, but what if it's not? What if something goes wrong? Brent and I would have to live with that guilt the rest of our lives, knowing that we could have done something and didn't.*

She could end up dead, and here we were, too worried about our livelihood and wondering if it was necessary to go. I couldn't bear the thought. God, help me!

Then a thought came, *In a multitude of counselors, there is safety.*

I certainly needed a multitude right now. I grabbed my phone, walked into the bedroom, and sat on the burgundy ottoman at the foot of the wingback chair, in the corner of the bedroom.

I needed advice. I knew who I needed to call. I pulled up Pastor Fernando Leite's number.

"Leite," as in, "late for dinner."

Pastor Leite was the new pastor at our church who had replaced Pastor Mark. I had never met him; I had not even spoken to him before.

We hadn't been to our church for the past year. We were "in the wilderness" after the church had gone through a tough time, but we had been enjoying another church within our denomination on Dr. Martin Luther King Drive.

I had to "grow up" and learn by experience what I had always known in theory, that not all people in the church were true representatives of God, as they portrayed themselves to be. There were the "tares" growing right alongside the "wheat." Though we knew imperfect people were there, we had been hurt, so we decided to pull back for a while to give us space and time to think.

So here I was without a pastor at a time when I needed one the most, someone I could trust for guidance and direction. Pastor Mark had left and was now on the other side of the country and here was this new pastor, that I did not know.

Pastor Leite had texted me a couple of times just to say hello and that he was checking on us. I had texted back, cordially, as I couldn't take what had happened out on him. It wasn't his fault. He seemed nice, and genuinely concerned about us, but going back to that church building was something we hadn't been ready for.

I took a deep breath and dialed the number.

"Hello, Pastor Leite, here," said a voice with a Portuguese accent.

"Hello? Pastor Leite, this is Destiny Harris. How are you?"

"I'm good, and you?"

"Not good, I'm sorry to say. I hate to call you like this, but our family is in trouble, and I don't know who else to call. I need advice," I said.

"Okay, what can I do?"

I explained everything that had transpired so far. He listened patiently and intently.

"So, my question to you is, should we go over there and get her? Should we do that?"

"You know," he said in his thick accent, "we are our brother's keeper. When it is in our power to do good, to 'elp someone, we do it! And this, this is your *dau-gh-ter*." He drew out the word softly and tenderly.

I began to tear up. I knew he was right.

"Now, what you need is a plan. Do you have a plan?"

"No, my plan is just to go there, grab her, and run!" I said.

"Yes, that is understandable. But think how your daughter might see it. She needs to see that you are willing to talk to his family. She needs to see that you are trying and that you care about what she cares about. She needs to trust you and if you just grab her and go, you may risk losing that."

"And if I stay and talk, I may risk losing her. I'd rather take action now and apologize later."

"Yes, this is a hard thing. It must be done with care. If you sit down and talk first, and show her you are trying to communicate, and find out what their reasoning is, why it is they brought your daughter there, then you can say, 'Well, we are taking our daughter home now, where we can make better decisions about this situation, and perhaps later we can come back at a better time, or perhaps he can come to the U.S., but right now is not a good time, as we were not prepared for this.' Maybe you can even tell your daughter that he can come with you, to get her on that plane home. That is Plan A. If talking doesn't work, you go to Plan B."

"And what is Plan B?" I asked.

"That's when you grab her and run!"

I smiled. I was liking Pastor Leite. He wasn't just loving, he had strategy. He understood this was a fight and I felt I could truly trust and rely on him for spiritual guidance and support.

He then offered to pray with me. He said a gentle prayer, asking God to give us wisdom, direction, and protection as we embarked on this journey forward. He prayed for Victoria as well, that she could see how much we loved her.

I thanked him and told him I would be in touch. As we hung up, I heard Mom calling my name and I quickly returned to the kitchen.

CHAPTER 6

VISITING THE FBI

"A lady called about buying a house and I told her what was going on," Mom said. I took a deep breath; she told everyone everything! I doubted that lady wanted to hear about our problems. "She works at a government office and told us we should check with the FBI."

"The FBI?" I asked.

"Yes, let's see if your dad will take us there. He just pulled up outside."

We told Dad the plan, then Mom and I got in his black Chevy and headed to the FBI to see if there was anything they could do. We took the letter Victoria left and I rode up front with Dad while Mom sat in the back.

We had just left the house when Seb called telling us he had contacted the Dallas International Airport to see if he could get any information on Victoria's flight or confirm her itinerary with times and dates. We didn't know exactly where she would be and when. We needed to know how much time we had. Somehow, he managed to get that information. He was trying to see if he could have her stopped in Dallas, so he could get to her, but it seemed she was already en route to her second destination in Hong Kong.

"There's a typhoon headed for Hong Kong," he told us.

We were excited at this news, hoping the typhoon would stop her plane from leaving Hong Kong for New Delhi. At least Seb had the itinerary and knew the deadline.

By this time, Victoria's letter was all over the internet, courtesy of Sebastion Reinhardt.

Looks like someone awfully close to you, is not on your side, a friend messaged me, having seen the letter, not thinking I would have given it out.

Kelli called. I hadn't had a chance to get back with her. "I've done some research and the boy's sister, she's not a real actress."

My heart sank.

"She may not even be his sister. Sometimes with things like this, girls will come along with the guy, acting like they are his sister or a friend to make the girl feel more comfortable going with them."

"So, she is an actress, just a different kind of actress," I said.

"Right," Kelli replied. "It could be that she was hired."

I felt sick. Dad offered to get me a baked potato at *Wendy's* to settle my stomach. I had not eaten all day.

Kelli continued, "My contact in India has a cousin who spoke with the sister and says that he feels there *is* something shady going on, as the sister is trying to get Victoria out of Immigration. I'll keep you updated on anything else I find," I thanked her as Dad pulled into the drive-thru.

Next, we parked at the FBI building downtown. It was a large, white building with black iron fencing and a large, black iron gate around it. A guard wearing a dark navy uniform was stationed just inside the gate.

We walked up to the gate and the guard asked me what my business was. I nervously told him while handing over my daughter's letter.

"I need help," I said distressed, but hopeful.

"I'll take it inside and I'll be back." We watched as he walked a long way to the white building behind him and all the way up the steps, as another guard stood nearby.

It wasn't long before he returned, handing the letter back to me through the gate.

"This is out of our jurisdiction; there's nothing we can do, but we've seen a case identical to this and it didn't end well."

Another blow. My heart sank another ten meters down. This was getting worse and worse. I thanked him and we headed back home.

> Meanwhile, Brent was at home texting Victoria, *Victoria, this is Dad. This is not the last memory we want of you. It is killing us to not hear from you. Please call. Please call. Please call.*

On the way back home, Claudia, Pastor Mark's wife, called and gave me the number of a friend of hers named Evelyn saying she could help. I called the number and a woman answered. As we began to talk, I realized she was also my friend from church.

I had known Evelyn Silva da Cruz for about a year, but we weren't close. She and her husband, Carlos, had two daughters of their own, one in middle school and one in elementary school, and a little boy around five years old, who was a handful. Belinda, was Carlos's daughter from a previous marriage and was a beautiful, sweet girl Victoria's age.

Evelyn had tried befriending me a whole year prior to us becoming friends, but we had just lost our family dog of twelve years and it was like losing a child, so I had put off us getting together.

She was looking for friends for Belinda, her stepdaughter, who had just come to live with them from her home on one of the islands. Evelyn thought it would be good if my children could befriend Belinda, so our families went canoeing together.

Evelyn's husband, Carlos, had worked with Brent and me as youth leaders at church while Evelyn worked with a younger group of children, and she was currently studying to earn her degree to work with children as well.

She and I had gone out to lunch together and her family came to our home many times for dinner after church. I liked Evelyn and was glad she was going to help us.

She told me about a friend of hers, Troy Garfield, who was a private investigator and who lived in another country. She said, "He's married to a man, but is good at what he does" and he had helped a lot of people.

I called Troy and left a message as we neared home. Just then I received a text. It was Pastor Mark responding:

Where she is headed is only thirty minutes from the Pakistan border. If she gets across that border, you'll never see her again.

A lump formed in my throat. Another blow.

CHAPTER 7

SEB'S WILD PLAN

When we reached the house, my dad's wife, Isabel, had arrived, as had Brent's parents, Jeannie and Charles. All seven of us sat down to put our heads together, leaving only three seats unoccupied at the long, black, rectangular table in our dining room.

As we did, Sebastion called again. This time he had a plan. Mom handed me her phone and I put him on speaker as I laid it down in the middle of the table. His friend, Quincy, was also on the line.

"What we need," said Sebastion, "is to charter a private jet so we can get over there fast. And we need machine guns so we can take this guy out."

Whoa, I thought. Then Quincy began to talk about the logistics of how we would carry out this plan. As he was talking, I received a call. It was Troy Garfield, the private investigator, Evelyn's friend.

I got up from the table, and went to another room to take the call, as Quincy continued to speak. Troy sounded nice as he proceeded to tell me how he could help. He gave me a list of things he would need from me. There were about thirteen different items and he said to e-mail them to him.

He also told me it would cost $15,000 and he needed $10,000 up-front. As I wrote down the list of things, he said he would be looking for my e-mail. I thanked him and hung up, returning to the dining room.

Sebastion was no longer on the phone and everyone looked dumbfounded.

"Sebastion said he needs $200,000 to rent a plane," Mom informed me. "When I told him we don't have that kind of money, he said, 'You don't care about your daughter, all you care about is money."

"Smh," I sighed. "Who does he think we are?"

"What I want to know is how he thinks he's going to get machine guns into another country," someone said as I turned to go to my office in the garage.

I needed to get that list of things together for Troy. I spent the rest of the afternoon gathering the information and documents he had requested and putting them into an e-mail.

During that time, Brent told me there was a Sergeant Stone from the Child Advocacy Center searching Victoria's room. Mom's friend, Fern, with *Eye Heart World* Human Trafficking Agency, had gotten in touch with him.

"He says the letter Victoria left looks just like sex trafficking and that he has seen letters just like this before… they all look the same," my mom and Brent told me as I entered the house.

I took a deep breath as I entered Victoria's room to say hello to Sergeant Stone and found him going through drawers and papers. He was wearing a tan uniform, was clean-shaven and seemed to be in his mid-forties, just a little older than us. He asked me a few questions, then I thanked him for what he was doing and let him get back to his job, as I turned to go back to the office.

On my way, two other officers showed up, also in tan uniforms, saying they were just checking on us as they had heard the call from my police report earlier. They told me they were sorry this was happening and wished they could do more. They looked as sad and as helpless as I was, lingering a bit before leaving.

"We hope you get your daughter back," they said warmly, and though it was heartfelt, it made me uneasy.

I thanked them as I continued to my office where I finished up a few hours later and saved the e-mail to Troy. I would send it in the morning after checking it over one more time to make sure I had everything correct.

I began to think of how I might be able to get the funds. Maybe on one of the credit cards, I had somewhere. But how would I even know if he had tried to get her back? He could just take the money and say he did everything he could and there's no way I would know any different. Plus, he didn't care about her as much as I did. She wasn't his daughter. After you're paid, where is the motivation or accountability?

Still, I had to consider it. My daughter's life was at stake.

Then again, I could probably do a better job.

I mean, I didn't have the resources, but I had higher motivation than any other human being on the planet. I was a mother. A mother bear who would seek after and protect her cub at any cost if someone threatened to harm her.

And mothers never give up.

CHAPTER 8
SERGEANT STONE'S INSTRUCTIONS

Iwas so tired; I could hardly see straight, much less think. It was getting dark and as I stood by the desk, Sergeant Stone entered the office.

He seemed very concerned, tired, and distressed. He was adamant that the first thing I do in the morning is go to probate and file a petition to the judge to get temporary, twenty-four-hour emergency custody of Victoria.

"It's only temporary, now. It's only for twenty-four hours just so you can have her deported back home and save you from going over there."

He gave me his card and the items he found in her room that he thought were of some importance: A Visa gift card in the name of some woman I didn't know, a letter Ranjit had sent to Victoria with drawings he made, and some notes Victoria made in preparation for going out of the country including where she was learning some of the language. There was also a piece of paper with an address written on it. The address was in Amritsar, India. Showing it to me, Sergeant Stone said, "That may be where she is going."

He looked sad and it made me sad.

I nodded, very tired.

He stated it again, "First thing tomorrow."

"I will," I promised and thanked him as he left.

As I walked towards the house, my phone rang. It was Luke, my youngest son, in Australia.

"Mom, what's going on? Uncle Seb called and said something about Victoria and India, and jets and machine guns.

"I asked him what he was talking about, and he said, 'What? Your mom didn't tell you? Your parents are idiots!' I was half asleep. What's he talking about, Mom?"

"I'm sorry he called you. I didn't call because I knew you were sleeping and had to get up early for your flight home to California." I filled him in on what was happening. He and Victoria were only fifteen and a half months apart. They were practically twins and since she was held back a year in school, that put them in the same grade, making everyone think they were.

Luke was the closest person to her, other than me. Victoria didn't allow many people to get close, as she had never trusted anyone. She and Luke weren't only siblings, they were best friends. They shared teachers, classmates, and friends, and experienced each new milestone in life together.

Now that Luke had moved on to pursue his life beyond high school and had taken a job in California on the other side of the country, it was a little strange and hard for her. She didn't have her "best bud" there. Things were different now, but she didn't comment on or share her feelings about it. Luke couldn't imagine that she had done this without telling him.

"I'm not sure what we're going to do, yet," I told him. "We're still trying to see if there's a way to get her stopped so we can either get to her or have her sent back here. I may need you. Get home and rest, if you can, and I'll be in touch," I said and hung up, as I continued walking towards the house. Dad and Isabel had gone home, and Brent was standing on the front porch with both his parents, Charles and Jeannie, and my mom. Brent's dad said he had been talking to Grant, Brent's youngest brother.

"Grant seems to think Sebastion set all this up to make money off it," Charles said.

Jeannie slapped her husband on the arm, "Charles!"

"It's okay, Jeannie," my mom said. "I'm not offended."

I laughed at the thought of it, "Seb may have been willing to capitalize on the situation, but he certainly didn't plan it all out."

We were all tired.

"Keep us updated. We'll talk to you tomorrow," Brent's parents said as they left.

Mom was staying the night and sleeping in Preston's room so she could be there early in the morning to accompany me to the courthouse, and file the petition to the judge. Dad had told us to call him and he would go with us as he didn't want us going downtown by ourselves.

Brent's other younger brother, Derrick, had called. Derrick said his boss had to go to India at times and he always drove in a bulletproof vehicle. He said it was no place for a young girl and "I would drag her home by the hair of her head if she were my daughter."

"Your dad said he would go to India if you needed him to," Mom said, which baffled me as much as it warmed me, as Dad never went anywhere. It really got me thinking, if Dad was willing to go, then maybe I should. He obviously thought somebody needed to.

Brent, Mom, and I stayed up a while longer talking. I went to bed at 10:00 p.m. That in itself was a miracle. But I was so worn out, and I knew I had to be fresh in the morning. I had more work to do. Plus, I needed to get some sleep in case Victoria called.

Realizing I hadn't had a chance to tell any of our friends the news, I sent out a group text. I told them the situation, asked for urgent prayers, put my phone on charge, and crawled into bed. As I closed my eyes, my phone rang. It was Sebastion. I didn't answer; I just let it go to voicemail. I'd deal with it tomorrow.

I slept soundly until 3:42 a.m. when I heard my phone "ding." It was Victoria! She had texted me!

> *My phone wasn't working until now. Mom, they wanted you to come with me and so did I. I had a lot of stress about it because they spent $1,000 on my ticket, and if your answer was 'no' then I wasted their money, and I was also afraid of you yelling at me or punishing me for even asking to go, but I really, really wanted you to come.*

I turned on the lamp sitting on my bedside table and dialed her number. No answer. I texted:

> *I tried to call you! Please answer the phone!*

I called again, no response.

> *Please stay where you are! Victoria, please let me come there! I can still go with you! I'd love to meet him and his parents! We'll ride the last flight together, baby! If he loves you, he would want to meet your family.*

> *Please don't go anywhere! Please answer the phone so I know you're okay. I need to hear your voice! Please!*

I tried calling several more times with no answer.

> *Your phone keeps going to voicemail without even ringing. I need to know you're okay!*

> Moments went by and I texted again, *Because you won't answer, I'm extremely worried about you. We don't mind that you went, we just want to know you are safe. Why aren't you answering me, baby?*

Finally, I received a text back, *I'm trying to call. My phone won't let me. Probably because I'm not in the U.S.*

I replied, *It's okay that you went. We just need to know you're okay.*

Victoria responded, *Mom, I'm sorry for hurting you and Dad.*

I then made a call to our cell phone company to see what I needed to do. They assured me that she should be able to call me.

The cell phone company said you could make calls from anywhere., no problem! Please, go to a desk and ask to use the phone. Call collect and I will accept the charges. I need to hear your voice. I need to know you're okay. Where are you right now?

Mom, I'm fine. Everything is okay. I'm trying to call.

It had occurred to me that I might not even be talking to her. How would I know? I needed to hear her voice!

By only texting, I don't know if I'm really talking to Victoria!

It's not working, she replied.

Go to a landline! Go to a desk!

So, you want their numbers? And talk to them? she texted, referring to the boy and his sister.

Yes! What are their names? Where are you? Please give me their numbers and their address. Make sure your phone is not in airplane mode. If it is, turn it off!

This is Tanvi's number. She is his sister and also wants to talk.

She must have been texting with them and me, and that was the reason for the long pauses. I tried calling the number she gave me. No answer.

Thank you, honey, but it's not working. I'll keep trying!

A couple of minutes later with no success in reaching Tanvi, I was getting fed up and determined to speak to Victoria one way or another. This was ridiculous. I texted Victoria again.

Go to a desk right now and ask to use the phone. Or ask someone to borrow their phone. I need to hear your voice to know you're okay!

I was adamant. Why was she withholding just hearing her voice from me? Why wouldn't she simply give me the peace of mind of knowing it was really her and that she was okay? Was that too much to ask? For God's sake, just find a phone! I was dying!

Instead, I got another text from her.

> *Their parents can't have a full conversation in English. Let me give you his number, too.*

> *Where are you, Victoria?* She still had not answered my question.

> *They said we will all video chat with you and Dad when I get there. I'm at the Hong Kong gate. Waiting for my last flight.*

> *No! Not video chats when you get there! I need to hear your voice NOW! You could be in great danger. None of this sounds right! I don't even know if this is Victoria.*

I was beginning to feel sick and had a sense of hopelessness and exhaustion; I wanted to cry. It seemed I was getting nowhere. She could be slipping right through my fingers. Maybe she was already gone. I needed to hear her voice!

Brent was sleeping soundly right next to me.

> *This is Victoria! Let me get them to call you.*

> *I can't believe it is you unless I hear your voice!* Why was that hard to understand?

Then a picture of her came through. She had the phone in her lap and pointed it up at her face as she stared straight ahead. She was wearing a black T-shirt, her hair flowing over one shoulder.

She looked beautiful, innocent, a little anxious and tired, but who wouldn't be, doing what she was doing? I hoped this wasn't the last picture I ever had of her.

I'm alone at my gate, was the message next to her picture.

That picture is not enough!!!

Please stay where you are and let me get there, so we can ride the last two flights together!

You can't come without a Visa, she texted me.

I have one.

Really.

Yes! Of course, I didn't, but I may as well have had one. Consider it done, gosh darn it! I would do whatever it took to get one!

Tell me something only you would know! What airline you are taking next?

Mom, if I stay in Hong Kong for twenty-two hours to wait for you, my phone will die. There is no American outlet on the wall.

What is the flight number? I need to see your itinerary. Take a picture of it and send it to me so I will know where you are. What time does your flight leave Hong Kong? Please don't get on it!

She sent me a flight confirmation showing the times of the two flights from Mobile to Dallas, and from Dallas to Hong Kong.

I need to see the next two flights.

Mom, please. I'm in line. I will send you a pic with proof, please trust me.

What? In line for what? I can't believe this is happening!!!! Everyone is worried about you, Victoria. Please don't leave us! Please!!!!

I lost connection, she replied after a few moments.

Dad, Grandma Priscilla, Grandad and Isabel, Grandma Jeannie and Paw Paw, Luke and Preston, Uncle Seb; they have all tried to text you. They want you to stop and come home! We are all worried sick!

Can you give us your Apple ID and password? It may help us call you.

When are you planning on coming back? You could be in serious danger!

You don't know that you're not in danger!

Haven't you heard about scams on the internet? Preying on young, beautiful girls? American girls?

India, especially the part where you are going, is known for that!

India is popular for sex trafficking. You could end up a sex slave. They won't tell you that, but it's their way of life over there and they think it's okay.

There's really not a law over there. They can do anything to you without getting in trouble or being found out!

Once you are in India, there is NOTHING I can do if this turns out bad! NOTHING!

Please listen to your God-given intuition. It is what naturally protects you, by letting you know when you are in danger.

But it's very, very quiet. You must listen.

When you feel it, run the other way! Like the little boy in the movie.

You left your Bible here. Isn't it important to you?

Please send me your itinerary ASAP!

That photo you left of his sister reading that book; they definitely influenced you. That's what I'm worried about.

You got a one-way ticket! Not a round-trip! They won't pay for you to come back! They may never let you leave!

When you are in a foreign country, everyone is smarter than you. You don't know anything about their customs or culture. You will be at their mercy to let you come back.

You are killing us! This hurts our hearts more than you could ever know!

I tried calling the sister. She texted me, but she will not answer, just like you are not doing! This is not right!

If something bad happens to you, and you don't come back, we will be sick!

We won't be able to work. We will lose everything!

Give me your passport number. Once you land in India, I may never see you again!

Why did you do this to us, baby? I kept telling you, you could go places, and I encouraged you to go, but to please talk to me first. I could have gone with you!

I believe you may have been deceived! You do not know people just because you talked to them on the phone or through the internet!

She was not responding. I tried calling the sister again. This time, I got an answer.

CHAPTER 9

CONVERSATION WITH A CAPTOR

"Hello?" a female voice answered with an Indian accent. "This is Destiny Harris, Victoria's mom," I stated firmly.

"Hello Mrs. Harris, how are you doing? Everything is fine, your daughter is safe with us."

"Let me talk to Ranjit," I said, and she handed the phone over to him.

Hearing my frantic voice, Brent was now awake. He sat up in bed as he listened to the conversation.

"Is this Victoria's mom?" a high-pitched, soft voice of a young man with an Indian accent asked.

"Yes, this is Victoria's mom. What are you planning on doing with my daughter? Why did you take her from me? From her home? Without telling us!"

"We just want to meet."

"Why couldn't you come here? Why did she have to go to you? The women aren't supposed to go to the men, you are supposed to come to her!"

"I cannot come to the U.S. unless I am married."

"You don't have a passport? You can't even come visit?"

"No, I can't come there. I assure you, Mrs. Harris, I am Hindu religion. I am not Muslim," as if it made any difference to me. His voice was very calm and docile.

"What do you mean? I don't know either one," I said, not sure what he was trying to tell me.

"Muslims are not good. I am Hindu, there is a difference. They are worse." I was sure he was trying his best to reassure me, but it wasn't working. I didn't know the difference, and frankly, I didn't care. All I wanted was my daughter back home and safe. I didn't trust these people. Not at all.

Then he added, "I love Jesus," for good measure, I'm sure, since he knew we were Christian. I was not convinced.

"You do not take a person from their family, from their home, and from their country! Good people don't do that! You are not good!" I stated angrily, my mind whirling.

"Mrs. Harris, we are meeting your daughter at the airport in New Delhi at 9:30 tonight so we can fly with her to our town in Amritsar."

"Give me your address!" I said starting to break down a little, but still holding it together. I looked at the paper on my bedside table that Sargant Stone had found in her room with an address in India written on it. He recited the address exactly as it was on the paper.

"You did all this without telling us! Is that how you do things in India? Because that's not how we do things around here!"

"Can I call you Mom?"

I was shocked and horrified. My daughter's abductor was asking me if he could call me Mom?

"No. No, you may not," I told him simply. "As soon as you see my daughter, I want a video chat with her! Do you understand? I want to see my daughter and hear her voice! I want to see that she is okay and unharmed!"

"Mrs. Harris, if anything will happen to your daughter, you can take action on me. As soon as we get to her, we will do video chat. Everything is fine; don't worry. She is safe," he said.

"I will talk to you when you reach New Delhi," I said as I hung up.

I looked back at the flight schedule Victoria had sent.

She had left the Mobile airport at 6:01 a.m. yesterday and had departed Dallas headed for Hong Kong at 10:44 a.m.

While I was at the gym finding out from her co-workers that she was going to India, she was already on a flight leaving the U.S.

It was now 6:30 a.m. I needed to get up and get dressed to go to the courthouse, but I was completely exhausted. I needed just a bit more rest. I closed my eyes and slept for what felt like another whole night but was in fact only about fifteen minutes.

VOICES
BEHIND THE SCENES

Meanwhile, text conversations were going on between Victoria and others.

Sebastion to Victoria: *Before you get on that plane to New Delhi, I want you to know I've researched everything, all those photos and letters they've sent you. This is a one hundred percent scam. It's all fake. New Delhi is a port for sex slave trade and you are walking into a trap. Look at this news article.*

I know things at home suck, but these men are going to get you in the car, and as soon as they are out of sight, they will drug you, and you will be tied down, raped, and tortured. They will sell you to people for sex. I bet they told you there will be three women there to meet you. It's part of their trade. They're all paid. My friend in California is doing a documentary on this exact scenario.

I have Homeland Security reviewing everything. They are looking for you in Hong Kong and will be waiting for you in New Delhi while your dumb a** parents are praying for the truth.

Let's talk this out. I'm coming to India to find these men. I'll go with you to meet them and visit, so we all know you're safe. That's all we want. You don't have to go with them, or home. Come stay with Sophie and me. If you ignore this, I want you to know I'll never stop looking for you.

Victoria to Tanvi (Ranjit's sister): *This is an article from my uncle. It's about sex trafficking in India. This is all wrong. I am safe with y'all.*

Tanvi: *Yeah! Okay!*

TUESDAY, SEPTEMBER 18, 2018

CHAPTER 10

S.O.S.

After speaking with Ranjit on the phone, I woke up thinking about what an awful dream I had. Then suddenly I realized it wasn't a dream. I lie next to my husband and confirmed it with him. Yes, it had really happened. Victoria was really gone. That sinking feeling hit my stomach again as I rolled over hugging the bed, and then slid out of it. It was about 6:45 a.m. Brent had to be at work at 7:00 a.m., so he jumped up and got outside to the garage.

I dressed in a hurry and exited our bedroom. Evelyn texted asking how things were going and I told her what had transpired the night before, giving her the address that Ranjit confirmed to me that morning, and told her I was leaving to file for emergency guardianship to have Victoria deported back home. I crossed the kitchen and headed towards the living room where I found my mom sitting on the couch in front of the big screen TV. My laptop was hooked up to it with my *Facebook* news feed on the screen.

I stood in the doorway looking at a post by my brother-in-law, Grant. It read:

> *My niece went missing. She left a letter saying she was going to meet someone in Amritsar, India whom she met online. We are obviously very concerned that this is actually part of a human trafficking ring. The boy's name is Ranjit Sharma. Any help would be appreciated.*

Oh, no, I thought. I felt bad for Grant and for the boy because Grant had stated his name. I didn't think that was a good idea. Soon, however, the post was gone. Maybe he had decided against it as well.

I appreciated the help. We needed to get as much help as possible, as fast as possible, but naming names wasn't something I felt good about since we didn't really know anything for sure yet.

Next, I saw my mom's post.

"When did you post that?" I asked her. She turned around and looked at me, "Last night before going to bed. I couldn't sleep without doing something! We had to get help!" she said looking at me with concern.

She had posted a photo from this past Mother's Day of Victoria. It had been the best Mother's Day ever. Victoria had prepared me a breakfast feast and given me, not one, but two dozen red roses!

This photo was one of Victoria and me in front of the vase of roses with the Mother's Day card. Mom had cropped the photo to show only Victoria and used it for her post which desperately read:

> *We fear my granddaughter is in great danger. She has a form of autism. She left a letter in the middle of the night and is flying to New Delhi (landing in Hong Kong in a couple of hours) to meet a man she met online. From all information we have, we believe it is very likely a human traffic ring has brainwashed her. If anyone knows anyone who can help in these areas, PLEASE let me know.*

Oh goodness. Did she have a form of autism? We hadn't had her diagnosed, but all the top symptoms were there, glaring at us.

It had taken us twenty-one years to figure it out, as it was so subtle. We lived with Victoria her entire life and although we all knew there was something different about her, something that didn't seem quite right, we weren't sure exactly what it was.

Then, about four months ago, while fasting and praying, I believe God had shown me not only what it was she had, but how she acquired it, and how to set her free.

I always felt that when something was going on with myself, be it a set of symptoms or anything I didn't understand, it was very soothing and comforting if I could define it. If I could put a name on it, I could wrap my hands and mind around it, and it didn't seem so big, or ambiguous, but small and something I could handle. It then became real, not made up or imaginary, but concrete.

As I fasted and prayed, I thought long and hard about Victoria's symptoms. Since she was a little girl, Mom and I had always felt she had a hint of autism because she didn't start talking until she was three years old, didn't like affection, and had social anxiety. I got out my laptop and Googled "symptoms of autism." Those three symptoms were at the top of a long list in which Victoria had almost every single one.

I had recently learned that a vaccine caused autism, but I never knew which vaccine. Then I was reminded of the day I took Victoria to the doctor when she was four months old to receive the MMR shot. Within minutes of receiving the vaccine, she broke out with red spots on her tummy. I was alarmed and asked the doctor's receptionist what was going on. She told me it was just a reaction to the vaccine and it was fine; it would go away.

God had never let me forget that day and only a few months after receiving the shot, I noticed changes in Victoria. She slept so much that she didn't nurse enough and we didn't get to bond quite like I did with the boys. While Victoria used to be a happy baby, she became fussy and frustrated even after just having a bath when most babies are relaxed. When she was only eighteen months old, she would get upset when Luke's overalls would fall off his shoulder and she would put it back correctly.

As she grew, she became very moody, and by the time Victoria was six years old, I realized this child was not pleasant to be around and it made me sad. We used to joke about how it was going to be when she came into womanhood and got her cycle; how we didn't know if we could handle more negative emotion. When that time came around, however, much to our surprise, we hardly noticed, which in itself was very telling. She was just the same as usual.

Thinking about all this, I just knew the MMR vaccine had to be the one that caused autism. I Googled "Which vaccine causes autism?" I took a deep breath and pressed the *Enter* key. *Bingo!* The MMR came up in my search. Putting two and two together; remembering Victoria's reaction to the shot and the symptoms that followed, and the result of this Google search, the mystery was solved.

I believed if I told Victoria what was plaguing her, and how she acquired it, that it wasn't her fault and it could have happened to any of us, that possibly, that knowledge, that truth, would be so incredibly powerful, that it would open a door in her mind and wisdom could enter, and God could heal her and set her free.

My hunch proved to be right.

Mom and I sat down with her one beautiful, sunny afternoon in the backyard in the brown wicker chairs underneath the canopy.

We each held her hand, my mom on her right and me on her left, as I shared with her what I believed God had shown me.

At first, she was angry, saying, "I'm not retarded!" as the only people she knew with autism had a severe form of the disorder. We had come to understand there is a spectrum with a multitude of little individual slivers along it, with varying symptoms and degrees. It is referred to as the Autism Spectrum.

I went on to explain, that "no, she was in fact, very smart; brilliant." I told her many people with autism are geniuses, and their brains work in a different way than the rest of ours, in ways that sometimes make it difficult for them to communicate with us the way we are used to doing. I explained that I believed she was on the *high-functioning* end of the spectrum, a part that made it incredibly difficult to detect, but no less real, as we all knew it had made life hard for her and us.

I went on to tell Victoria I believed it had been given to her through a vaccine called the MMR vaccine which, from my research, had been shown to cause brain damage that leads to things such as ADHD, ADD, paranoia, and schizophrenia as well as other illnesses, including autism. I told her everybody gets that vaccine and that we had all gotten it as children; that her dad and Preston had ADHD and learning problems, and that I even may have a tiny bit of autism myself, as I am not a very social person, I'm quiet and not a very outwardly emotional person.

I had always told Victoria that she is a lot like me, but to a higher degree. That day in the backyard, I tried to help her see that this was something that came from *outside* of her, it was not *a part* of her; that it *was not who she was*, that it *was something that happened to her*.

I had asked her at least twice as she was growing up what she thought these symptoms were. Both times Victoria stated she believed it was a chemical in her brain, and I agreed.

She knew she had anxiety. Specifically, social anxiety. She had a very hard time in social settings. In first grade, Victoria became the class clown, and at her birthday parties, she would act super silly. I didn't know it at the time, but she didn't like all the attention being on her and this was her way of dealing with it.

As she grew older, most days she would come home from school and sleep for several hours, then after she graduated high school, Victoria

63

would come home from work and do the same. I had often asked her if she was anemic and if I needed to take her to the doctor. I would later come to realize that she was so worn out from the intensity of socializing that she had to sleep off the exhaustion.

She didn't seem to know how to express herself, and we rarely knew what was on her mind. She kept everything bottled up inside and when she did let out some relief, it came in the form of anger, frustration, or laughter. Victoria mostly seemed to lack empathy. If someone was expressing their feelings to her or was upset with her, her face was expressionless; she was unmoved and sometimes she would even laugh. Later, we would come to understand that Victoria couldn't handle her own emotions, much less anyone else's, so she either clammed up or laughed to relieve herself of the pressure.

As a teenager, she would often borrow things from family members and not return them. It frustrated us because we were always looking for our items. One day her brother, Preston, was desperately searching for his laptop and when her dad finally found it, she was sitting in front of it at her desk. Her dad asked Victoria where Preston's laptop was and she replied she didn't know. When her dad pointed it out to her on the desk, she didn't respond. She was lying even when the evidence was right in front of her. She was six years old when she told her first lie and what bothered me the most about it was, it was a case in which she didn't even "need" to lie, and still she had. It didn't happen often, but it happened from a young age.

She didn't like to play family games or watch movies with us, but mostly spent time alone in her room. Victoria just didn't seem to enjoy being around us. Maybe it took too much mental energy to play the games, although she was good at it, and maybe too much emotion was required for the movies. I know she loved us; it just didn't feel like it.

I asked her one day, feeling frustrated, "Don't you love us, don't you care?" and to my surprise, she got extremely angry and shouted, "Yes!" her brow furrowed. Being upset by my questioning her affection for us, in itself, gave me comfort, and I knew she really did care.

Victoria wasn't an affectionate child. She certainly didn't seek it but mostly tolerated it. She had allergies and her skin was sensitive, which I later figured may be the reason for the lack of human touch.

And then there were the nightmares. The sleepwalking. The bed-wetting.

She had been slow at developing as a child and had a hard time in school. Victoria's kindergarten teacher was very concerned that she may have a learning disability. She repeated the first grade, even after attending summer school, and then was later put in a learning program.

She was gullible, not always understanding things; it just didn't seem she had matured for her age. The message I kept getting from teachers was "Victoria just needs more time."

Holding her back ended up being a great thing because it put her and her younger brother in the same grade and he was able to be there for her the whole way through school, helping her navigate everything from the hallways to schoolwork, teachers, and friends. Now looking back, I know that having someone there to share the whole experience with was truly the best thing for her.

I homeschooled both Victoria and Luke during eighth grade because I knew how bad middle school could be. I enjoyed being with and teaching them that year. We ran laps at the college track at 5 a.m. for "P.E." a couple times a week. They went back to public school for ninth and tenth grades. Then Victoria begged me to put her in private Christian school because the students at the public school were so mean. Luke went with her so they could stay together. After her eleventh-grade year in private school, she again begged me to homeschool her for twelfth grade and ended up graduating from homeschool.

I learned how to make green smoothies and started cooking healthier meals. I made three meals a day, five days a week, all four years of the children's high school and it made a huge impact on all of us. I was asked to teach smoothie classes and cooking schools at our church. Except for the occasional backtalk, we had no memorable problems with any of our children as teenagers. There were no drugs, alcohol, smoking, partying, sneaking out, getting into fights at school, or even cursing. They didn't date until they were older and didn't have a cell phone until they could drive. We felt blessed to have weathered what was supposed to be most parents' biggest storm.

Victoria was very good at knowing how to care for her anxiety. She knew what she needed. It's why she loved exercise, long hot showers. and sitting outside bathing in the sun. It was the reason she had become a vegetarian on her own at the age of thirteen and why she loved to laugh. It was all good medicine for her, that gave her relief and eased her struggles.

"I just always thought you were a lazy, selfish, brat," I had told her, holding her hand that day in the backyard under the canopy with Mom and telling her about autism, "but I sought first to understand, before being understood myself, and that's when I figured it all out! Instead of telling you how you were making all of us feel, I tried to understand you, and I'm so glad I did!" I smiled with tears in my eyes and a whimper in my voice. I could see she was taking in all my words, wide-eyed. She stayed silent as she listened.

That was only four months ago, and we were still getting used to and enjoying the new Victoria. We had not had a chance to have her diagnosed and now didn't feel the need to.

Within hours of telling her what I believed God had shown me, she was acting differently. She was in a good mood, coming up with ideas, wanting to go grocery shopping and cook with her boyfriend, and talking about their "future," even talking about having children. She always said she would never have children, that she couldn't handle it.

Within two days, she told me her anxiety was completely gone, and over the next four months, there would be so much to prove it.

Now this post my mom had put out there for the world to see made me a little apprehensive and uncomfortable with putting the word "autism" on her. I cringed, wondering what Victoria would think when or if she saw it. However, right now all that really mattered was getting help to save my daughter's life, the daughter who left her home, the home she rarely ever leaves. The daughter who couldn't find her way an hour to the beach from our house. The daughter who hardly came out of her room. The daughter who was now on her way to the other side of the world to meet someone she did not know!

What in this world could have possessed her to do such a thing? Something was not right about this. She had been naïve in the past, and she may not understand the gravity of her actions. From her letter, it surely didn't seem so. I knew what my mother knew: that we needed help, and we needed it fast, whether she had autism or not, but if she did in fact have it, it made the situation all that much graver.

I looked underneath my mom's post. It read *35,000 shares.* Just overnight, in less than twelve hours! Tears came to my eyes.

"That many shares! That's unbelievable!" I cried as I came around the couch and flung my arms around my mom, hugging her. "I can't believe it. We have that many people helping us!" It blew me away.

Mom was crying, "I've been getting calls all morning, private messages, and comments on the post. My friend, Tessa, called me early this morning. She knows someone high up in Homeland Security who's going to help. Also, Richard, from the Church Conference, who used to be a Director of the Conference in India (the one Claudia told us about), I spoke with him this morning. He is going to help us. He got me in touch with a human trafficking attorney named Amanda Rodriguez. She works with legislatures to get bills passed to help save girls. Then a lady who works with the airline, private messaged me and gave me Victoria's route information!"

"Really? That's incredible!" I cried, trembling.

I couldn't believe it! I was utterly overwhelmed. How could it be that this many people were coming to our rescue just like that? Just ordinary and some not-so-ordinary people, showing up to help us in our greatest time of need? It was an indescribable feeling. Help was coming from everywhere, some from people we knew, some we hadn't heard from in years, and many we did not know at all, but here they were, offering their help in whatever capacity they could. Some were offering prayers and scripture, while some gave us words of encouragement, comfort, and hope.

Mom put out a cry for help, and people answered.

I had never seen anything like it and it humbled me greatly as I began to praise God for sending us His love and care through these people!

I then shared with my mom what had transpired that morning, about my conversation with Victoria, and the boy and his sister.

"I guess we need to get going," I told her. "Are you ready?"

CHAPTER 11

SEEING THE JUDGE

We got into my black Honda. It was time to go to the Mobile County Probate Court to file the petition with the judge to see if we could gain temporary, twenty-four-hour custody of Victoria, so we could have her deported back home, as Sergeant Stone had suggested we do as soon as possible.

We had nearly left the street when Seb called. I could hear him talking to Mom on the other end.

"We are trying, Son, but we must be wise about it. We can't just do whatever comes to mind," she told him. "We're praying to God and we have a lot of people praying with us and for us right now! People we don't even know!"

"*God*? God deserted this family a long time ago! You pray to your God, but I'm going to *do* something!" he said, and he hung up.

"He thinks we're not doing enough," she said.

"Not doing enough?" I shouted. "I have not stopped *doing* since I found out. I'm trying! I'm trying everything I know to do! As if he thinks he could care more about her than I do! Nobody could. He thinks I don't care because I won't fork over two hundred grand? I would do whatever it takes!"

"Yes," Mom replied resolutely, "We must work as if everything depends on us and pray as if everything depends on God. We must pray while we run, and run while we pray, and that's just what we are going to do!"

The phone rang again, it was Dad. In the rush to leave and then talking to Sebastion, we had forgotten to call him. He hadn't wanted us to go downtown without him.

When Mom answered the phone and told him we were on our way, he laid into her, angrily. She handed me the phone.

"Dad, I'm sorry! We were going to call! I don't need this right now! Please!" I was beginning to cry. It was just too much.

"I'll meet you down there, and don't you go anywhere without me!" he shouted as he hung up the phone. "Okay," I said to the air, still sobbing. I hardly ever remembered him speaking to me that way.

"I can't believe him!" I cried, wiping the burning tears from my eyes, trying to drive while Mom handed me a tissue from her purse. I knew he only had our best interest at heart. It was clear we were all stressed, emotional, and overwhelmed by the magnitude of what was happening.

Soon, we were pulling into the white gravel parking lot behind the courthouse. It was 7:50 a.m. The courthouse opened at 8:00 a.m. In no time, Dad's black Chevy pulled in beside us.

As I walked towards the front door, I got a text from Evelyn asking what the boy's last name was.

Sharma. Or could be Samrat. Not sure, I texted back.

She then sent me a flight confirmation.

This is the flight she is on. I have a friend in Switzerland who is a computer wizard. He is doing everything he can to hack into her computer. The confirmation showed the time she left Hong Kong and the time she was to land in New Delhi.

How long do we have, Evelyn?

About an hour.

Any luck with the custody thing? she asked.

I'm about to file now, I texted as I walked into the courthouse with Mom behind me as Dad waited outside.

I'll check out this address; did you get everything sent over to Troy? Just then my phone was ringing. It was Victoria! The first call from her since she left!

"Victoria! Honey! What's going on? Where are you now?" I asked, leaving Evelyn's text unanswered.

"I'm in the New Delhi airport. There's a long delay."

She had landed earlier than Evelyn's estimate.

It was about 7:00 p.m. New Delhi time. Ranjit and his sister, Tanvi, were supposed to be meeting her in two-and-a-half hours.

"How long are you planning on staying in India?"

"Two months. Then I'm coming home. My manager, Rachel, said she would hold my job for me until I get back. I just want to meet him and his family."

"They told me they would video call once they were with you," I said as I walked back and forth down the hallways, looking for the place I was supposed to be, with Mom in tow.

"Victoria, call me back in a little bit, okay honey? Call me once they get there. I love you!"

71

"Okay, Mom. I love you, too." It was incredibly hard to hang up that phone. All I wanted to do was talk to her, but time was of the essence and I still hadn't found the correct office.

Once I found where I was supposed to be, I told the lady behind the window what my business was and she handed me a form to fill out and made copies of all my identification. There were several things she needed from me such as Victoria's birth certificate and something showing that Victoria had a learning disability in school or a doctor's note, anything showing she may not be capable of making the best decisions. All those things were in my office.

Dad drove us back home, and he and Mom waited outside while I rummaged through filing cabinets where I kept all the children's school and employment information. In no time, I found Victoria's documents from the learning disability programs in school and the comprehension skills testing they had done. As I was about to leave, Evelyn called.

"I spoke with Victoria," she said, "I tried to reason with her. I told her that I had done the same thing she did. I left home and left my country at eighteen years old, and I was raped. I told her it's not safe and she will be drugged and raped by thirty men in the same day, and she told me, 'It's worth the risk.'"

"*Worth the risk?* Oh, my goodness, then she is out of her mind! She is not thinking clearly, Evelyn!"

"I know. It's sad," she said. "She just doesn't believe that anything bad could happen to her with him. Love is blind."

"It sure is," I said, taking a seat on the edge of my desk for a moment.

We talked a bit about what we could do to help Victoria once she was home.

"She could live with me for a while. Later, maybe she could apply to the University in Seattle, and room with Belinda there. It might be good for her," Evelyn proposed.

"I agree, that's a good idea. She may want some space away from home when she returns. If she was interested in going away and rooming with Belinda, that would be great as well." We chatted a bit more, then I told her "I've got to go. If I can get emergency custody, I might be able to have her sent back home before Ranjit and his sister arrive there to meet her."

Once back at the courthouse, the lady behind the glass window made marks and signatures on the papers I had given her and handed me the petition to have it notarized, telling me there was a bank on the corner where I could have it done.

Back outside, I informed Mom and Dad of the next hoop we had to jump through. All three of us began walking downtown looking for the bank. We were having trouble finding it. I walked up one side of the street, while my mom walked down to the other end.

Then Evelyn texted me.

That address doesn't exist, Destiny. It's a bakery!

My stomach sank for what seemed like the millionth time.

I desperately texted Victoria, showing her the address.

THIS ADDRESS DOESN'T EXIST!

VICTORIA RUN!

GET AWAY BABY, PLEASE!

This is the address he gave me this morning! He's lying!

WE HAVE TONS OF PEOPLE LOOKING FOR YOU, BABY! TONS!

I quickly searched for the human trafficking hotline and sent it to her.

Text 233-733 or call 202-657-4006 FOR HELP NOW!

I then got very desperate. I called Congressman Bradley Byrne's office. I don't know how I knew to call them; I just did. I explained my situation, crying and short of breath as I paced up and down the street.

"I'm sorry ma'am," a young lady on the other end said, "but that's out of our jurisdiction. Call the FBI."

"I already talked to the FBI! They said it was out of their jurisdiction! Please help me! Please!" I cried desperately.

"Oh? Alright. Hold one second." She quickly came back on the phone.

"Ma'am, where did you say she is right now?"

I regurgitated all the information I had and texted her the flight information Evelyn had sent me.

"Okay, ma'am we're going to get you some help. I believe we have people over there right now. I'm going to call you right back, okay?"

I thanked her profusely and hung up.

I was beginning to feel disoriented, and a little sick. It was now about 9:30 in the morning. The street looked like a ghost town. There was absolutely no one anywhere. Either everyone was busy in their offices or I was completely unaware of any other person around. I was getting blisters on my heels. I sat on some steps and removed my shoes to rub my feet.

I looked down the street. I was on one end, and Mom was on the other end, looking around and talking on the phone. Dad was right in the middle between us both, nervously smoking a cigarette and looking back and forth at Mom and me. It was like he was watching a tennis match. I'm sure he was thinking, *How in the world am I supposed to keep up with these two women and make sure nothing happens to them?*

We were trying to stay together and I could still see them in the distance several blocks away.

Kelli then texted and I gave her the flight confirmation Evelyn had sent me.

What do you think about calling the airline and claiming she is a terrorist with chemical weapons? They would have to detain her at the airport. Were you able to put an alert on her passport? Don't have the number, I texted back.

I have someone en route to the airport now to find her! she texted.

I just spoke with the Congressman's office at the State Department and they are supposed to be sending someone to her as well, I texted. *I'm also trying to get emergency guardianship, so they can actually do something. Since she is of age, all the State Department can do is stall her,* I replied.

Maybe we can get enough people to show up, to scare off the people picking her up, Kelli texted. My contact has senior people in Immigration and Customs in India. He has someone at the airport now, on their way to find her. He needs her passport number or social. I completely trust him, if you are willing.

I sent a photo of something that looked like it could be a passport number along with her social security number.

I'm not sure, but these notes could be something, I texted back, still sitting on the sidewalk.

Evelyn then texted me,

Did you send Troy, the private investigator, the address and the information he asked for? I just spoke with the State Department,

Congressman Byrne's office. They are sending people to the airport to find her, I texted back. Ask them if they can stop her and tell her to video chat, so you can see her. Just then my phone rang. It was the lady from Congressman Byrne's office.

"Hello, ma'am? We have U.S. Marshals in the airport in New Delhi where your daughter is. We are sending them to check on her. Don't you worry, Mrs. Harris, we will try to delay them and ask them questions. Maybe she will get the picture, this is serious."

I felt as if she had told me she was sending an army of angels to help my daughter! I'm sure there *were* armies of angels there as well!

"Oh, and Mrs. Harris," she continued, "we are also able to expedite your passports and visas in case you may need to go over there."

I couldn't stop crying. I felt like I had just won the lottery. After being told countless times that no one could help me, that it was "out of their jurisdiction," finally I was getting real, physical, authoritative help! From the U.S. government!

Up until this point, it had never entered my mind that there could be people already there, in India, who could help stop her, let alone *our* people, from *our* government. I had never had to concern myself with international affairs. Of course! They had people already there! How wonderful! They were also going to see to it that our next step was already underway in getting us there as quickly as possible. I could never thank her enough for what she had just done.

Hopefully, we wouldn't need to go. If I could just find this bank and get this petition notarized, we could have her sent back here before she got on that last flight.

I caught up to Mom and Dad and told them the good news. We then turned a corner and found the bank we had been looking for, and the petition was signed.

We returned it to the lady behind the glass window and then sat in the parking lot to wait for the judge.

Evelyn texted, *Did you get custody?*

> *Waiting now. We were told it may take four hours. Pray the judge will give it to us if it's God's will.*

> *Amen. Here is the flight information for the last flight from New Delhi to Amritsar.*

> *We have six hours.*

We didn't want her getting on that last flight to Amritsar if we could help it.

Mom, Dad, and I sat in the truck ruminating back and forth through everything when Grant and Kelli called.

"We've been talking to Victoria, the boy, and his sister," Grant said. "Our next-door neighbor is from India and speaks Hindi. He was willing to translate. I offered to put them in a hotel if they would stay in New Delhi just one night until Victoria's family or someone can get there, and we can discuss this. They were not willing to do that, saying their parents wouldn't want them staying in New Delhi and they weren't willing to leave Victoria unattended, saying they had to take her with them. They were uncooperative and Victoria didn't seem to think she had a choice, saying she had to ask them what to do.

"My neighbor says they were being impolite and very unbecoming of their culture, and he told them, 'Indian people don't act like this,' and told them this isn't a safe situation for Victoria.

"Here's what really disturbs us," he went on. "We asked to speak to the parents, and the parents won't talk to us. Maybe the kids aren't letting them, maybe the parents don't know what they are up to; we're not sure. The kids gave the excuse that their parents don't speak English, but we have an interpreter, and they still won't talk.

"If they care about her, they should want to talk to Victoria's family, and if they don't want to look bad, because this looks bad. When we asked to talk to their parents, they hung up on us and we haven't been able to get them to answer since. It's scary that the only way we can talk to her is on his phone."

We talked a little more and Grant mentioned, "Maybe this could be bringing the family back together." There had been a rift between Grant and Kelli, and Brent and me. Even though the rift started over twelve years ago, things had not been the same since.

It happened one night while on a family beach vacation. There was a disagreement between Brent and Grant, and then again between Brent and Kelli. Both times I told Brent not to argue with them; they're stubborn; you can't win. Grant overheard it and the second time I said it, he got offended and shouted something with the F-word. Grant said this in front of our then eight, nine, and twelve-year-old children as well as his parents and our whole family. Then he and Kelli stormed off to their bedroom and the night of fun was over. The next day Grant unexpectedly charged us $550 for our short weekend stay in a tiny bedroom with his parents and our kids (seven of us) crammed like sardines in the small room. We felt it was done in spite and we never stayed together again.

Now that we were working so hard together for Victoria, and Grant mentioning it might mend the rift, I was beginning to feel God could be using this tragedy for good.

Before long we got a call that it was time to see the judge. We told Grant and Kelli we would be in touch as we made our way back to the courthouse. Once there, the lady behind the window opened a door for us that led to a large office.

A man came in and sat down behind a desk. He was wearing a light blue button-down shirt and dress pants. He had short gray hair and blue eyes. He looked like a judge. As he sat at the desk, he informed us that he was not the judge, but the judge's clerk. He then said something that surprised us.

"I already know about this case. I know your story. I heard about it last night. I was at a social gathering and a young policewoman told me about it, so it's very interesting that you are sitting here before me today." He seemed very surprised by the fact himself.

"Where is Miss Victoria right now?" he asked.

"She's in New Delhi, India, sir," I piped up.

"Well, unfortunately," he said, "Since she's in India, we don't have jurisdiction over this matter; she would need to be in Mobile County for us to be able to do anything. I'm sorry."

Boy, if I had a nickel for every time I heard that the past two days.

Just then my phone rang. It was Victoria. I barely had a chance to talk to her earlier.

"It's my daughter!" I interrupted excitedly, as Dad was asking the clerk some questions. "Thank you for your help; please excuse me!"

The clerk nodded with a smile. I exited the office into the hallway with Mom behind me.

CHAPTER 12

NEW DELHI

"Mom!" Victoria exclaimed. "There are guards all around us! They are asking Ranjit questions. They are questioning all of us. Mom, they are going to send me back home; you've got to tell them I'm okay. Tell them I'm safe," she said anxiously.

"Victoria, they are only making sure. They are there to protect you," I said trying to sound calm, quenching any excitement in my voice.

"Mom! They are going to make me come back home!"

"They are just checking on you," I said trying to calm her down. *I wish they could take you back home,* I thought. I looked wide-eyed at my mom who was listening as I gave her a thumbs up. "Victoria, please do not leave that airport!"

"I have to go; they are talking to me," and she hung up.

Mom and I looked at each other in wonder, then smiling from ear to ear, we let out a sigh of relief, accompanied by a chuckle, "Oh, thank God! They're there!"

Any news? Evelyn texted.

> *We didn't get custody. The U.S. marshals are surrounding and questioning them. We believe Victoria is starting to feel concerned and barriers are being broken down with all the attention they are*

getting. I then told Evelyn what Pastor Mark said about the danger of the area and about the conversation with Grant and Kelli earlier about them not wanting to stay in New Delhi for one night.

How much time do we have now, Evelyn?

About three hours. Three hours until that plane departed New Delhi.

We should know something soon then, I texted.

I texted Kelli and Grant what was happening.

Is she willing to come home?

No, she thinks she's fine, but I think the guards' questioning is showing her how serious this is.

We spoke with her also, and she still couldn't believe they could harm her, Kelli texted. *I told her regardless of what she decides, to not let them take her phone from her. If she makes it to the Amritsar airport, we have a group that will be meeting her there.*

It seemed that we had given in to the fact that she was going on to Amritsar and we were preparing ourselves for that.

Any news on the court order? Kelli asked.

It didn't work. They told me she had to be physically in Mobile. I informed them we had three hours until the plane departed New Delhi and told them I'd be in touch.

Again, Brent texted, *Victoria, please call us. You are killing me and your mom. This is not how anyone wants to spend their birthday.*

We don't care if you're going, we just want to go with you. We want to make sure you're alright. Please let us come with you!

I hope you know your mother and I are not going to survive this. You're literally ripping our hearts out. We can't even function.

✦   ✦   ✦

It was now a quarter to three in the afternoon and we were famished. So, Mom, Dad, and I set out to eat at one of the restaurants downtown.

It looked as if someone would be going to India to get her after all. At least we already had the process underway. I just needed to wait for Congressman Byrne's letter to expedite our passports and visas.

We drove to *T.P. Crockmier's,* a nice place with a piano and a sax playing jazz. There was a winding black iron staircase towards the back and it was a relaxing atmosphere. Dad came there sometimes. He ordered a seafood platter, the one he always gets. My mom, a sandwich and fries, and I had a bowl of black bean soup with hummus and bread. Even though I was hungry, my stomach was still in knots and I couldn't eat much.

After the waiter came and took our drink order, my phone rang. It was Luke. I stepped outside the front door of the restaurant into the crisp autumn air.

"I really wish Grandma wouldn't have put 'autism' in that post," he said as the cool breeze blew across my face. The fresh air felt extra good.

"I know, but I can't control Grandma," I told him. "We have gotten a lot of help. Did you see how many people shared it?"

He said he had. "What are you planning to do, now?"

"Well, it looks like we may be going to India. We just need to decide *who* is going. Her plane will be landing tonight, in a few hours, and I'm not sure how all this will play out. You need to pray, Son. I'll call you later."

"Let me know what you need me to do." He had made it home from Australia to California. I told him I would and we hung up.

CHAPTER 13

"DON'T GO WITH STRANGERS"

We made it back home and settled down in the living room for a bit of peace. The past two days had been a blur. The phones had been constantly ringing and texts coming through with Human Trafficking Agencies and Homeland Security asking questions or offering other information. Family and friends were calling to check in; some had new insight and some just wanted to say they were praying for us. The house had been in a constant state of buzzing, the dining room table filled with papers, and notes being made all over the place. It looked and felt like one of those police detective shows.

"This feels like a movie," we had all said at one point or another. It was the most surreal thing any of us had ever experienced.

Our day's work was done, at least outside the house, and we needed to rest our legs. I had two big blisters, one on each heel, from walking up and down the street. Dad's wife, Isabel, was on her way over.

"Dad sure had a time rounding us up today," I said with a tired smile. He peered at me over his reading glasses. Mom looked at me with pursed lips. Everything was so intense today.

"I would tell you if I was going to India," Dad said, "and I'm a grown man."

"Thanks, Dad," I smiled. "She thought I wouldn't let her go."

"And you probably wouldn't," Mom said. "At least not without talking about it first, and planning it out, to make sure it was safe."

"That would take me at least a year to plan, and if she was serious, her dad and I would want to go with her. I wonder if the reason the airline was delayed is because of her?" I asked.

"Could be," Dad said. "They were checking things out."

Then Mom's friend, Tessa, called saying Homeland Security had also been in the airport in New Delhi and was surrounding Victoria, Ranjit, and Tanvi, asking them questions. They were trying to cause a delay and make a big enough scene so that if anything *was* going on, maybe the attention could stop it from happening and scare them out of executing any plan that might be in play. They would try to discourage her, but couldn't stop her from getting on the next flight.

Then she said something astounding, "My friend, in Homeland Security, who has stood next to President Trump, said he put his eyes on Victoria and that she was unharmed, but they don't know what will happen once she gets on that plane and reaches her final destination."

"Wow!" I exclaimed, "U.S. Marshals *and* Homeland Security!"

Just then Brent came in to take a break. "What's going on?" he asked, hearing me about to cry.

"Someone who has stood next to the President had his eyes on her!" I told him, feeling incredibly grateful. Brent was taken aback by the enormity of the situation.

"I forgot to tell you earlier this morning, I missed a call from Vance. I just wanted to let you know," he said.

"Does he know?" I asked, slightly cringing, as Brent sat down next to me on the brown leather sofa.

"I'm sure he does, with it all over the internet," he replied. "I didn't call him back. I was too busy."

Vance had been Victoria's boyfriend. She asked her dad and me to help her break up with him just six weeks ago. He was Christian, handsome, an only child, and had a golf scholarship. He had his insecurities, and I'm not sure he was the best fit for Victoria, as they both seemed to have some of the same weaknesses, but that boy was smitten with her. She had broken his heart into a million pieces and I wasn't sure he would ever be the same.

We met him at the local café one night to execute the break-up and as we stood in the parking lot, he told us he believed she was cheating on him with someone on social media. He had urged her to stay off it, telling her it wasn't good for them. I had told him, "If she's cheating on you, then you don't need to be with her anyway." He didn't deserve that, nobody did.

I felt sorry for him to have seen it online. She not only left him, *She left me, too,* I had tried to text, but he had blocked me. It made me incredibly sad. I would have welcomed being there for him. My heart crushed and ached for him and for myself, and I wished Brent had answered that call.

Dad was looking at *Facebook* and got upset. "What is it, Dad?" I asked.

"People are saying ugly things," Mom replied.

"What ugly things?" I asked. How could there possibly be anything ugly being said about this situation? With all the outpouring of love and support we had received; it had not occurred to me that there could be anything other than sympathy for parents who had their child taken from them.

But apparently, Victoria had a whole other team of people out there supporting her "decision to be an adult," to find love, do what made her happy, and not let her parents try to control her or tell her what to do. Never mind the fact that this was a life and death situation, a mistake she may not live to learn from. I had given birth to her, raised her, loved her, and was looking out for her best interest. I was pretty sure this Ranjit person who had never met her, could not possibly feel the same way I did about her, no matter how much he said so on social media.

The comment Dad was referring to came from some guy here in the U.S. "Well, look at her! Why wouldn't he want some of that? I would, too!"

How insensitive, I thought. *Just a bunch of kids making fun. They think this is a joke. They think it's funny.*

There would be plenty more of it to come… enough to make us all want to vomit. From then on, we tried not to pay too much attention to it.

"Try not to look at it, William," Mom said to Dad, "It's just going to upset you. We've got to stay focused." Isabel had come in and sat next to him and agreed with Mom.

Al Gore, the ex-U.S. Vice President, commented on the situation, posting on *Facebook,*

> *Clearly, this guy is a loser. There are 1.3 billion Indians, and he had to obsess online over a girl from the other side of the planet. Trafficking is a for-profit enterprise. This type of "love" is like buying a car to have all to yourself. Ever watch 90-day fiancé? Sad and desperate.*

Calls and texts had slowed, but information was still trickling in. Mom's phone rang. It was Richard from our Church Conference in Washington D.C. He was from India and used to be in charge of the India Church Conference. He wanted to tell Mom about the plan for that night when the plane was to land in Amritsar, Ranjit's hometown, and Victoria's final destination.

As Mom spoke with Richard, I thought of all that had transpired in the last two days. Kelli and Evelyn had been so involved with helping, bringing their expertise to the table, and I was grateful for it. Now it was almost time for the big showdown. How this was all going to go, we weren't sure.

Our friends, Keith and Anne Thompson had been in touch with us after receiving my text the other night. They were some of our closest friends. They went to our church and we had known them for ten years. The day we met them, they felt like family. They loved us and our kids; they had dog-sat our little Maltese for us and had grieved with us when she died. They taught us a lot of new things and we loved them.

Keith had gotten me in touch with Chris and Laura Cotton, other friends of ours from church who had moved away. They were both nurses who owned their own clinic and had been to India on mission trips for months at a time and had just recently returned from there. Keith thought they could offer us some helpful advice.

We got word from Chris, that the amount the family paid for her plane ticket was equal to one year's rent, a substantial investment. He also said American girls with her characteristics: young, fit, beautiful, and pure, were worth about one million dollars. She was a lottery ticket. It was not sounding good at all.

We learned that President Trump had visited India the past summer, to have talks with them regarding the sex trafficking that goes on there. Someone told us India had recently been testing *Facebook,* the social media site where our story was taking place and they were sure it was getting India's attention.

"Okay, here is the plan," Mom announced, ending the call with Richard. "Richard said there is a family that are members of our church in India. The man is a doctor. He and his family are willing to go to the airport and pick Victoria up and let her stay with them if she is willing until you or someone can get there. The doctor, the pastor of the church, the youth minister, and their wives were called and are getting out of bed just now to go to the airport to meet her. It's 3:00 a.m. their time right now. If she gets on that last flight, it should be landing in Amritsar about two hours from now."

"Really? There are people getting out of their beds at 3:00 a.m. to go help my daughter?" I cried with shock and joy. God was surely working!

"That's what he said," my mom smiled.

"Wow," my dad and Brent replied simultaneously.

"That's crazy," Brent said. I could tell he was holding back tears.

"Thank God!" Isabel said, putting her hand on Dad's shoulders.

We were all in shock. *Thank you, once again, God, thank you.*

"Now," Mom continued, looking at me, "Richard said once the family gets to Victoria, the doctor is going to call you and hand the phone to Victoria so you can tell her that it's okay to go with them until you can get there."

"Okay," I said, "We have one hour left. Let's do this!"

Just then, Evelyn texted saying her younger daughter found Ranjit's profile on *Snapchat,* another social media app and she sent me a picture of it.

His screen name was *Bad,* and he had $$ signs in his eyes. Earlier in the week, Grant and I were looking through social media profiles and found another of his with a machine gun on it.

"Bad, huh?" Dad asked.

"Yeah, apparently a bad money-maker," I said with a frown.

I texted Evelyn, *Can they drug test Victoria in the airport? With her telling you she was willing to take the risk, maybe they gave her something to make her not care.*

Evelyn said she didn't know the laws in India and that we would have to check. She was texting Victoria, telling her to not get on that last flight.

> *Sounds like Ranjit is threatening or manipulating her by acting sad and hurt so she will do what he wants,* she texted.

Victoria's phone was not working. It seemed she was able to text, but not call, and had to rely on Ranjit and the sister's phone. Evelyn told her to go to a desk and call. The plane was scheduled to leave around 6:00 p.m. *our time,* 5:00 a.m. their time. They had been waiting in the airport since 9:30 p.m. the night before.

> *What are the plans of your group?* I asked Kelli who was having someone meet Victoria once she landed. *Because she is at the desk now, getting her boarding pass, and says she is going. She hung up on my friend twice. She won't listen to her.*

Kelli replied, *Our people are going to arrive before the plane lands, but they can't do anything to Victoria if she isn't willing to go with them.*

She sent me a photo showing plane tickets in the hand of Tanvi, and a caption that read:

'*We are coming Tor Tor!*' with a kiss.

This was on the sister's Snapchat, Kelli said.

It must have been from earlier that day when they left to meet her.

A tear came to my eye.

That's what we call her. Tor Tor. I put a sad face with a teardrop.

Now they had not only taken my girl, but they were calling her by the name we called her. My heart balled up like a fist, and at the same time, it was melting with hurt. But I was determined to stay focused and not let it deter me. I could cry later.

Kelli informed me that the flight had been delayed until 6:30. It was now 5:55 p.m. They probably had already boarded the plane for Amritsar.

There was a unanimous feeling that we were about to be a part of something big.

I informed both Kelli and Evelyn about Richard's plan to send the doctor, pastor, and youth minister, with their wives, to meet Victoria once she landed. Both Homeland Security and the U.S. Marshals had fended off or thwarted any plan or transaction that might have taken place in the red-light district of New Delhi. Now that she was headed to Amritsar, we would have these families from our church waiting to offer her a place to go instead of with Ranjit and Tanvi.

She has a choice, I told them, *She is either going with Ranjit, or she is going with the people we are sending.* What she would choose, only time would tell.

Lynette was in touch, making sure Richard had told Mom the plan and that everything was a go. She had been instrumental right from the start. If it wasn't for her getting us in touch with the Conference, we wouldn't have found somewhere safe for Victoria to go, and thus be leaving her in the hands of Ranjit and his sister.

Amanda, the human trafficking attorney near Washington D.C., had been watching Victoria's plane every step of the way and had been working behind the scenes coordinating the plans with Richard and the families who were on their way to the airport. She had been in touch with Homeland Security and was also watching for the plane to land.

We were all sitting, waiting. Evelyn and Kelli were waiting in their respective homes. We had ceased to hear from Sebastion since early that morning and didn't expect we would anymore after his remarks. Brent was keeping his parents informed and I was in touch with Preston and Luke. Everyone knew what was about to go down.

We still weren't sure if they had actually gotten on that last flight, we only knew when the plane would be landing, and Kelli had contact with a police officer who would intercept them on the ground once they did.

> *He said although he could not do anything to her, he possibly could to him, and said he 'would take care of it' whatever that means, and sounded very concerned, Kelli texted.*

Thank God we've got some authority on the ground, I said, but reminded her that the police there can be bought, yet she assured me this was a family member of a reputable contact.

I assume this is why they delayed the flight, Kelli texted with a photo showing some type of communication within the airline which read:

> *The poor woman doesn't know what kind of danger she is in.*

> *Thank you,* the airline worker responded, *we have sensitized our relevant departments, and are working on it.*

I then got a phone call from Victoria. She, Ranjit, and his sister had just boarded the plane for the last flight to Amritsar.

"Mom! There were hundreds of guards trying to stop me from getting on that plane. They asked, 'Are you sure you want to get on that plane?' They were scaring me!"

"Victoria, we have people meeting you on the ground there in the airport when you arrive. A doctor, two pastors, and their wives. They are going to let you stay with them until we can get there. Please go with them, okay?" I could hear her talking, but the phone was breaking up.

"About……leave……" I could hear her say.

"You're breaking up, honey," I said. A few more crackles on the phone and then silence.

"I'm not sure she heard me," I told everyone. I was sitting on the edge of the recliner in the middle of the living room, and Mom was in the one next to me. Brent was getting a quick shower, and Dad and Isabel were sitting on the brown leather loveseat, diagonally across from Mom and me.

"I think the plane must have been about to take off," I told them.

We waited an hour for the plane to land. Brent was now sitting next to me. Kelli had her police contact there to find Victoria as soon as she got off the plane and our people were already there waiting in the tiny airport.

It's in flight and landing in thirty minutes…all we can do is pray the police can intervene, Kelli texted.

Then a little later…

It's on the ground, taxiing now.

Evelyn was also watching the flight.

Arrived. She texted.

Fifteen or twenty minutes went by after landing when Grant called us. In the background, we could hear Kelli talking to Victoria on speakerphone.

"The police have split them up," Grant said. "He is questioning Ranjit and the sister and another policeman is questioning Victoria."

They were questioned for about twenty minutes, then I heard something strange. The sister said to her brother, "It's not worth it, it's not worth it. Let's go!" Kelli then repeated to me what Tanvi said. "She said, 'It's not worth it, it's not worth it."

"I heard that," I frowned, looking at my mom.

"*It*?" Mom mouthed, disturbed. I nodded; my brow furrowed.

"What does she mean by '*it*?'" I asked Kelli. "The plan? The plan's not worth it? Or is my daughter '*it*' and not worth it?"

"Yes," said Kelli. "I think the police and the questioning wore them down a bit and they seemed to be getting nervous. I think they were about to bail. At least the sister wanted to, but he was not willing." After a long pause, Grant said they would call us back.

He then texted me that Victoria was waiting to talk to the church people but couldn't find them.

Let me ask, I told him, then texted the doctor's son.

They are by the gate outside, I texted Grant.

Okay, Victoria is inside. She said she is willing to let them go with her to Ranjit's house.

After some back and forth we were finally able to get the two parties to meet.

Several minutes later Mom got a call from Richard in D.C. and she put him on speakerphone. I was prepared to talk to Victoria and tell her to please go with the church people.

"Okay," said Richard, "I talked to her. I talked to Victoria, and said to her, 'Victoria, the people there are from your church. Your parents want you to go with the doctor and pastors to make sure you're safe until they can get to you."

"I told her," he continued, "Now you have a choice. You can go with these people your parents sent, or you can go with Ranjit and Tanvi. You don't know these people, Victoria. *You don't go with strangers.* Go with the people your parents sent from your church.' She then agreed to go with the doctor!" he said.

"Oh, thank God!" I cried, letting out a deep breath, trembling.

"Thank you, Jesus!" Mom cried and we both profusely thanked Richard. There was no way I could ever thank him enough. He might have literally just saved my daughter's life.

"Yes," said Richard, "she was only worried that they had her luggage. Praise God we had success!" We said goodnight to Richard, thanking him again. I was grateful for his art, skill, and tact in dealing with her.

"Her intuition must have kicked in!" I cried, wiping away tears. "She trusted Richard and the church people. She must have sensed that it was safe to go with them and not with Ranjit."

"When he told her, 'Don't go with strangers," Mom said, "something must have resonated with her as if she sensed the danger or at least *questioned* her safety with them."

"Yes," I continued, "with all those guards surrounding them all day and at the last minute trying to get her to *not* to get on that plane, then hearing '*the church people*' and '*your parents*,' all of that must have come together for her and clicked." She had *listened*. She had heard the *still, small voice. Thank you, God, thank you for saving my little girl.*

The doctor Victoria would be staying with was named Mustafa. His son, Sanjay, texted me saying they had Victoria and were headed to take her to their home.

Kelli and Grant called and we talked for a little bit about what had just transpired. "Now you guys need to decide who should go over there," Kelli instructed.

"I think Preston and Luke should go," I said, thinking Victoria would listen to them and may not want to face us, the parents.

"Definitely, Luke," everyone agreed. Luke was her lifeline. Luke was her "Best Bud." She would listen to him.

"We think you and Brent, the parents, should go," Kelli said.

"I don't know… can we? Can we do that, Brent?" I asked him. We had to keep the doors to the business open. Somehow, we were going to need to pay for all of this. We rarely ever closed and this would be abruptly and perhaps for a couple of weeks. There would be appointments that would need to be canceled and, of course, losing half a month of income in addition to the cost we would incur and who knew how much that would be? But we had resolved to do whatever we needed to do.

"Let us think about it," Brent told them.

"Yes, we'll call you back," I said. "I'm going to call the doctor and see how things are going. They should have made it to their home by now."

Dr. Mustafa's son, Sanjay, answered the phone.

"Hello, Mrs. Harris," he said. He was probably in his thirties, very polite, with a soft, mild tone. I'm sure they were all very tired after having gotten up at 3:00 a.m. at the drop of a hat to answer the call from their pastor to help an American family. These were truly incredibly unselfish people.

"Hi, Sanjay. Did you make it home with our daughter okay?" I asked. I felt like we had just labored for her all over again and she was alive and being brought home safe just like the day we brought her home from the hospital after being born. In a sense, she was resurrected, born again, by being kept alive.

"Yes, ma'am. Victoria is fine. She is here." He then put her on the phone with me.

"Mom? Are you coming here?" she asked sounding a little anxious and impatient as her vacation had been interrupted and put on hold and she wanted to get back to it as quickly as possible.

"Yes, we are trying to figure that out. We are thinking Luke will come and maybe Dad and me."

"But you don't have passports or visas," she said concerned.

"I know. We're working on that," I explained. "Let me talk to Sanjay for a minute."

"Okay, but…."

"Hello?"

"Sanjay, we are trying to figure out which of us will be coming. We were thinking her two brothers, but maybe my husband and I should come. We have a business that we will have to shut down. We're just not sure," I said.

"Mrs. Harris, it will be good for the parents to come because our government always sides with the parents. She is of age, but in our culture, it is customary to do as the parents wish, so I think it will be a better outcome if the parents are here. The officials will listen to the parents on this," he said assuredly.

I explained to him the hurdles we needed to jump. "We will get there as quickly as we can," I said, hardly believing what we were about to do.

"Okay, Mrs. Harris, but Victoria isn't wanting to wait. The boy and his sister followed us home."

"*What?*" I could not believe what I was hearing. I thought for sure Ranjit and his sister would not know where they were taking her and would have no clue how to find her. I thought the plan was to escape. They didn't need to know where she was. We were supposed to be able to get to her, and then *if* and *only if* we wanted to talk to him, we would arrange it. *Our sole objective was to keep her safe until we could get there.*

"Sanjay," I said swallowing hard, "I didn't know they were going to follow you." Brent and Mom frowned.

"Yes, Ms. Harris, but Victoria is safe here with us. She is fine. You guys just plan to get here as soon as you can. We will be happy to keep her and we will not let her go as far as it is possible for us. We cannot force her to stay against her will, but as long as she is willing to wait for you, we will encourage her in that," he replied.

"Thank you, Sanjay. Thank you and your family so much. We will be more than happy to compensate you for your trouble helping us. You have done more for us than you know. We are so grateful, and we could never repay you for what you've already done for our daughter."

"No problem, Mrs. Harris. You don't owe us anything. Nothing is necessary. We are just glad we can help."

I asked to speak to Victoria again so I could tell her we were coming.

"Victoria, honey. Dad, Luke, and I will be coming. Just give us time, okay?"

"When? How long is it going to be?"

"Soon, honey, as soon as we can." She was pressing me for a time, so I said, "Give us two days. Can you stay at least two days?" I had no idea what I was talking about, I just wanted to give her some kind of time frame until we could figure some things out. Maybe it would get us down the road a bit.

"Okay, Mom I'll stay two days," she said.

"Thank you, honey. We love you so much! You get some rest and I'll be in touch."

"Love you, too," she said, as we hung up.

We then called Grant and Kelli and told them about our decision for the three of us to go and that Victoria had agreed to stay for two days until we could get there.

"Maybe that will hold her over a bit and we will see what we can get done in the next two days," I said.

Then Grant chimed in, "Uncle Frank says he can go with y'all as sort of an escort and help with talking to the family."

"That would be wonderful," I said, and Brent agreed. Frank was Brent's uncle and he had lived all over the world working as an engineer, so he knew about different cultures and as a businessman had done plenty of negotiations in foreign countries as well as had a lot of experience with travel. He would be a great help.

Now for the next step…. Kelli texted.

What next step? I asked.

Getting her home!

We thanked them for their help and were so glad for the success we had that night. We told them we'd be in touch and said goodnight.

WEDNESDAY, SEPTEMBER 19, 2018

CHAPTER 14
EVELYN'S VISIT

Wednesday morning came and it had been almost two days since we had gotten the news. After speaking with Victoria on the phone the previous night, I stayed up until after 2:00 a.m. trying to find the correct website to acquire the visas, finding out what documents we needed, and what procedures to take.

I got a little sleep and then was back up at 6:00 a.m. to see if I could either get a call through to the embassy in India to make the purchase or go through the website. I just wanted to make sure I was getting the visas from a legitimate source. I didn't need anything to go wrong; we were already behind the eight ball.

For the rest of the day, I was planning on getting a little rest and recovering while I waited for the e-mail from Congressman Byrne's office to get the expedited passports and visas.

I never sent the e-mail to Troy, the private investigator, with the list of things I had gathered for him. I also never heard back from him, which I found eerily interesting. I had fully expected that if he had not heard from me, he would be calling to find out why. Who wouldn't be, if they were about to receive a $10,000 deposit? I had given him no indication that it wasn't in my plans. I, myself, had been seriously considering it. Not hearing back from him made me think I might have scarcely dodged a bullet. Evelyn also never asked about it again.

There was still a lot I had to learn as we had never been out of the country before. We had hardly been anywhere. Our travels had mostly been in the southeast area of the country and except for visiting my brother out west a couple of times, we rarely left the nest.

I was a homebody by nature. I loved home and wasn't all that adventurous. I could say the same for my husband, but even more so. He could care less about going very far, he just had no interest in it. Suffice it to say, we didn't get out much.

So, there was a big learning curve ahead and I didn't have much time.

Just days ago, I was deep into my business, training a new manager, really digging in, to lift it to a new level, and it was as if I had been plucked up by the roots and suddenly thrown into a whole new world, one that I surely hadn't seen coming. But when life throws you a curve ball, you've got to swing or get pelted.

Monday seemed like a lifetime ago now.

Evelyn texted saying she wanted to come by; there was something she wanted to talk to me about. She also said my mom should take down her *Facebook* post now that we had found Victoria and she was safe.

She can delete it. I've deleted mine.

At about 2:00 that afternoon, Evelyn showed up and we both sat in the living room on the chaise lounge together. Evelyn began with some small talk, "I talked to Victoria last night as she was arriving there in India and she said it was like Disneyworld."

"Disneyworld?" I asked shocked. "What part?"

"Yeah, I know right," said Evelyn, "but that's what she said. Anyway, um, you should try to video call her." Evelyn showed me an app on her phone called *Whatsapp*, where you can make international phone calls, video calls, and send texts, all without costing anything.

"Well, I'm going to need that! Thanks!" I said.

"Yeah, no problem. Download it and you can go ahead give it a try."

I downloaded the app and video called Victoria. She answered but it was dark. I couldn't see anything.

"Mom, it's in the middle of the night. Everyone's sleeping."

"Okay, sorry honey. I'll text you." I hung up. I had completely forgotten about the time difference.

She was now on the opposite side of the world, making it about eleven hours ahead of us. So, if it was 2:00 p.m. here, I figured it was around 1:00 a.m. there, just change from day to night, and back up one hour, was how I calculated it.

She texted me first:

> Grandma's post still makes him look like a threat, and it's not helping. I'm trying hard to be open and honest with you, but you're making this hard for me. I made a decision BY MYSELF to come here without anyone forcing me, and I'm not under any influence.
>
> I'm just asking for a visit. Not a permanent stay. Grandma doesn't understand how much she is hurting him. Ranjit is in danger of prison. The police and the doctor I'm staying with, trust Ranjit and his parents and say they are good people.
>
> The only problem now is the mess Grandma created. I'm so heartbroken. This wasn't how it was supposed to go. We planned on doing so many fun things together with his sister and parents. Not everyone in India is a rapist.

My heart ached as I read the text. I didn't want her hurting. I didn't want to mess up her plans. God, I only wished she would have informed us so none of this would be happening, but there was no way to know if the family could be trusted.

Then I was reminded they had given me no reason to trust them. They had done the exact opposite. They had taken my daughter from me without my knowledge and had not provided her a way back home. She may have believed she was only visiting, but it sure looked permanent to me.

If they thought we were going to just sit here, on this side of the world, and let this happen, they thought wrong.

They had messed with the wrong family.

Furthermore, no authority had guaranteed me anything. No one had spoken to me about Ranjit's family or tried to calm my fears. I doubted any authority had spoken to Victoria either. She only knew whatever Ranjit was telling her. I simply responded to Victoria by telling her to get some rest, that I didn't mean to wake her, and assured her that it would all work out in the end.

I did, however, tell her we needed to talk to the parents, and that we had been trying to call. *If someone calls, they need to answer!* I told her.

She asked how we would be able to talk to them when they didn't speak English. I reminded her of Grant and Kelli's neighbor who speaks their language and who had spoken to Ranjit and Tanvi in New Delhi.

As I laid my phone down next to me, Evelyn proceeded.

"Victoria also told me Ranjit is the only one who understands her. He's the only one she can be herself with."

Those two statements sent shock waves through my body, and I looked at her wide-eyed and replied, "Well, *that's* not healthy!!!" This was *not* good. Not at all.

After waving those huge red flags, Evelyn went on, "I've also been video chatting with Victoria and Ranjit. Now I'm beginning to think this is not sex trafficking, it's just two people who fell in love. I ran away from home and went to another country when I was her age, as I told you, and married a man from a different culture and country. My mother didn't approve."

I was beginning to feel uncomfortable.

"Evelyn, I can't go by what you *think*. This is my daughter's *life*. We don't know the intentions of this family and Brent and I are going there to make sure she is safe."

Sitting there, I texted Grant and Kelli. *Has your neighbor been able to speak to the parents? I told Victoria they are not answering our calls.*

No, and Victoria has been ignoring our calls, too, Grant replied. We tried last night after her plane landed, which was early in the day for them.

I wonder why the parents are staying away, or why their children are keeping them away? I texted.

That's been the biggest RED flag for us, texted Grant.

They finally said they would talk to us after midnight. Kelli texted, but our friend had already gone home. We're trying to arrange a time with them, but they always say, they 'will be sleeping', as if we haven't all lost a ton of sleep over this. They are very selfish people and are not willing to compromise at all. We're going to try again tonight. They say they will call, but I'm guessing they will have another excuse.

Evelyn's thinking he's not that bad, I texted back, That he just wants to get married, so he can come over here. I believe there are too many suspicions to think that way. I must be prepared for the worst.

Even if it's just for marriage, Kelli texted, He has gone about this completely the wrong way and made the wrong decisions, even when we gave them options to make the situation better, and it would still mean they are only looking at her as just a way to the U.S.

I know. I'm trying to prepare myself for the fact that I may not be able to bring her back. She thinks she is coming back in a month or two, I replied.

Do you think someone from Eye Heart World who has dealt with these situations could meet with y'all to prep you for how to approach Victoria and interact with her? They may have some tips since her guard will be way up, texted Kelli.

I had spoken with Pastor Leite and had a plan, but coaching would be valuable as well. We also had Brent's Uncle Frank going with us. I had almost forgotten about that. I believed he would be the one doing most of the talking. Since Brent and I were younger than Ranjit's parents, and would not be in our own country, or our element, it would be nice that Frank, someone much older with experience in foreign relations, would be there helping walk us through the situation.

"Frank will be with us, but I will check with someone at *Eye Heart World*."

I told them to let me know as soon as they spoke with the parents and thanked them for their efforts.

Soon, some of our family including my mom and Brent's mom showed up with food, which was wonderful as I hadn't had time to cook or hardly eat, for that matter. Today was a day I could catch up. Evelyn stayed most of the afternoon and had lunch with us. It was mostly quiet now that Victoria was safe.

Fern called from *Eye Heart World* saying she found that Ranjit repeated the tenth grade four times and his parents say he is a problem child and a burden to them. Also, he didn't have a passport and had never left the area.

"That boy hasn't learned anything but his own plan," Mom said, "Fern said she could go with you to talk to Victoria if you wanted her to."

"That's very generous of her. Kelli asked me about having someone to coach us. I don't know. I don't know how this is all going to go."

I was thankful people were ready, willing, and able to step in and help. I was overwhelmed and wasn't sure how to manage it all. We had Uncle Frank, and I didn't want too many people there. It might get confusing. I also wasn't sure how Victoria would act with a stranger being with us. It could be good, or it might not be. I was unsure.

I shared Mom's initial post on *Facebook,* but I had not yet made a post myself, so that day I posted an update for all who were concerned and who had been faithfully praying for us. It simply read, "Victoria is safe, but please don't stop praying!"

Later that night, Belinda called Brent, and said the exact thing to him Evelyn had said to me earlier that day. We had a strange and unsettled feeling about it as we discussed it. It was as if they were trying to change our minds, to quell our fears, and make us feel safe in the face of danger. I saw a change take place in them that day, and I didn't understand it.

An e-mail popped up on my phone. It was the one I had been waiting for, from Congressman Byrne's office. I sent the attached letter to my printer as I trotted out the sliding glass back door, down the porch steps, and through the backyard to my office to read the letter.

Beautiful, I thought as I picked it up from the printer. With Congressman Byrne's letterhead and seal, and his charge to "expedite The Harris' passports and visas to the issuing office." This was all so surreal.

Brent and I would be heading to New Orleans, a two-hour drive from Mobile, first thing in the morning to get our passports. After that, I could focus on the visas. Just then I received a phone call. It was our friend, Chris Cotton.

"Hi, Chris Cotton here, Keith said you needed some help."

He and his wife, Laura Cotton, had recently returned from India after being there two months. He told me some things I would need to take with me, how I would need to contact my bank to let them know I'll be international so they will allow charges to my account, about logistics like taking an Uber using the app, and how to exchange dollars for rupees.

"A lot of people there speak decent English or at least understand it, so you shouldn't have a problem, but there's an app for that. You already know about *Whatsapp* for communicating."

He then told me about the culture. "In India, you are not considered an adult and not allowed to marry until you are twenty-one years of age. Almost all sons live at home with their parents their entire lives. When they become grown men, they will take on the role of the household, providing for and caring for their parents in that home, so essentially reversing roles, but never leave the home."

I had learned India was in a caste system, and how much money you made depended on the caste you were born in, and you couldn't change that. You were stuck; you couldn't move up to make a better living, so many people either moved to another country, or found other means to provide for their families, which weren't always kosher.

We also heard there was so much violence and disrespect against women in India, that they weren't even treated like human beings, but like animals, and weren't buried when they died, but left on the side of the road.

Chris reassured me that Indian culture is big on family and largely stands behind the parent's authority over what their children do, even after the they reach adult age. "Even though it's not law, it's culture and most will almost always side with the parents no matter what the age of the child."

That confirmed what Sanjay, the doctor's son, had told me the previous night. I felt much better after that talk with Chris. He also told me he would have a friend of his named Phillip, meet us there to help with logistics when we arrived. I was feeling more equipped for the journey.

Just then our friends, Hope and Nelson, walked into the office, escorted by Brent. I thanked Chris and hung up the phone.

"Hey guys!" I smiled. Boy was I happy to see them! After days of being knee-deep in harrowing details, it was refreshing and brought a waft of normalization to my life. I got up from the black leather chair and came around from behind my desk to give them each a big, tight hug.

"We just thought we'd stop by to check on you," said Hope sweetly, closing her eyes with a sad smile.

"Aww, thank you," I said, as Brent returned to the house where many family members and friends were gathered.

"Getting anything done?" Nelson chuckled.

"I think we're finally getting somewhere," I said, "Getting all my ducks in a row." I then went on to tell them what had transpired over the last two days and what we had planned next.

Just then Brent returned, "Finally got word from the mother. She claims her son told her Victoria was being abused, and they believed they were rescuing her from an abusive household."

"What?!" I exclaimed. "That's ludicrous!"

"Yep, just wanted you to know," and he walked out.

"That's insane!" said Hope, and Nelson agreed.

"Let's go inside. I'm done here," I told them. They followed me through the backyard and into the house to the dining room where my mom, Dad and Isabel, Brent's parents, and a couple other friends were gathered; where the stress and solemness of the last two days seemed to be replaced with relief and everyone was enjoying being together. It was a comforting scene to know I was not alone through all of this.

"Please sit down and help yourself to something to drink and food or snacks," I told them, as I went to answer a knock at the door. As I opened the door, there stood a boy about Victoria's age.

"Hi, I'm Austin, Victoria's friend. I saw what happened on *Facebook*. I just wanted to stop by and see how things were going. I sure hope she's gonna be alright." I remembered him now. He really liked Victoria and had one time brought her a stuffed blue bear and candy and left it at the door, "just because."

It was sweet of him to think of us. I thanked Austin for stopping by and told him I would let Victoria know. Our lives were truly on display more than I realized. People were watching this unfold.

"No, problem. Have a good night," he said as he left.

It was getting late and soon everyone was ready to go home. I thanked them all for coming, as they headed out the door.

I got a hot shower to soothe my tense muscles and laid down in bed to rest a bit, just thinking things over, and about what needed to be done the next day. It was getting close to midnight. Then Victoria texted. It was 11:00 a.m. her time.

Mom! The FBI is here at the doctor's house. They are investigating Ranjit. They were here and at Ranjit's house all day yesterday, and now they are back this morning. They're going to arrest him! I don't want him to go to prison. It's all because of Grandma's Facebook post. Tell her to take it down.

The FBI?! I asked. She must have meant the Indian FBI, I knew our FBI said they weren't able to do anything.

Yes, and the President is here and his high official.

The President of India? that certainly couldn't be right. Maybe she meant the mayor, or someone else.

> *They need Grandma to send a letter to the embassy saying it was a misunderstanding, and not human trafficking, and she needs to delete that post.*

> *Victoria, they don't arrest people for something someone said about them on social media.*

> *This is not a joke; you need to listen to me. Newspapers and police have been calling Ranjit's dad. We're really in a big mess. This is making my life a nightmare. I don't want to go back to the U.S. I've been planning this for months and I didn't want to meet them with inspections and police. Grandma needs to say he is not a threat, the officers are asking. Please fix everything!*

Okay, Victoria, I said, trying to appease her.

Thank God! Now everyone will be happy!

Mom, Ranjit is not going to be able to go to school tomorrow because of all this! And it's going to look bad on his record if he ever gets into college.

You mean he's still in high school? I asked, baffled.

Yes.

What? He's twenty, right?

Yes, but he failed his test to graduate. It's not his fault. It's the government. They made it hard for him to pass.

This was certainly news; although Fern with *Eye Heart World*, did say he had repeated the tenth grade four times. Twenty years old and still in high school. As if there wasn't enough already, here was one more strike against him. One more reason for him not to be with my daughter. This was not a person who was going to be a good provider. Even if everything was kosher, this certainly wasn't a characteristic I would want anyone courting my daughter to have, no matter who he was, American or otherwise.

I hope you can get here soon, she texted.

We are working on it. Dad and I are going to New Orleans tomorrow morning to get the passports, I assured her.

I can't wait for you to get here so you can meet them and see they are okay.

Me, too, Victoria, I told her.

As I lie there in bed, I thought back to what Ranjit's mother had said.

I wondered if when he told his mother we were abusing our daughter, if that is how he got the parents on board to pay for her tickets? It was plausible.

Or was it the parent's idea? Since their child was 'a burden to them.' I wasn't sure how the plan came about, nevertheless, they had executed it over a two-year span.

They had gotten her where they wanted her……almost.

THURSDAY, SEPTEMBER 20, 2018

CHAPTER 15

NEW ORLEANS

Thursday at 5:00 a.m., Brent and I headed to New Orleans to acquire our passports. It was a two-hour drive from Mobile and we wanted to be there when they opened. We left the shop in Norman's hands, the new manager, even though he barely had a week on the job. We would only be gone for the day and he had experience running his own business, so we figured he should be able to handle it.

With Congressman Byrne's letter, and our birth certificates in hand, I slid into the passenger's seat as Brent got behind the wheel and we headed for the interstate.

Luke would not need to get a passport. He already had one. All our children did. We had gotten them so they could go on mission trips at the end of their course of study.

Having never finished her course, Victoria ended up not using hers to go on the trip. However, it had fit perfectly into this plan. The passport was one step we had already done for her. It was sad that what we had meant her to use for good, was now being used against us.Some people had sent us checks in the mail and others were asking how they could help with the expense of getting to Victoria, so our friend, Keith Thompson, started a *GoFundMe* donation page called, "Bring Victoria Home."

We had just turned a corner when Evelyn's text came through.

Good morning, Destiny. I've been talking to Victoria and I need to talk to you and Brent. Is it okay if I come by?

Sorry, we're on our way to get the passports, but I can call you when we get back.

Okay, I have a plan to get her back, but we must be smart. Your mom, brother, and the Thompson's need to get those posts and GoFundMe page down, because that is just making her more rebellious and upset because you guys are hurting Ranjit and his family. Even though she understands why you have done it, she says it's not right to hurt and accuse people of being something you have no proof of. So please tell them to get those posts down.

Evelyn, you can relay to Victoria that the GoFundMe is to help get her family to her, I texted back.

I sure will. We are checking out Ranjit and the family again. Will let you know. The important thing is to get Victoria home.

Then a few minutes later.......

I have good news! Ranjit offered to send me a ticket to go with you guys to India!

To get us to India, you mean? I was confused.

You and I both.

We had just exited to the I-10 West ramp. As I was reading her texts out loud, I frowned at Brent.

We have means, but thanks for the info, I texted back.

I wanted *nothing* from him. He wasn't going to pay for *anything* for me. If he thought he was going to manipulate me, he was wrong.

He had paid for Victoria's ticket, which was a substantial investment, but now he was going to also pay for mine, Brent's, Luke's, and Evelyn's? This was a ploy, a tactic. I wasn't buying it, and if Evelyn was, she wasn't being smart.

> *He wants all of us there, including me, so we can meet his family and see his country.*

> *I bet,* I texted back.

> *Exactly, lol. I was like 'Nope.'*

> *Thank you,* I replied.

> *Anytime.*

> *Evelyn, another huge red flag is that the parents aren't talking to us. We have a Hindi translator, my brother-in-law's neighbor, and they won't compromise on even arranging a time to talk to us.*

> *If we were really ruining their reputation, they would have gotten rid of her, given her back to us, so this would go away, and not continue to be a problem for them. They could've let her go back when they were in New Delhi, and we were trying to get them to stay in a hotel so we could get to her, but they wouldn't cooperate. They have made their beds.*

> *I agree with you,* she texted.

This was a family situation. It was already complicated enough with the three of us going. I didn't need anything to make it more complicated, and I didn't like the way this was sounding. Evelyn was talking to him too much. *Way* too much.

Keith Thompson texted saying a reporter from *NBC 15 News* wanted to talk to us. She had contacted him via *Facebook* after seeing the *GoFundMe* page. Ever since he posted the page, he had become sort of a spokesperson for us, as we were busy making arrangements to get to Victoria and didn't have much time to talk to anyone. He asked if he could give her my number, and I agreed.

At 8:00 a.m. the passport office opened, and Brent and I walked down the street, hand in hand, to obtain what we needed to leave the country and get our daughter back. It was the first time we had been together all week. Brent had been finishing customer vehicles and rescheduling upcoming appointments so we could take off the week after returning from India to rest and spend time with our daughter.

As we turned the corner there was a large glass building with tall doors and a brick walkway in front of us. We followed the signs and took the elevator up to the third floor. As we waited in line, Kelli texted.

> *An informant said Ranjit and Victoria tried to get married at the temple today, but they wouldn't allow it until they hear from her parents. Have you spoken with Dr. Mustafa today? Do you know if she's been able to leave?*

> *The informant can only speak Hindi and isn't willing to give out his number because he is supposedly a cousin of Ranjit. He is willing to provide any information and will notify us of any movement. Hopefully, you can confirm that she is still with Dr. Mustafa.*

I will try to call him, is all I could text back. This was unbelievable. Trying to get *married?* I looked at Brent, reading him the text, and he could only shake his head. We couldn't comprehend what was happening. It wasn't registering. This was all so unimaginable. Sunday night we were having dinner, Monday she was gone, and now she's on the other side of the globe trying to get *married* in an *Indian temple?*

Our daughter, a Christian? Who only six weeks ago had a boyfriend, *here. This was utterly insane.* This was *not* happening.

We were next at the window.

I handed over Congressman Byrne's letter along with our birth certificates. Brent's was not an original copy. I hadn't thought much about it when I grabbed it from the file that morning.

"We must have an original copy," the lady told us.

Oh, no! I'm not believing this! If we have to drive all the way back home and order a copy from the Health Department, then drive all the way back, we may not get this done before they close today. Time was ticking. *Please, God!*

She took a moment and then, to our relief, said,

"We can give him a passport, but it will only be good for one year, instead of ten."

"Thank you so much!" I said, gratefully.

"I only need it for the next ten days. I'm never going to need it again!" Brent said as I elbowed him.

Now we just needed our photos taken and our passports would be ready at 2:30 p.m.

As we were on our way back down the elevator, Kelli texted a news article from the *Tribune* in India with a photo of Victoria on the front sitting between two ladies. It spoke of someone named Esha, who was Kelli's contact, who brought the matter to a Deputy and a Police Commissioner. A District Administration had sent a team to Dr. Mustafa's residence where Victoria was staying. I wondered if these were the people Victoria had spoken of when she kept saying the FBI and the President were there.

The article went on to say that Victoria would like to go back home, as her parents would arrive, and Ranjit's dad stated he would go by what the parents wanted. I skimmed through it. They had gotten a lot of details wrong, such as her age and state of residence, but that was to be expected as the media didn't always have all the facts straight.

Kelli texted again, *Esha visited Victoria twice today. She doesn't think Dr. Mustafa would've let Victoria leave and Ranjit was also there.*

Esha was a politician. *She is next to the President,* Kelli told me. *A high official. She's the one who helped us get the police there the night Victoria landed.* She then pointed her out in the article's photo.

Thank God, they didn't let her leave, I texted, as I was sure Dr. Mustafa wouldn't have let that happen, but still there was rumor they had tried to get married, making me wonder what else they had planned.

When I spoke with Esha, she said Victoria's well-being is in the hands of the state, and not to worry because they are watching her closely. Also, Ranjit is not of legal age to marry there, so that shouldn't be a concern. I have more information I received from her today, so just call me when you get done with the passports.

We exited the elevator and found the photo station. As we took the pictures, it was a strange moment for us. We knew these photos would capture all we were feeling that day. Even though we were told to use a neutral facial expression, we could not have smiled, even if we had wanted to. Our faces were solemn with the corners of our mouths turned down, and our eyes like deer in headlights.

Our passport photos taken that day

As we sat in the food court waiting on the photos, I received a text from the reporter. Keith had spoken of earlier.

> *Good morning, Destiny. My name is Mickie Benz, I'm a reporter for NBC 15 News. I saw your post about Victoria. I can't imagine how terrifying this must be for your family. I would like to help get Victoria home by telling her story and to raise awareness among our viewers who may be able to help with the GoFundMe.*

> *This could be anyone's child and trafficking is a terrifying and dangerous thing that many people don't realize is very much happening. Would you be able to meet and tell us how the community can help?*

We set up a news interview for 6:00 p.m. which would give us just enough time to get home.

She sent me a mock-up of the report that would go on the news preview for that evening so I could approve it. It had the word 'autism' in it, from seeing my mom's post. I immediately texted back:

MICKIE, IN YOUR ARTICLE, DO NOT PUT IN THE PART ABOUT AUTISM! It is not necessary. You can say she is introverted. We certainly didn't need that going on the television nightly news! Mom had put it online, but it didn't need to be brought out further.

Done, she replied and sent me the new write-up.

You will be meeting with Gracie tonight to do the full story. I wish I could meet you personally as well. I'm passionate about doing whatever I can to help. I can't imagine how scary this is. I am praying. Thank God you guys didn't wait. I have hope, and I hope I can meet Victoria when you come back with her from India.

Just then Evelyn texted.

Any news? Are you still in New Orleans?

NBC 15 News wants to talk to us when we get home.

Do you think that is a good idea?

It's the very first thing I wanted to do when I found out what she'd done. Communities need to know and the police couldn't help me.

Yes, I remember that.

At about 2:15, we headed back upstairs to retrieve the passports that would've taken months to get if it hadn't been for Congressman Byrne.

We took a number and sat in one of the rows of gray, plastic, bell-shaped chairs. As I did, my phone rang. It was not a number I recognized. I decided to answer it.

"Hello, this is Amazing Facts," a man's voice said cheerfully on the other end. "We were just calling to see if there was anything we could pray for you today."

They must know what's going on, I thought.

"Oh," I said, surprised, and about to cry, my heart was warmed. God was sending me help. "Do you know what's going on?" I asked.

"No," he said. "We just like to call our donors from time to time and see if there's anything we can pray for." Now he was the one who sounded a little inquisitive and his voice toned down a little, hearing the angst in mine.

"Oh, my goodness," I cried as I got up and walked over to the three-story window to look out. "Yes, yes, I desperately need prayer! My daughter got on a plane in the middle of the night to go to India to see a man she met online. Now my husband and I are in New Orleans waiting to get our passports so we might be able to get her and bring her back safely! We are so afraid of what might happen to her. I thought maybe you had seen it on the news or heard about it."

Amazing Facts was a Bible study ministry. Luke attended their Bible school after high school graduation, and Brent and I had been donating to them for the past year.

"*Oh my,*" he said soberly. He seemed to be thinking deeply about what I had just told him. "We're having a meeting tonight and I will be bringing your story to the attention of the group. We will say an extra prayer for you tonight but let me pray for you now."

He prayed a prayer of protection over our daughter and us, and for God to give us wisdom, and see us through the days ahead, then gave me some final words of encouragement. It was amazing to me how he was able to come up with words to say to someone in a time like this.

I hung up and sat down next to Brent. I told him what had just happened and he was surprised and thankful. He squeezed my hand. We both knew God was working on our behalf. I knew that call hadn't come at this point in time by mistake. It came to encourage us.

Evelyn then texted me.

This is my latest information:

I video-chatted with Victoria and Ranjit this morning. Victoria feels her reputation is ruined in the USA, but Ranjit told her to go back because things are not going well for their families.

She said she would come back with you guys, but to please stay one week to get to know Ranjit and his family. She said she feels bad you guys are missing work, and she would be happy if Luke stays with her for a week, and then she could come back with him.

Ranjit apologized many times and understands that the way they did things wasn't right, and he had told her to let you guys know about him. She now knows it would've been better to have told you, like they'd asked her to do.

He offered to pay for you guys' tickets to come there and get her. Furthermore, he said you guys could stay in his house, while he and his family stay in a hotel, or to put you guys in a hotel if you prefer.

She continued, I also talked to the doctor's son and he said Ranjit seems like a nice guy, and they wanted to take Victoria to Ranjit's house to visit. But Ranjit said, 'NO', very firmly, and that until you guys say she can, he doesn't want her to; his family has enough trouble as it is because of the decisions he and Victoria made, and he doesn't want to cause any more problems for anyone.

Ranjit told Victoria that her leaving with her parents is the best thing to do for everyone involved. And, once again, he was sorry for the whole mess, but that he really loves her, and wants the best for her, and said he would do whatever we told him to.

Evelyn wasn't finished. *He said he would video-chat with me later today so I could see their home and take screenshots so you guys could see it, and that his parents don't speak much English, but they are excited to meet you guys.*

Now that we have worked so hard to make Victoria see the error of her ways, and come back to her senses, and say 'yes' to coming home, we must be very careful how we proceed because anything that makes her mad and upset again will only push her back into his arms, and further away from you guys, and we don't want her to, out of anger or hurt, decide to stay in India.

I don't believe him, I texted back. The doctor's son gave me FIRM assurance that he would let her go NOWHERE without my permission.

Well, yesterday the doctor's son told me they were going to Ranjit's house, but because Ranjit said 'no,' they didn't go.

I believed it was probably the other way around, but just in case it wasn't, if she was telling me the truth, I was going to have to make some changes. I was beginning to get very concerned.

I will call the doctor because that concerns me. I have another place she can stay, I challenged her, letting her know I would find out if what she was telling me was true, calling her bluff.

I had a cousin who knew people who lived near there, and Kelli also had people she knew. We could find somewhere else for her to go.

If we moved her, maybe we could do it when Ranjit wasn't around. Then we could get her somewhere without him knowing, so he wouldn't be able to visit her until we were there. His knowing where she was, was such a huge risk to us. She could leave with him at any time.

Sanjay, the doctor's son, told me they had to let Ranjit visit. He said it was a law in India, that if someone was in your house that another person wanted to see, you had to let them in.

I thought it was the craziest thing. Sanjay reassured me they had the doors locked and the back gate locked, and that he, himself, or one of his family members, stayed with Victoria all day and they wouldn't let her leave as far as it was possible. Again, it was her choice, they could not stop her from leaving, but they would do everything they could to encourage her to stay.

He told me Ranjit and his sister, Tanvi, came every day and stayed all day long, sitting on each side of her, talking in her ears. He explained to me that by allowing Ranjit to visit, it was helping to keep her there and keep her calm, otherwise, she would probably already have been gone.

Just then, our number came up, and I went to the window.

Evelyn responded, *She is fine there, Destiny. I told them not to let her go anywhere until you guys get there, and I said it in front of Ranjit.*

She was pushing me.

I was very clear. I think moving her around would make Victoria even more defensive than she already is towards you guys, and I don't want that to happen.

Pushing.

We are just getting things back on track with her attitude and decisions, any little unthought could put us back where we were in the first place.

Pushing, pushing, pushing.

I call her many times during the day and Belinda does too. So we know where she is, and we keep her in her senses, and on track with our plan to bring her back.

I felt like I was being pushed against a wall. I felt a heaviness on my chest like I couldn't breathe. I was being put in my place. What was my place? Who was the parent here?

Didn't I know what was best for her? Wasn't it my decision? What do I feel comfortable with?

I was making all the sacrifices to get there, not Evelyn. I didn't need anything to risk Victoria leaving and ending up God knows where, and then we get there, and she's gone.

I needed her to stay right where she was, where I felt she was safe. And here was Evelyn, pushing me out of the way. I felt she was coming into my territory and taking over. She could be putting my daughter's life at risk.

If something went terribly wrong, it needed to be my fault, not Evelyn's. It needed to be because of my decision. I would take responsibility for my daughter; I didn't want it to be because of my having listened to Evelyn.

I would not be able to forgive myself for not going with my gut, my parental instinct. I trusted my instinct, and Evelyn was not sounding too good to me right now.

None of us knew how to handle this situation. We had no professional, seasoned counselors. We were taking it as it came. I didn't feel she was giving me advice anymore, but that she was now *telling* me what to do.

I am the parent. I will take your advice, but please respect my position also, I texted, as the lady in the window was ringing me up. She had us sign for our passports and gave me the receipt which included extra money to expedite. It had been made possible, but it came with a price.

Oh, I do Destiny, please don't take me wrong! I'm just trying to help get her back. I apologize if I overstepped! I will take a step back and stay out of the whole situation if you prefer......I was only trying to help.

I know you are trying to help, Evelyn, and I don't want you out of the WHOLE situation, I only asked for you to please respect my position as you help guide me! Please!

I do, Destiny. Always, she texted adding two kisses.

One step back, thank you, I replied with a kiss and heart eyes. *I'm just letting you know I do have other people she can go to, but I believe I'll be able to get there and bring her back. If she will not come with me, I am fully prepared to leave her with the consequences. I am not trying to force her, only woo her.*

I had come to the hard conclusion that, in the end, I may have to leave her there. I fully did not believe that would be the case. However, I had to come to terms with that being a possible outcome. After all, it was ultimately her choice, and if that's what she wanted to do, then I may have to let her face her fate, but I was going to do *everything* in my power during the time that I had there to make her see the light.

If I could talk to her long enough, I could talk some sense into her and she would at least get on that plane for the time being until we could get back home and discuss this. Then Ranjit could come later or we could go back to him later. But if, after doing all we could to reason with her, if she still wanted to stay, then all I could do was put her life completely in God's hands and trust that He would bring her to where she needed to be. But the time for that was not now. Now I had a work to do, and a fight to fight.

You are an amazing mom. I truly admire you! You are making all the best decisions to help her! Evelyn texted with a smile.

CHAPTER 16

FINAL PREPARATIONS

Wwe got back in the black Honda and turned onto I-10 headed home. I called both Keith Thompson and my mom, asking if they could be at the house to let the news reporters in so they could set up.

As we drove home, something had been bothering me. It was Tabby, my other sister-in-law, Derr ick's wife. She was always posting things on social media to get awareness, asking for support, or prayers for those in need, and now that our family was hurting, there was only silence. I had recently sent her daughter money for cheerleading, but she couldn't even text me that she was praying. I believed she was holding a grudge and it bothered me that she didn't seem to care what was happening to our family.

Grant, being a family-oriented guy and the baby of the family, really wanted to fix this between her and me, and I was grateful for that.

Maybe God is trying to bring us all closer, He had texted. *When this is done, we will all be talking, because I just can't have this. Family united is stronger, so please, in your heart, find forgiveness. We need to be a family again. I've got this. If anything, believe in me to make things right, over time. I love you both! Family means so much to me!*

Us, too, Grant! We love you! I texted back.

He was like my little brother. He was only nine years old when I came into the family. Brent took Grant almost everywhere with him including our high school football games when he was in elementary school and showed him a lot of attention. He and Brent had always been close and were much alike. I was glad he wanted to work on our family and keep us united.

When we pulled into the driveway of our home, the news van was already there. We had no time to be nervous or think. It was lights, camera, action. When we walked in the door, we found Keith and Mom talking to the reporter, and the cameraman setting up his equipment, lighting, and microphones.

The reporter came over to shake our hands with a smile. She was pleasant and professional. "Hi, Mr. and Mrs. Harris, I'm Gracie," she said extending her arm to us.

"We're so glad you decided to sit down with us and tell your story. Is it okay if we use these photos?" she asked pointing to the three eight-by-ten picture frames sitting on the back of our piano in the foyer of the living room. The pictures were of each of our three children in their high school graduation gowns.

"Yes, I think that would be great," I said looking longingly at my daughter's photo, her clutching her graduation cap against her chest, smiling. I hadn't stopped to look at that picture in a while.

"And these, also?" she asked pointing to the sofa table in the middle of the living room with family photos of us on vacation.

I nodded.

"Great, we'll just have you sit here on the couch."

As we sat, the cameraman attached microphones to our shirts while Gracie briefly asked a few questions to get us prepared for the interview. She made us feel comfortable seeing that she was very compassionate about our situation. Keith and Mom sat in the two recliners in the middle of the room while Gracie and the cameraman stood in front of us. The lights came on and Gracie began.

The entire interview only took about ten minutes. Gracie's questions were short and to the point, to make sure everything came across clearly. I was able to tell them I had spoken to Ranjit in the middle of the night while Victoria was on her way there and about how he asked if he could call me, "Mom." We also told them of our plans to go to India to get our daughter.

After the interview was over and the news reporter left, we relaxed, taking off our shoes and curling up on the furniture. Mom and Keith settled down in the living room with us and soon Brent's parents came over. Brent's mom, Jeannie. had brought some homemade salsa and chips, our favorite. We hadn't eaten all day, but again we really couldn't eat much. This was just right to settle our stomachs.

The reporter had just left when we heard on our local news channel that in Orange Beach, the son of one of the famous restaurant owners had been charged with sex trafficking in that town, just an hour and a half away. This was unbelievable. We had never heard of anything like this anywhere near us, much less practically in our hometown.

"That just goes to show you, if it can happen here, it can happen anywhere," said Keith.

"It's getting bad," I said. "We can't be too safe, even here."

I had told Kelli I would call her when we were home, so I dialed her number.

"How did the interview go?" she asked.

"Well. Just finished."

"Good, do you have the visas yet? I'm being told that you must present to the embassy for the urgent visa. Frank tried filling his out online and the soonest date for entry is Monday."

"I can get the visas online. I needed to have the passports first, but it looks like I'll need to have my flights arranged as well, so I'm going to work on that tonight."

She offered to help me with it if I needed. I then told her about my conversation with Evelyn, and how I asked her to please respect my position as the parent. Kelli didn't comment on it too much. I wouldn't think Kelli would disrespect my position, but just in case she did, I was letting it be known where I stood. I wasn't that close to Kelli; sme, but she had been in the family for fifteen years now and I felt I could trust her.

She was well-studied, liked research, was capable, had a good job, and had contacts that I didn't. I greatly appreciated her help. Kelli was also a mother and I felt she understood where I was coming from.

"Luke flies in tomorrow afternoon," I told her. "I should check in with Victoria. She is probably wanting an update since it's been two days. That's the time I told her to give us, but this is complicated. It's not just a drive across the country. I'm thinking we'll be leaving the day after tomorrow.

Victoria was calling.

She wanted to know how things were going and I told her we got the passports, and we were getting our visas tonight.

"Mom, you have no idea how long it takes to get a visa. You don't know what all I had to go through. It takes months."

That statement gave me pause. The thought of that, the thought of all she went through, behind my back, planning all this, doing it all without my knowledge, made me feel pain all over again, but I quickly shook it off. I had to stay focused.

"Yes, Victoria. I had them expedited, the visas and the passports. Luke will be here tomorrow and then we should be leaving here on Saturday. I just need to schedule the flights."

She seemed very calm, at ease, and satisfied with the progress, to my surprise. I thought she was going to be upset, that it was taking longer than I initially told her.

"Luke just came home a couple of days ago from Australia. He had to get back to California so I can fly him here to Alabama, so we can go to India." I was sitting in the recliner next to Keith. He was also on the phone with Laura Cotton, Chris' wife, our church friends. Overhearing part of my conversation, he looked at me and gave a chuckle. I shook my head. The insanity and surrealness of what was happening were hitting us. Sometimes you had to laugh to keep from crying.

"Yes, I remember," Victoria said, "I don't feel good. I think I'm getting a fever. I'm going to lie down."

"Okay, baby. Get some rest. I love you. When we get there, we're getting a hotel with A/C. Just know Dad and I are doing everything we can, and we will be there soon!"

"I love you, Mom, and can't wait to see y'all." She said as we hung up.

Keith handed me the phone saying Laura wanted to talk for a second.

She and I chatted a little and she offered to go with me. I thought that was extremely generous of her. She had a business and two children. I thanked her and told her I would let her know, handing the phone back to Keith. Right now, we had Uncle Frank and I wasn't sure how it was all going to go, but having another woman with me who knew the ropes wouldn't be a bad thing.

Later, Kelli texted, telling me what Brent had relayed the other night, that Ranjit's parents said they thought they were rescuing Victoria from a mentally abusive household.

> *It's not clear how much of this Victoria portrayed to them or how much it was skewed by Ranjit. My guess is, it's a combination of the two,* she texted.

I was pretty sure it was all Ranjit putting these thoughts in her head. Making her think she had it bad at home, so she would want to leave. He needed her to hate her parents so she would come to him.

> *They were also told that you did not approve of her coming to India, but that you didn't care what she did now,* Kelli texted.

> *Well, that's another good reason to get her out of there. They have a lying son,* I texted. *I would love to know if they have toilet paper in that home.*

We had a pastor from India visit the previous year and a lady from the lifestyle center where Preston was studying had lived in India for years. I heard things from both of them about what life was like there.

"People use the bathroom in the streets; there is urine and feces all over the sidewalk. We don't have toilet paper, people use their hands," Pastor Amos had said.

I couldn't believe what I was hearing. How could this be possible? This was a person who was born and currently lives there. He had to be telling the truth, but I still had a hard time comprehending it.

Pastor Amos said that they didn't have a sewer system, therefore paper products of any kind were not allowed, but I still couldn't imagine the hand wiping part.

Knowing how Victoria took two long, hot showers a day, basked in the sunshine taking in the fresh air several times a week, spent hours in the bathroom primping, rested hours in bed, and mostly ate fresh fruits and vegetables that she made into food art before eating, if this place was as these people said it was, with no toilet paper, India and Victoria were not going to get along. This was not a place she would enjoy.

As Brent said, "The girl cleans her face with avocadoes." He was referring to the cleansing masks she made. She used a lot of natural recipes for her skin because it was sensitive and she liked experimenting with different things to see what worked for her. I would say in some ways she was spoiled, but again, I had learned these were her coping strategies and most of us had not understood what all she had to go through mentally just to be prepared to leave the house every day.

Anytime we were going somewhere as a family, we would be sitting in the car for at least ten to twenty minutes waiting on her. I would tell her everybody is in the car and she would be one hundred percent perfect, every hair in place, just staring in the mirror.

"You're beautiful; let's go!" I would say, frustrated with her for making us wait and making us late, and we went through this *every single week*.

"Waiting on the queen...." I would tease the guys, as I came out to the car. It didn't dawn on me that even though she seemed to be self-absorbed and obsessed with her appearance, it could be that she was paralyzed with fear. She was procrastinating and it took her a long time to get ready to face the outside world, but she never tried to explain herself or take up for herself. It was such a relief to solve all these mysteries about her that she couldn't seem to tell us.

So, if they thought we were abusing our daughter, just the environment there would be abuse to her.

FRIDAY, SEPTEMBER 21, 2018

After taking our photos for the visas and having Luke text me his, I applied for them around midnight. I then spent the next three hours looking up flights for the three of us and trying to figure out which ones would work. The screen kept changing as flights were taken. It was tedious and nerve-racking.

I also had to schedule Luke a flight back to California after we would come home from India, and I needed to figure out which credit cards to put it all on. I also gathered the credit cards I would take with me and made sure I knew the limits on each.

At about 3:30 a.m. I went inside to fill a glass of water and then returned to my office to get a second wind and print all the itineraries. I had booked one-way flights as I was not sure exactly when we would return.

We would be leaving the next day, Saturday. I had spoken to Pastor Leite to get his guidance about us flying out on a Saturday. I didn't want to make anyone work on that day, as the fourth commandment stated, but I also knew this was an emergency. I knew if we waited one more day, God could certainly work out any problems that arose; I would rather obey and leave the consequences with Him, I needed His blessing on us. Pastor Leite assured me that while this was true, it wasn't necessary because God provided an exception in these situations. "Go get your donkey out of the ditch," he said, referring to the scripture where Jesus says it is lawful to do good on the Sabbath.

So, having that settled in my heart, I proceeded to buy the tickets.

Our route would be:

Mobile>>>>>>>>Dallas>>>>>>>>Qatar>>>>>>>>Amritsar

1 Hour   14 Hours   3 Hours

It was now early Friday morning, about 6:30 a.m., and Brent was just coming into the office for work. "Did you ever come to bed last night?" he asked.

"No," I said, as I took the cash and checks from the drawer and made out a deposit slip. I was making final preparations; a deposit at the bank, instructions for the payroll company, and paying all the bills for the next two weeks. I had moved money around where it needed to be, from savings or credit cards to checking. I had not begun packing yet, so that was next.

"I need you to call Frank," I told him, "and ask him if Qatar is a safe place."

"Why?" he asked.

"Because it's right next to Iran. And that's where we're flying into."

Just then my phone rang. It was Victoria. She was very sick. She had an upset stomach, a fever, and was vomiting. I felt bad for her to have to go through that in a strange place, without me there to help her. Esha, the high official was there, and I spoke with her briefly. She said she needed to take Victoria to the medical office and was asking my permission. I told her that was fine. She told me Victoria didn't want to take any medicine, but finally accepted some.

"It's probably because you're out of the country and not in your usual environment. I've heard of people getting sick when they travel to other countries. It's just your immune system needing to get adjusted."

"Well, it's awful. I've never been so sick in my life," she said. I told her I had our visas and flights, that we were scheduled to fly out tomorrow, that I loved her, and we hung up.

Then I got a text from her.

That woman you were talking to on the phone, Esha, is helping me. I hope you'll talk to her tonight. You really need to listen to me. I think it's funny how I was forced to stay with 'good Christian people' because Ranjit and his family are believed to not be good, but it's completely twisted.

You brought me to an unsafe place with fake Christians when I would've been in wonderful hands in the beginning. These people are just using me. They are uneducated and are getting a lot of money from the government because of their religion. Believe what you want, but it's sad y'all brought me here, thinking you're helping.

So, you like Esha? I asked. This was good information.

Yes, she wants me out of this house.

Where does she want you to go? I never got a response. That gave me a little more insight. Esha wanted her out of the house? Maybe she wasn't on our side. I thought she was at least a neutral party; she was Kelli's contact.

It sounded like Victoria had been talking to Ranjit again. He was making the doctor and his family look bad, and themselves look good. How in the world did she think Christians, especially in a non-Christian country where Christians were the minority, were getting paid for their faith? Pakistan was thirty minutes away where Christians were *killed* for their faith. How could she possibly think the doctor was getting *paid* for being a Christian? Ranjit was feeding her nonsense. He was trying to get her to distrust them so she would leave.

Victoria put a post on *Facebook* that day, admitting the way she and Ranjit went about this was wrong, that they should have told us, and not gone behind our backs. She explained how his father had already purchased her plane ticket *before* she got the courage to tell us about it, and how she hadn't wanted to waste his money. Someone posted a news article showing Ranjit admitting the same thing.

When I finished my errands, I began packing for the next two weeks since I didn't know how long we would be staying. Halfway through packing, Brent came in and laid down two heavy-duty military-looking backpacks, one tan and one black.

"Those look awesome! Where did you get them?"

He told me as he began showing me all the neat things about them. We would use these as our carry-ons. The best thing about them was they had straps that buckled across the chest and waist, helping bear the weight, keeping it off our shoulders and backs.

He also picked up three battery packs, one for each of us, so we could charge our phones without a power outlet. He had some extra-long USB cords for charging and found some electrical outlet adapters. On one end the adapter had an American port and on the other end, an Indian port. This way we would be able to plug into their outlets.

He then threw a couple of neck pillows on the bed.

"These are for the flight." It would be a long flight, and they would prove to be very helpful. Brent had two neck injuries, so he especially needed this.

"Wow, honey, you did great! These are nifty!" I said, leaning over to kiss him. It would be so good to get life back to normal. We had barely seen each other lately.

I stuffed a bag of dates and cashews, and other snacks down into one of the front zippered pockets of my backpack. I had chosen the tan one. I placed the battery pack and extra charging cords in another pocket. I slid my laptop into one long, thin pocket. I would need it to check on bills at home and whatever else we might need.

"Put some overnight clothes in there, too." He knew I wasn't the best when it came to packing. I had all my clothes in the checked luggage. I decided to put my purse inside my backpack so I could have another personal item. I took my driver's license, debit card, and passport and put them on me for easy access. It had been sixteen years since we had been on an airplane, and never an international one, so I had a lot to think about.

"Oh, and Frank said Qatar is fine."

I nodded. Everything was just about ready.

ᴧ   ᴧ   ᴧ

Do you have your flights now? Kelli texted.

I sent her a photo of our itinerary and told her to keep it confidential.

Very important that you protect this info. Limit to immediate family only. We aren't taking any chances.

She sent a thumbs up and texted, *Understood.*

I drove around the corner to our cell phone company and got an international plan as a backup. I had the *Whatsapp* and made sure all our family and friends downloaded it. I told them it was going to be the way we communicated, both calls and texts.

I also had our family download a flight app so they could see exactly where our plane was at all times. I knew my dad would especially enjoy using this. He liked tracking things, and our flight would certainly be no exception.

I asked Grant and Kelli to make sure my mother-in-law, Jeannie, had the app downloaded since she wasn't used to technology. I tried to explain it to her and help her with it, but we were in a hurry to leave and she kept saying she would get Grant to help her. Anytime we left her house, just a thirty-minute drive home, she always asked us to call her when we got there to let her know we had made it safely. Every. Time. So, I knew she would want to get in touch with us as soon as we landed on the other side of the world.

Now we only needed Luke to arrive.

All our customers were taken care of and their vehicles were picked up. Many of them had seen us on the news and were telling us to be safe and to please make it back. Some said they were praying for us. I put a sign on the office door, as we locked up that read:

DUE TO A FAMILY EMERGENCY
WE ARE CLOSED UNTIL FURTHER NOTICE
PLEASE PRAY FOR US!!!

I took a photo of it and posted it on our business *Facebook* page. Once we had closed, and our customers knew, it all seemed very, very real. Everything we had done all week got us to this point and we were about to see everything unfold. We were finally going to get our baby, and I was so happy I would see her soon. I thanked God, we had made it this far. I had not seen how it would be possible just four days ago when I found out she was gone. Now here we were, about to go to a foreign country, to get our child!

A third time, Brent texted, *Victoria, this is Dad. I don't know why you haven't talked to me, but I want you to know I love you, and we miss you. I miss you. I'm praying for you every moment I can. I'm so sorry you feel the way you do. I don't understand why you could never talk to me, or us. I can't wait to see you again! I love you!*

Brent went to the airport to pick up Luke, and Mom came over to spend the night with us. She was going to take us to the airport the next day, and all our family plus Keith and Anne Thompson were coming over to see us off.

I got a text from Mickie at *NBC 15 News, Keith said you guys are leaving tomorrow.* She asked us to keep her updated and that she would be praying for us.

When Luke came in, I was so happy to see him. I wrapped my arms around him in a big bear hug. *I have one child back in my arms*, I thought.

When I suggested that he and Preston, my only other two children, should go to Victoria, I don't know what I was thinking! At the time, I don't think I realized what I was suggesting! As apprehensive as Brent and I were about going, and we were adults, I couldn't imagine a twenty and a twenty-four-year-old going alone; even boys were not safe over there.

"BB wants to talk to you," Luke said. BB was the vice president of the company Luke worked for and who he had just gone to Australia with. He had been in the hotel room when Luke got the call from Sebastion.

I had never spoken to BB before; I'd only seen him in videos.

"Hey, Mrs. Harris. I just want to let you know how sorry I am that all of this is happening and how upsetting it is for me. I can't imagine what you are going through and are about to go through. When Luke told me, it reminded me of the movie, *Taken.*

"You're not the first person to mention that. I haven't seen it," I told him.

"Well, you should. It's just like your situation. Well, you shouldn't watch it now, but you know, later, after everything is better.

"I'd like to go over there and get a hold of this guy," he said.

"Thank you, BB, that means so much to me. And thank you for letting Luke go with us. I know he's only been on the job for a couple of weeks.

This is a great company; you guys are the best. Luke going will help Victoria tremendously. She looks up to him so much."

BB was the first person I had spoken with from the outside looking in, from an everyday-person standpoint, who didn't know us. It gave me great comfort to hear this guy, a stranger, being truly upset about what was happening to me and wanting desperately to fix it! It gave me perspective about what was happening and how others may be viewing it. I didn't yet truly understand the "audience" we had.

"You got it! You guys have a safe trip! We need Luke, bring him back, too!"

"This *does* feel like a movie," Luke sighed, his eyes wide as I handed the phone back to him. It wouldn't be the last time we would have that feeling.

An email popped up on my phone saying our visa applications were processed and would be ready on the day of our arrival. I sent the email to the printer and went back to my room to finish packing.

Later, as I was walking through the house to get a bar of soap, I overheard Brent talking in Luke's room. He was on a three-way call with his two brothers, Grant and Derrick, and Luke was also part of the conversation.

As I walked by, hearing them, something told me I wanted no part of that conversation. It may have been because there were so many people talking, and half of them were on the phone, it just seemed complicated. Or it may have been that I, myself, was so emotionally drained from the night before, having never gone to sleep, getting the visas and flights, that I knew I may say something or someone may upset me, and I might snap.

I needed rest for the next two days of flights. We had a lot ahead of us and I, at this point, had nothing left in me. Everyone was stressed and upset, and I knew two people in that conversation didn't know how to communicate well. It was a disaster waiting to happen. I still had to finish packing and I needed to go to the office to get the visa confirmations.

My mom, on the other hand, chose to walk into that room. If it was already a bomb about to go off, my mom being emotional right then, was the match that would light the fuse. I knew I should've grabbed her by the arm and stopped her, but I didn't. That's how tired I was. I didn't have the energy to fight with her or try to explain why she shouldn't, so I just went to my office. If I wanted to know what it was all about, I would soon find out.

"Victoria told me if she didn't go to India, she was going to kill herself," Grant said. He then asked Brent, "What would y'all have done if she had told you she was going to kill herself?"

"I guess we would have to get her help," Brent said. "As a matter of fact, Victoria did say it about a year ago. The counselor we were taking her to for anxiety told us if she ever says it again to tell Victoria we would call 911, so Victoria wouldn't say it unless she meant it. The counselor observed that she was a little depressed and anxious, but not suicidal."

Then my mom chimed in. She had been listening, but they didn't know it, and it startled them.

"She has autism, too," she blurted, her voice strained, holding back tears.

"Don't label her like that," Grant firmly shot back. "Did you have her diagnosed? If you didn't, you can't say that. You're not a doctor."

"You don't have to be a doctor to know your own child. Every symptom she has is the exact same as people *who have* been diagnosed with it. So, it's plain common sense to put the two together You can call it whatever you want, but she has a problem and a list of symptoms."

"I don't care if she has autism or not," Derrick said. "She's somewhere she doesn't need to be and I would get her on a plane back here as fast as I could."

I got in the shower to soothe my aching shoulders. After sitting at the computer all night, they were knotted up and on fire. I got dressed and could barely see straight as I stumbled toward the bed.

> *How are things going? Any news from or about Victoria? I saw the news last night! You guys did a great job!*

It was Evelyn.

As I burrowed into bed, I told her Victoria was sick, but was feeling better after having taken some medicine. I added that she was very upset with us and had posted on *Facebook* that she was not coming home.

I'm sorry she is sick. How are you guys doing? When are you leaving?

We are packing. Flying out tomorrow. Get there Monday, I texted her.

Yeah! Good news!!!

That would be the last time I spoke to Evelyn.

* *

VOICES
BEHIND THE SCENES

Earlier that day...

Victoria to Sebastion: *Believe whatever you want, but this article isn't true. Y'all have ruined my life, my reputation, and this sweet family's, too. Everyone in India; the police, the media, the NGO, even the people I was forced to stay with, know these people are safe. Y'all made assumptions that it was human trafficking when it wasn't. I know y'all are my family, who just care for my safety, but what you did was wrong. I'm on the news in India and in the U.S. and what's being said is all a lie.*

Sebastion: *I'm glad you're safe, and I'm sorry you're upset with me. I'd love for you to come stay with us, and bring Ranjit if you want. Our home is always open to you both. No one knew whether his family was safe until our connections had them checked. If they have nothing to hide, then there is no reputation to ruin.*

I want you to know I ran just like you did. Priscilla was always verbally abusive to me like your mom, telling me I had mental issues. I was malnourished as a child because no one looked after me. It was rough. Priscilla worked multiple jobs. Making money was more important to her than parenting was.

Our family thinks fear and control are the way to encourage your children to grow, but it's when parents educate and empower their children to reach their dreams...that's parenting.

I understand why you left, and fully support you. I see the happiness in your face, and I'm glad you got away from your parents. I no longer believe in God or any of that nonsense, and since I've separated myself from this family, my life has completely changed.

Spread your wings and fly Tor, and when your family gets there, be firm. Let them know you're your own person, and they don't have control over you. Their religion is a cult in my opinion, and I hope you stay far away from their influence.

⅄   ⅄   ⅄

Oliver: *Hi Victoria, Evelyn Silva is my best friend.*

I'm horrified by what is going on. I need to give you some unsolicited advice now, and I hope you hear what I'm saying.

You have found love. On your terms. Living in a home where you were stifled.

Your mother is doing everything possible to destroy that and you, and the man and his family who are good people. We were all told this story of sex trafficking, and it's nonsense.

You've got to put an end to this, darling. I don't know if you and he will work out, but I do know if you go home, your mother will rule your life on levels you cannot even imagine.

So, my advice: Contact the Mobile TV station. Say that you want to do an interview and explain you fell in love with a good man, from a good family, and your controlling, unsupportive family are doing everything possible to have you home to find white men to be with.

Because let's be honest, Christian or not, if you were at a Vanderbilt's house right now, sex trafficking would not be a question.

You need to stand up to them. You are a brave person.

You love this man. So, tell the world.

Be authentic. Be honest.

Your family has already scammed three thousand dollars out of people who are trying to save you from the sex trade.

A trade you are not at risk of being a part of.

Please end this madness and get back to getting to know that amazing man you went to meet.

They are ruining it all.

Don't let them.

SATURDAY, SEPTEMBER 22, 2018

CHAPTER 17

AN INNOCENT MIND
AND A MYSTERIOUS LOOK

Our flight was to depart at 3:00 p.m. We were up early to make sure we had everything ready.

Kelli texted me at 7:30 am.

I missed the conversation last night but heard there were some heated moments. I just wanted to reiterate that none of us are judging your parenting or placing blame. Anything we have told you about what Victoria is thinking is only to help you understand where she is coming from. Whether or not there is any truth to it, it is what she believes. She wants to mend this relationship.

I asked her, 'You don't want to not ever see your family again, do you?' and her response of course was, 'No', and she became tearful. She wants this to work, and I know you do, too.

Also, since human trafficking has been ruled out, there won't be a police escort now. They said it is safe for you to travel around there. If you want to talk, give us a call. We are driving out of town right now, going whitewater rafting for the weekend. Love you guys and we'll be praying for you during your travels!

Human trafficking had not been ruled out, but I didn't have time or energy to argue with her. I told her I understood and thanked her for all they had done to help.Grant then called and we chatted a bit. He told me that he knew Victoria wasn't his daughter, but he loved her like one. I told him I believed that because he was a family guy.

"We're going to get her back, don't worry," he said as we hung up.

I was in my closet getting a few more things together when I received a private message from a boy named Johnny, whom Victoria had dated once. He sent me a screenshot of Victoria's *Facebook* page.

> *Hello Mrs. Harris, I thought you might want to see this. Be careful on your trip over there.*

It appeared she had just opened a new *Facebook* account because she only had two friends at the moment: Ranjit and Johnny. She had deleted all her social media accounts since leaving. I friended her and was accepted immediately. Although I did have certain parameters in place for our children's internet usage while in high school, I had never been a friend of Victoria's on any social media. I never worried about it. Victoria was a good kid. She wasn't wild, and didn't go out partying. She stayed in her room and was quiet.

I thanked Johnny. He was a great kid, too.

We then got a text from Brent's Uncle Frank who was accompanying us to India. He had been working on his visa the night before.

> *I'm not going to be able to go with you guys. I'm sorry, and I know it's last minute, but the travel arrangements aren't coordinating with my work schedule.*

> *Remember you'll need a round-trip ticket to get to India. I will keep my phone with me 24/7, so call me anytime. Love y'all and GODSPEED.*

I replied,

What do you mean we need a round trip to get to India??? Victoria didn't have that.

I don't know the details of her visa, but yours is short-term. If you land in India without a return flight, they will make you buy one before you can enter the country. These can be very expensive.

I didn't know mine was short-term, I only knew it was expedited. I checked my visa confirmation. It said 60 days.

Frank texted again, *If she had a 60-day visa, she would need a return flight, or else the family is standing for her with the Indian immigration.*

I didn't know what that meant. I remembered one of Kelli's contacts saying the sister was "trying to get Victoria out of immigration" and that he felt something shady was going on.

I texted Victoria, *Are you still planning on coming back in a month or two? Can you send me a pic of your visa? Wasn't it for 60 days? I'm being told that because my visa is only for 60 days, I must have a round trip! I may have to change my flight! I wasn't sure how long I needed to stay. Evelyn said you wanted us to stay a while and spend time with you around the city.*

Meanwhile, behind the scenes, Victoria was texting Tanvi:

Victoria: *My mom is asking about my visa and if I am still coming back home in a month or two.*

Tanvi: *She is trying everything to take you back.*

Victoria: *I know. I see the trap.*

I never received a response from Victoria. I remembered some preparation notes Sergeant Stone had found in her room. I went to get them. *Apply for a ten-year visa* was written on a notepad. This whole time I thought she had a 60-day visa because she told me she was coming back in two months and her boss was holding her job for that long. *Why on earth did she need a ten-year visa if she was only going to meet them? Why had she written this in her notes? Had they told her what to do?*

She has a ten-year visa, I texted Frank.

He texted back, *Then the family is planning on them getting married.*

A shot went through my heart. I felt dizzy. I walked it off, then went into the living room and laid down on the cold leather couch where I had been folding laundry.

"NOOOOOOOO! This is insane! What is happening?????" I cried.

What were these people up to? Did my daughter not know?

Brent had seen the text and so had my mom.

"We don't know for sure that's what it means," Brent said.

"Frank is an engineer. He's a smart man. He builds buildings all over the world. Frank knows what he's talking about!" I shouted.

"We've got to call Grant and Kelli, maybe they can find out through one of their contacts!"

I made several attempts to call both of them. Neither were picking up their phones.

I texted them, forwarding Frank's message.

This is from Frank!!!! Please answer the phone!!!! Frank says we need to change our flights!!!! We need to talk to your contact at the embassy!!!!!!. CALL US ASAP.

"They were driving out of town. They probably don't hear the phone," I said.

"I've got to change our flights."

So, I was back to the office once more to hunt for another flight, one with a round-trip ticket.

We had planned to close the business for two weeks, one week for India, and one to recuperate after returning home. We didn't need to forfeit any more income than that and our employees needed to work. I was able to find our exact same flight with a return flight added. I called the airline and made the change.

人　　人　　人

Brent's parents, my dad, Isabel, and our friends, Keith and Anne Thompson all came over to say goodbye.

I stood in the kitchen and asked Brent and Luke to come stand beside me so I could take a picture.

I uploaded it to my *Facebook* page with the caption, *We are Coming to You, Baby!* to let Victoria and everyone know. We were so excited to finally be leaving! We were going to get our girl!

As we were about to walk out the door, our story came on the T.V. news:

This situation is a horror. One local detective and sex trafficking experts say this could happen to anyone in our community.

It's a race against the clock to bring this daughter home. Loved ones say Victoria Harris left in the middle of the night Monday. No parent, no victim thinks a conversation online could end in sex trafficking or a fight to save a loved one. Experts targeting these crimes in Mobile say you parents need to be alert.

We walked to Mom's vehicle parked out front, ready to take us to the airport. Keith looked at us, "You know what I said about God being able to use anything."

"For His glory," he said pointing to the sky.

"Amen," Brent and I smiled, as we put our luggage in the back of the red SUV and climbed in with Luke. We said our goodbyes as Mom drove off.

We arrived at the airport early, and Brent held all our passports so we wouldn't lose them. As we went through security I gave the lady my I.D. and boarding pass. She handed them back to me and smiled, "Have a good trip!"

I paused. I realized she didn't know this wasn't "a good trip."

I just smiled and headed down the line to the conveyor belt placing my electronics and articles of clothing in the bins. Another lady in a light blue TSA uniform behind the conveyor belt smiled and asked me where we were going.

"India," I said plainly.

"India? Wowwww. That's far away," she said kindly.

"Yes," I replied. "We're going to get our daughter. She went there to meet a man she was talking to online and we're afraid for her, so we're going there, hoping to bring her back home." I blurted it out so unexpectedly that I surprised myself.

Her face then turned serious. Her brow furrowed.

"Ooooooh Girrrrl! You better go take care of yo daughter! Oooooh, If that was my daughter, I'd be doin' the same thing! You know what you gone hafta do? You gone hafta do whatever you gotta do! You know what I'm sayin? You understand me? Hmmmm!"

I smiled and nodded.

"Yes, girl!" she said nodding her head as I put my shoes back on and gathered my things together.

"You have a good one, and go get yo girl!" she said with a smile.

"Thank you so much," I smiled as I walked away. It felt good to see someone fighting with me. Feeling what I was feeling. *I wasn't alone. I was understood. By a TSA officer.*

Our flight was delayed several times due to work being done on the engine. The delay was going to make us miss our connecting flight in Dallas.

I texted Victoria, *Our flight out of Mobile keeps getting delayed. We are coming to you! I said sending the photo I took of us at home.*

Mrs. Harris, Sanjay here, Dr. Mustafa's son. It's early here. Victoria is sleeping, a text came back. (I texted her on the phone she had last contacted me from, which must've been Sanjay's.) Can you tell me the flight number, and when you will be reaching, so that we can pick you up at the airport? He replied.

I'm not sure when we'll be arriving yet, but it was originally 2:10 a.m. Monday. I sent him my itinerary.

I got the details, don't worry we'll be there to pick you up. She is doing fine. Just waiting on you guys to get here. Have a safe trip. If there are any changes, please do update us. Will keep track of the given flight number.

I plan on compensating your family for helping us, I texted back. You are wonderful people. Thank you for all you've done. We'll get a hotel as soon as we arrive. I don't want Victoria to leave until I'm there, and we don't want to see the boy when we first arrive.

That's alright Mrs. Harris, we are just trying to help and do what we can. Yes, we'll make sure of that.

As we sat in the airport, people were commenting on the photo I posted, telling us they loved us, to be safe, and giving us scripture.

Have you seen this? It was our friend, Anne Thompson, posting to my page.

It was a picture of Victoria and Ranjit in the airport when he met her in New Delhi. She had on a pair of jeans and a cream-colored cardigan over a black T-shirt. She was leaning on his shoulder, smiling big. She looked excited to finally be with the person she had talked to online for so long.

He had thick, jet-black, wavy hair, and a black beard. He was peering through dark eyes, his lips pursed together, and a smug look on his face. There was something mysterious; handsome, yet diabolic about him. He didn't look anything like the guy in the pictures she left. The guy in those pictures looked like Mickey Mouse. He had big round eyes, a plump nose, big ears, and a shy smile. He didn't look like he could hurt anybody. But the guy here, sitting in the airport with her, was different.

"Even the captives of the mighty shall be taken away, and the prey of the terrible shall be delivered; for I will fight against those who fight against

you, and I will save your children," Isaiah 49:25 was the verse everyone kept posting to us.

After being delayed two hours, we finally boarded the small plane for Dallas International Airport. It was about 5:30 p.m. As I took my seat, I saw a comment by Mr. Eddie Upchurch under the photo of Victoria and Ranjit. Mr. Eddie was a father figure to me growing up. He commented, "Looks like a devil. Bring her home!"

We landed in Dallas an hour later, and after waiting in a long line to get our instructions for the next flight, were told it was scheduled for 5:30 p.m. the next day, Sunday, and they were putting us in a hotel for the night.

We were now a whole day behind.

We took a tram to the hotel, and after getting into our room, we went to the restaurant downstairs. It was about 10:30 p.m. and we hadn't eaten all day. We ordered a tortellini dish and as we sat there, I replied to messages from friends asking about our situation. One commented,

Praying for your protection. Victoria's mind is so innocent.

She didn't know Victoria, but she could see the innocence; not only in her photo, but also in her posts.

When we returned to our room, I called Victoria. She spoke again about human trafficking and I told her if she had gone to Florida or Tennessee, or any state in the U.S., we wouldn't have thought that, but she had chosen to go to the most violent city on the planet for women.

"I can't help where he lives!" she replied.

I updated Sanjay that we would now be arriving Tuesday at 2:10 a.m. *You don't have to tell Victoria; I don't want her to be upset. Just tell her we are coming.*

SUNDAY, SEPTEMBER 23, 2018

CHAPTER 18

DALLAS

At 3:00 a.m. my phone rang. It was a number I didn't recognize. I answered it.

"Hello? Mrs. Harris? This is Jagdeep. I'm Sanjay's brother. I live in Los Angeles. My parents and brother in India can't get in touch with you, and they need to speak with you. Victoria is giving them trouble."

Jagdeep said his family would need us to write some sort of letter. We chatted for a bit, and I assured him I would straighten it out.

I then saw where Sanjay had been trying to call. We all must've been completely passed out not to hear it.

Then I saw Sanjay's text:

> *Hi Mrs. Harris, I just wanted to let you know Victoria has been posting a lot of incorrect information about my family and Christians in Amritsar, Punjab.*
>
> *She is saying we're keeping her by force and that we may get some financial benefit out of it. We need an authorization letter from you stating that she should be staying with Dr. Mustafa Azad family until you arrive. I hope you understand our situation. We don't want to be in any trouble. We are just trying to help. Thank you for understanding.*

At this point Brent and Luke had woken up, hearing me on the phone with Sanjay's brother, and I was trying to explain what we needed to do.

> *Mrs. Harris, I got a call from Victoria's Uncle Grant and he is accusing us of keeping her captive. He is asking us to not listen to you guys, so I guess we must let her go. That was wrong for him to say that. We are just trying to keep her safe until you come here, but I'm sorry things are getting out of our hands.*

I texted back, *If it wasn't for you, she would be gone by now, and in great danger, or worse. And that couldn't be Grant. It may be a fake. We'll call him.*

He then forwarded a text he had received from Grant:

> *This is Grant Harris, Victoria's uncle. Victoria is an adult and can make the decision to go where she wishes. She should be given her passport and allowed to leave.*

I then texted back, *It's okay, I understand, just hold fast, we are calling Grant. We know you can't completely hold her against her will, but please use all the authority you have to do so. We were told that in India, the authorities are strongly on the side of the parents, no matter what. We hope this is true.*

> *Mrs. Harris, even the government can't hold her. I guess Esha would be the best person to talk to, as she is involved with the authorities.*

We're calling Esha now. You are an awesome family. You have done EVERYTHING to help us! I reassured him.

I wrote the letter as Sanjay stated. I then thought about how I could let the authorities know it was really from us since it wasn't like I could get a notary at 3:00 a.m. in a hotel room in Dallas.

"Let's take a picture of you holding the letter," I said to Brent. So, with his hair disheveled, and sleep still in his eyes, in his white T-shirt, he held up my pink clipboard with the letter attached next to his face as I snapped the photo and sent it to Sanjay.

I then forwarded the texts Sanjay sent me to Grant and Kelli.

Sanjay is saying that Grant told him to let Victoria go and to not listen to us.

Whatever you guys did, you should do nothing without talking to us first. We are her parents. Please explain.

She's twenty-one, too, Grant responded.

I understand, I replied.

They told us they were having issues because of what she posted. They said y'all told them she couldn't leave, Kelli texted.

You do not do anything without talking to us first, if there is to be trust, I texted.

We then called Grant's phone.

"We feel like you are holding your daughter hostage," Grant said.

"Holding her hostage??? We are trying to keep her safe until we get there! We're on our way. We've done a lot to make it this far. We're almost there!" I exclaimed.

"We didn't claim they were holding her captive," Kelli said.

"Grant just said we are holding our daughter hostage!"

"I heard. The words. That came out. Of. His. Mouth." Kelli said, quite sharply.

Holding my tongue, I simply said, "We'll call you back," knowing I would not be talking to them again for a very long time. Once we, the parents, were on the ground in India, we would take it from there. They would have no reason to be involved any further because they wouldn't know what was going on.

I was shocked and appalled by what they had said and by them wanting her to go to Ranjit's house, just like Evelyn had wanted. *What was the rush?* We were on our way as fast as we possibly could get there. What was *one more day?*

If we went through all of this and lost her before we could get there, it would be like having the rug pulled out from under us and our hearts ripped out of our chests.

We were the ones sacrificing to make this trip, not them. She was *our* daughter. *We* were the ones whose lives would be changed forever if anything happened to her, and *we* would be the ones to have to live with that.

Victoria needed to wait for us, as had been the plan from the beginning. They needed to encourage her in that, not tell her to leave right before we got there. What on earth was the problem?

We saw a change in Grant and Kelli that day, just like we had seen in Evelyn, and we couldn't understand it. They had been so good at helping us. We didn't know where this was coming from.

I called Victoria. After several attempts, she finally answered.

I told her I understood she wanted to leave the doctor's house and go with Ranjit. I explained how we had worked so hard to get to this point. We made sacrifices, we closed the business, and we spent a lot of money. I asked her to please let us get there and meet his parents before she went anywhere. I told her we would be there tomorrow night.

I also told her it was her choice to either stay at Dr. Mustafa's house or leave, BUT that we did NOT want her to do that, because we did NOT believe it was safe.

"What is one more day? We're almost there. We are coming as fast as we can!"

"Well," she said, "You have done so much for me, the least I can do is stay here until you get here. My decision is to stay here at Dr. Mustafa's home."

That was music to my ears.

I would later see the post she had put out, but right now we had another plane to catch.

"Now you can call Grant and tell him *that*!" I told Brent as I headed to the shower.

As I stood under the hot spray of water, I could hear Brent talking. The conversation sounded pretty heated.

"You don't know our religion or what we believe…….we let Victoria do what she wants…..she's grown……just not go across the world to meet a stranger without telling us….....she's never lived outside our home…...we didn't know Ranjit existed.....she had a boyfriend here!"

As Brent sat on the bed next to Luke, he continued the conversation with Grant:

"You know you can't put her in a mental institution," Grant said.

"What are you talking about?" Brent asked.

"When Kelli's brother was putting a gun to his head in front of the police, they still didn't take him to a mental hospital." Grant and Kelli were in the process of getting custody of Kelli's brother's daughter.

Once I was out of the shower, Brent relayed the conversation to me.

"Where is that coming from?" I asked, referring to the mental institution.

"I have no idea. Maybe because I told him we would have to get her help; when he asked me (the other night) what we would do if she told us she was going to kill herself if she didn't go meet this guy in India."

"Well, that's not what you meant," I said.

"I know. I don't know what he's talking about. He was also saying a bunch of stuff about our religion and what we believe and none of its correct. He says he knows all about it because he got information the internet. I told him if he wants to know what we believe, he should ask us. You can't believe everything you read online."

Grant spoke of those who attended church as doing "the God thing," and believed the church was full of hypocrites.

"Grant somehow thinks because of our religion, we're being too strict with Victoria and not letting her live her own life," Brent said.

"That's certainly a change," I said. "What happened since yesterday? They were just as scared as we are, and they were helping us. She may be trying to live her own life, but I'm afraid she may not live to learn from this mistake if we don't get there in time. Let's get going. We're going to miss the plane."

I would later learn Sophie was asking Mom the same thing saying, "Are y'all really going to put her in a mental institution?" It was absurd, and Mom was busy talking with Homeland Security at the time, so she didn't answer her. Sophie had told Mom, "You're not educated. You didn't go to college. And you're not a doctor. You can't diagnose."

Soon we were waiting in the hotel lobby for the Uber to take us to the airport.

That was good, that talk you had with her, Sanjay texted me. She is a good girl; she has been cooperative. We had dinner together and she is fine. Hopefully, things will be okay. We will pray for your family. As you said, God is working in different ways!

Just then the van showed up, and we were on our way to board our fourteen-hour flight to Qatar.

CHAPTER 19

14- HOUR FLIGHT

As I rode in the van on the way to the airport, I thought of what loomed in front of us. We still weren't sure this wasn't an attempt at human trafficking. We still weren't sure of the intentions of this family. We didn't know them, and didn't know if they were good people, and since they didn't speak our language, how would we be able to?

The big question in my mind was, *Why did they meet her in New Delhi? Why not wait until her plane landed in their hometown of Amritsar?* What the intentions in Ranjit's mind were, that night in New Delhi, *we will never know.* And unless he told someone, or someone comes forward, *no one will ever know.* We believe a plan was thwarted that day. Now he was just settling for Plan B.

We had been told by more than one person who lives in India that the authorities in New Delhi are corrupt and easily bought off, and we didn't know if things were being covered up to protect people in high places. Governments have their *own* interests, and *we* must look out for the interests of our families.

It was beginning to look like Ranjit was a kid with no education, had no work ethic, and who was not making anything of himself. It was possible that someone powerful, in a high political position, with money, or a middleman, had approached him with the enticement of making a lot of money and all he had to do was follow the script; their instructions, and they could make him and his family wealthy.

His parents would probably jump at the idea, seeing that they didn't have a son who would be able to care for them in their old age, but who would be "a burden to them." So, one way or another, whether it was getting an American girl enticed into coming over, selling her on the black market and receiving a one-time windfall, or if it was by getting their son married to her as a chance at citizenship in America, either would work.

Or, better yet, get her to feel guilty about everything they lost because of her and her family, and coerce her into sending them money every month. Which in that case, would make them far richer in their own country than even coming to America, because of how far the dollar would go when exchanged for rupees.

What would be better? To be one of the richest people in your own country, one you knew, even if it *was* a third-world country? Or be an average person, in a first-world country, such as America, but one that was foreign to you? Maybe it didn't matter, whichever one they could pull off, would do.

Above all, I still had that nagging feeling that the way this whole thing started, on the wrong foot, with deception, a one-way ticket, without our knowledge, Ranjit's dad purchasing the tickets, "before I had the courage to tell my parents," and the fact it didn't jive with what she kept insisting, "They wanted me to tell you, but I didn't, and that was my choice."

No. She didn't have a *chance* to tell us. How would she know the parents wanted her to tell us, anyway? They didn't speak English.

She had been keeping him a secret for two whole years. Cheating on Vance that whole time. "I'm sorry for doing that to him. That's something I'm going to have to live with," she had told me. Then making her feel guilty about "wasting their money" if she didn't go. No. I couldn't trust them. From the moment they sent my daughter a one-way ticket, they could not be trusted.

Something else kept gnawing at me. Something about the ten-year visa. Something didn't add up. I just couldn't put my finger on it.

The van pulled into the circular drive and we exited to make our way to the airport lobby. Once inside the Dallas International Airport, I looked up to see the massiveness of this two-story airport. Looking at the hustle and bustle, the three of us were overwhelmed. As we zigged and zagged to make our way through everything, up and down escalators, combing the data on the big screens for our flight information, and then rushing through different hallways and subways to find our gate, my mind could not comprehend how in the world Victoria could have made it through all of this.

This was a girl who could not find her way to the beach an hour away from our house. A girl who repeatedly asked me simple instructions about everything. A girl who couldn't call the bank when she had a problem with her account but needed me to do it for her. A girl who got upset at the post office when picking up a package because "the postman was making fun of me." God forbid she needed to stop and ask someone for information or directions. It was truly unbelievable how she ever made it through that airport. Had he been helping her? Coaching her?

She would later tell me, "Everything went so smoothly for me. I don't know what I would've done if I had gotten a layover and had to stay in a hotel like you did."

We had a fourteen-hour flight ahead of us. I loved flying and had wanted to be a pilot since I was thirteen years old, but I had never been on an airplane for that long before.

In no time they called our seating row. As we boarded the plane, and I settled into my seat, I thought about how I would have loved to be in the cockpit instead. This plane couldn't get there fast enough.

It was a huge jet. The largest I had ever been on. There were three rows of seating. On the right were three seats, five seats were in the middle, and another three were on the left, with two aisles and three bathrooms. The seats were covered in crimson fabric with a wide, gray embroidered stripe down the middle.

I put my carry-on under the seat in front of me and soon the flight attendants were making their way down the aisles. Their crisp uniforms matched the fabric of the airline seats. Crimson with gray piping. They wore matching hats that looked like boats. They were even wearing crimson gloves. It was quite distinct from the American stewards, and I found it very professional and elegant looking.

They were assisting passengers and handing out little goody bags filled with things to make our flight more comfortable since this was going to be an overnight one. flight attendantherme a gray flannel blanket with "*Qatar Airways*" embroidered in crimson on the corner.

Our seats were in the middle of the plane. I was on the aisle, Brent was to my right, and Luke was to his right. There were a lot of empty seats as only about a third of the plane was occupied. I looked over at Luke. This would be his second trip to the other side of the world in less than a week.

There was a TV screen on the back of the seat in front of me showing a GPS of where we were on the map. I could see our itinerary. The flight attendant returned, handing out meal cards and taking drink orders.

I asked for water while Brent and Luke had juice.

I slipped off my shoes, put the gray fleece blanket around me, and settled down a little. Soon we were in the air and on our way.

It was about 7:00 p.m. and was getting dark. After the flight attendants served dinner and we had eaten, Brent and Luke found movies to watch, but my eyes just stayed glued to the GPS map as I kept watch on the little red airplane with red dashes behind it that symbolized us moving North towards Canada.

The screen soon became blurred as I began to doze off. I thought about all the things that had happened before Victoria left. It all was beginning to make sense.

A few weeks ago I was sitting in her room questioning her about her bank account. There was hardly any money in it. I printed out the last eighteen months of bank statements to see where all the money had gone. We had an agreement that she would save money each month so she could one day leave home and be independent. I had no complaints about my daughter. I only asked that she respect us, clean up after herself, spend some time with us now and then, and save some money while she lived in our home.

Of the $18,000 she had made, it looked like it was all spent on clothes, skincare, make-up, and car stuff, and she had very little in her savings account. I tried to check in with her on the progress every six months, but it had obviously gotten away from me.

As I went over the bank statements with her, there was a check she had written to "Cash" for $500 with "Travel" written in the memo line. I questioned her about it, but finally wrote it off as her just pretending and fantasizing. There was a $300 charge to a place I had never heard of, but assumed it was a clothing store. Later, after she left for India, I discovered it was where she purchased her visa. If only I had dug a little deeper.

Brent and I had been working 60-hour weeks for the past six months. We were excited about revamping the garage. We were doing all the work ourselves and there was a lot of physical labor involved in making the improvements, and at the same time, we were still working on customer vehicles, while I also stayed on top of paperwork. I had been exhausted.

That day, I questioned her for two whole hours while she completely stonewalled me, staring at me with a blank face, not answering a single word. She knew she was leaving in two weeks and she wasn't about to give up anything. There was an obvious friction in the room, her lips were airtight, and I was getting nowhere. It wasn't unlike her to clam up and not talk to me, but she was a block of ice, impenetrable, making me very uncomfortable. I could never have imagined what she was about to do.

I remembered how months ago she commented on the Mobile airport wondering if it was an international airport. I was a little taken aback by it and wondered why she would want to know. She was asking me questions about airports and flying. I thought maybe she was interested in flying like I was. We had taken all the kids on Discovery flights to see if it tickled their fancy, telling them we would pay for their schooling if they were interested, but none of them had been.

Then I thought about how she had come into my room one night a couple of months ago as I was getting ready for bed. It surprised me because she rarely came into my room unless she wanted to borrow something.

I had just gotten under the covers when she came and stood by my bed and asked me something that gripped me with an unfamiliar fear.

"Is there anything I could ever do, that would make you not let me live here anymore?" she asked.

I swallowed hard as I sat up. *What are you planning to do?* I thought.

Paralyzed, I just said, "No. Nothing. Why?"

"I was just wondering."

"What are you planning on doing?" I asked concerned.

"Nothing."

Then why ask?

But I dared not ask any further. I was afraid to know.

What was this about?

I felt a nightmarish feeling come over me.

That was my cue to do something. But I was so overcome with fear, I didn't know *what to do* with that information. It was like holding a boiling pot of something in my hands and I didn't know what was in it, or where to place it. I just knew it wasn't good.

Now I could hit myself upside the head over and over for not having the courage to unravel all of what that question meant. I should have searched a little deeper. I should have immediately begun a conversation with her, to get inside her head and find out what she was up to. I tried to think of things she might be planning, but I never could have dreamed it would be on a scale such as this. That it would be anything remotely this life-changing. Instead of having a conversation, I began to rationalize: *she stayed in her room all the time; she was the last person I had to worry about; what could she possibly do?*

Now I understood why she was upset about the mailbox. We had installed a new mailbox that had a lock on it. Being that it was at our business, we wanted it more secure. She was quite disturbed by this, saying she should be able to get into her own mailbox.

"There's a key right there in the desk drawer," I showed her in the office, not knowing what the big deal was.

"I need my own key," she huffed as she walked out of the room. We always checked the mail when it came to the office during the day, so there was really no need for her to unless she just wanted to.

That's the way he sent Victoria the plane tickets, through the mail. I never saw them so she must have gotten them at some point without us knowing. He had also sent her a letter through the mail, also of which we hadn't seen.

I opened my eyes again and tried to turn on my side to get more comfortable in the airplane seat.

So, Victoria was planning on coming back home and wanted to still live with us. Even more reason for me to feel responsible for her. She couldn't live on her own. When I had taken her to look at apartments, she wasn't interested, and though I was excited for her, I could tell it was stressing her out. "I can't do it, Mom," she had told me. "I need at least $10,000 before I can move out."

"No, Victoria, you need a deposit and first month's rent. And maybe a little savings," I had told her, but she clearly didn't feel she was ready. She seemed anxious about the future and about money. I had always tried to help guide my children in their finances and had helped Victoria open a Roth IRA account at age twenty, showing her how much money she could save by the time she retired by starting now. She was contributing to it monthly and seemed confident, happy, and secure doing something for her future.

I told her she could go live with Luke in California and study nutrition and make a career. It seemed like the best of both worlds. She could get out of the house and test out being an adult, but still be right alongside her brother. She would still have to pay her way, but I thought she would jump at the idea.

Was this my fault? Had I pushed her too hard? Maybe her plan was for this boy and his family to take care of her? No. She was only going to meet them, and then she was planning on coming back in two months.

I closed my eyes again and thought way back to the time when she and Luke were in middle school and we were all sitting at the dinner table waiting for her to come eat, as we usually did. The boys said something prophetic. As young as they were, they sensed something.

They both said, "When we grow up and she leaves home, we don't think we'll ever see her again. We won't know her husband or her kids."

I nodded, sadly "I think you're right." Her dad agreed. I knew what they were saying was very probable. She was not close to us, she didn't seem to want to be a part of the family, and none of us understood it. If isolation was the first step in taking someone from their family, she had already done half of Ranjit's work for him. And she had been doing it her whole life.

I thought back to when she was a little girl, how she had started sleepwalking and wetting the bed again. I would get her up so she could use the bathroom, and much to my horror, she would get down on the floor and crawl on her hands and feet, stretched out like an alligator, her belly barely touching the floor, and her face distorted into something that no six-year-old possibly could have, all of this while still asleep. I thought maybe she was having a nightmare, and she was mirroring what she was seeing, and it absolutely terrified me, my mom, and Brent.

Other times she would walk all the way to my bedroom, shivering with her teeth chattering, as if it were snowing. I would ask her if she was cold, and she would shake her head, "No." In the morning, she never remembered any of it. It began happening so often, I was afraid I would have to take her to a sleep doctor, and then suddenly, it stopped. I felt that whatever that was, had been terrorizing her, her entire life.

As she grew older, I finally realized something was truly wrong. It wasn't just slow development, or behavioral, or just her personality. Something was physically wrong. In eleventh grade, she told me she would wake up in the morning with her heart beating out of her chest.

"I feel nervous and have anxiety, and nothing has even happened yet. The day hasn't even started," she told me.

"You know this isn't normal, right?" I had asked her. I wondered if it was only now that she could verbalize to me what had been happening all those years. Maybe she was having nightmares, but couldn't remember them, and that's why she woke up with her heart racing.

Then my mom and I held her hands that day in the backyard while I told her what I had discovered, and she changed. She was a totally new person. Brand new. I felt like she had been born all over again. I had a new girl. Every day when I woke up, I had to ask myself if it was real. I felt like I was living a dream. It was truly bliss. It happened the week right before Mother's Day and that would be the best Mother's Day ever. One I would never forget.

Things were different. Like when I would knock on her bedroom door and open it, before she would always have a frown on her face and ask me angrily, *"What?"* but now she would raise her eyebrows and say, "Yeah, Mom?" in a pleasant "how-can-I-help-you" voice.

She got dressed and out the door easily instead of taking hours. When leaving the house, it used to take a long time to get her car turned around in the driveway, now she just backed straight out fast with no problem at all. It made me laugh as I watched from the window, amazed.

She used to come home from work and sleep for hours, but now she came home, put down her bags, and came and talked to me about her day, which she never did before.

She used to be rigid and robotic when I hugged her, but now she leaned into me warmly. She wasn't the same child I had all those years. These seemed like little things, but they were huge.

Victoria used to think people were always judging her, especially women. If she ever thought someone was looking at her, or talking about her, she was horrified. If even I or her dad looked at her, Victoria would get upset and ask, "What are you looking at?" "I'm just looking at my beautiful daughter!" we would exclaim. She hated women and felt they were always competing with each other.

But, now she talked about how everyone at work was so nice! She told me she had no anxiety at all anymore and had great days at work. She was really a miracle. I had been given a gift, a precious glimpse into what could be, otherwise you could have never convinced me it was possible.

One day Victoria said something profound. She told me, "A lie cannot live on its own, it must become a parasite on the truth in order to survive." In other words, there is always some truth to every lie, or else the lie cannot exist. Astonished, I told her she had bought gold from Jesus.

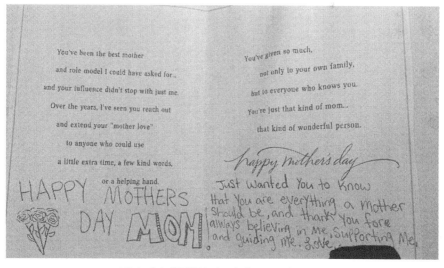

Victoria's 2017 Mother's Day card to me

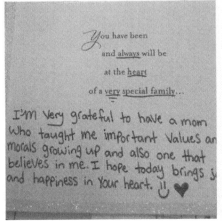
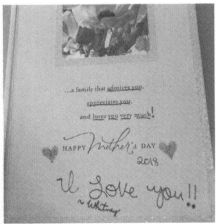

You have been
and always will be
at the heart
of a very special family...

I'm very grateful to have a mom
who taught me important values and
morals growing up and also one that
believes in me. I hope today brings joy
and happiness in your heart. 😊 ❤

...a family that admires you,
appreciates you,
and loves you very much!

HAPPY Mother's DAY
2018

U love you!!
~Whitney

Victoria's 2018 Mother's Day card to me, four months before leaving

I enjoyed two months of that wonderful change in her, followed by two months of ice-cold friction in the house to the point I was so uncomfortable, that I stayed in the office late at night working just to avoid being in the house with her. I hate to say it, but as soon as I realized she was gone, my very first thought right before thinking she was as good as dead was, *Well, good riddance!* She never wanted to be there anyway and the previous couple of months had been almost unbearable.

Then I had a revelation. It's as if the enemy had taken the change in her and used it against us. Her newfound confidence allowed her to do something extremely confident, yet extremely dangerous. In a way, I couldn't help but be proud of her. I didn't think she was capable of all this! Shoot, I didn't think *I* was capable of this! It had to be an incredibly maturing experience for her.

Two years of him grooming her, and she had never left. Then four months after this change, she was gone!

I awoke and sat up straighter as the GPS screen in front of me came into focus. It was late at night and we were now directly over snow. Nothing but white on the GPS. I looked at my husband, "Are we going over the Arctic?!"

He looked away from his action film, "Wow, yeah. I would have thought we would go completely east, horizontally around the globe, but it appears we are going straight north, vertically up the pole. How about that?"

I had not really been sleeping, but just drifting off into my own thoughts. I closed my eyes again.

Then I remembered something else. I knew this guy...this Ranjit. About a year or so ago, when she was being disrespectful, I had taken her laptop and phone away. A *Facebook* message popped up and it was from him. I responded, telling him to never contact this phone again.

Another time, I distinctly remembered her phone ringing around 5:00 a.m. "Who in the world is calling you this early?" I questioned her. She didn't answer me and I took it to be a wrong number, but still thought it strange. Later, I learned that part of the grooming process is to be the first person their subject hears in the morning and the last person they hear at night so that they start and end each day hearing the groomer's voice. The victim becomes conditioned to it, and then dependent on that person. As can be seen in the letter Victoria left, he drew her in and established a bond with her by creating an illusion of connection. He did this by sharing childhood memories of watching the same movies, having her same interests such as going to the gym and eating a specific diet, showing her his home, family, and pet, and romantically and artfully sketching her. He made her feel safe with him. He made her feel like she knew him; like she had always known him.

I had also seen where guys were messaging her and asking her to do inappropriate things. At the time, I was taking her to the counselor because of her anxiety and depression. I told him about the *Facebook* messages and we both explained to her how dangerous this was, and that she shouldn't be talking to people she didn't know. She said she understood, and I thought that was the end of it.

Everything had happened right under my nose! She had even printed out the letter she left on *my* printer in *my* office and then came and got it before I even had a chance to notice. How was it that everything had seemed to slip right by me: from the purchase of the visa on her bank statement, to the mail, to her printed letter, to even the morning she left with me waking up at 4:00 a.m. and looking towards her bedroom, two hours before her flight?

If I had just gone to her room; I would have seen she was gone. I would have seen the letter and gotten to the airport before she left. I would have talked to her and she would have stayed. I would have gladly paid Ranjit's family their money back, even double their money, to have her stay and cancel her flight. We all could have re-booked together later when we had a plan.

Oh God! Why couldn't it have happened that way? I thought. *I was all over it. It was all around me.*

Any little thing, a snag, one wrong move, and her plan would have been *over*!

But this happened so that the works of God might be displayed, a consoling, not to mention sobering, thought came.

It was supposed to be this way.

There was a reason.

I would see this pattern continue over and over again as things unfolded.

As the plane landed in Qatar, a message from one of Victoria's *former* Bible study teachers popped up on my phone. He taught the high school Bible study class at church and Brent and I had sat in as assistants because Victoria asked us to. She didn't like the teachers and wanted us close by.

Why don't you leave your daughter alone? he asked.

Wow. I had plenty I wanted to say to him. He was one to ask such a question. I wanted to ask, "The way you left yours alone?" but I didn't need any more contention.

Another crack in my heart. Attacks from the enemy. Some people are so ignorant.

I also had a group text invite from my mother-in-law, Jeannie, but no message. She must have figured out how to use *Whatsapp* and was set to communicate.

. . . .

VOICES
BEHIND THE SCENES

Oliver and Victoria:

Victoria: *Thank you for all your help, Oliver!*

Oliver: *Anytime, sweetheart. I am so proud of you. Your post ...took my breath away. You're a fantastic human being. Hope things don't get too stressful with your folks arriving.*

I hope after they calm down, they can see the beauty that is in India. It's an incredibly amazing place.

Victoria: *I'm really hoping they leave here with a whole better perspective.*

And a closer family.

Oliver: *I hope so, too! I took care of those people on Facebook who were attacking you. I want to post your letter, but I fear your mother's head will spin like a top.*

Victoria: *I ignored those people just for you. Thank you for intervening for me.*

. . . .

PART II

INDIA

TUESDAY, SEPTEMBER 25, 2018

CHAPTER 20

SAFE IN MY ARMS

We had a four-hour wait until our next flight to Amritsar. The Qatar airport was impressive. And empty. It had walls entirely of glass windows that reached more than fifty feet high.

It had been almost dark when we left Dallas and now it was getting dark again. This was the first time I had a chance to text my parents. I let them know where we were and that it wouldn't be long now. One more flight. Thankfully, we had Luke, our own personal posture therapist, who led us in some stretches to get us ready to sit for a few more hours.

Mom texted back that a friend at last night's prayer meeting said, *'You will be attacked this very night. Know that Victoria is going to come home, but it may not seem like it until the very end.'*

You were attacked last night by Victoria putting out that post, she texted. I still hadn't read it yet and didn't understand what she meant. I just knew she had caused problems for Sanjay's family, and something had changed in Grant and Kelli.

Around 2:00 a.m. we boarded our flight for Amritsar. The flight was only three hours long, so we got in a quick nap.

As we landed, and my phone came back on, a message from Grant came through.

Are you there? Grant had set up a group text he named, 'Family' and included Brent, Luke, Kelli, and me. I had not expected to hear back from them, but now believed they still wanted to communicate and this group text would be the place.

Yes, just landed, I replied.

As we went through customs, they asked for the address where we were staying, and who we were coming there to see. They wanted a name and a photo. I gave them Ranjit's name, and a copy of the letter Victoria left, along with Ranjit's and all his family members' photos. I explained what happened and why we were there; to see their family, and to take our daughter home.

After picking up our luggage at baggage claim, we exchanged dollars for rupees to have some cash on hand.

"This was the airport she was in that night," I said to Brent. The night she made that fate-filled choice to go with the doctor and not with strangers.

Soon Sanjay was outside to pick us up. It was 5:00 in the morning and the whole family had come. Sanjay's parents, grandmother, aunt, and cousin. They told me Victoria was at home by herself, waiting for us. I was a little surprised they had left her, and sadness came over me as I thought about her waiting by herself. We took pictures with everybody and hugged each other; then the three of us got in the car with Sanjay. He was a young man in his thirties, and nice-looking. He had a very sweet and gentle demeanor and was soft-spoken.

We drove through winding back country, red dirt roads. As Sanjay drove, he told us he was supposed to have returned to his home in Thailand by now.

"You don't live here in India?" I asked surprised.

"I left India for a better life. I'm just here visiting my parents. I can't stand to be here for more than two weeks. I live in Thailand with my wife and little boy. I arrived here the same day Victoria did. It's fortunate for you guys I'm still here because I'm the only one in the family who speaks English. I leave in a week."

God was already working on our behalf! Sanjay had been our contact, the one we had been conversing with the whole time. I found it interesting he was going to be here for the exact two weeks we needed him.

As the car pulled up to the small house in the country and we stepped outside, we noticed the stench.

"What's that smell?" I asked, holding my bags and wrinkling my nose. I didn't smell it back at the airport.

"It's the sewer," Brent replied under his breath.

We walked inside the little home into a room containing a full-sized bed, a coffee table, and a couch. The walls were raw, white, and missing sheetrock in some places. Victoria was sitting on the bed in baggy, gray, sweatpants and a maroon T-shirt. Her long, straight hair was pulled into a ponytail, and her face was natural and fresh.

Brent walked in first and embraced her, then Luke hugged her as I snapped a photo. Next, I leaned over the bed and wrapped my arms around her tight.

"How are you?" I asked with tears in my eyes as I sat on the bed.

"I'm okay," she said.

I looked to see tears in Luke's eyes and Brent's were red.

She seemed like her normal self. Not too happy, but not upset either.

Sanjay's family all seemed interested in us. They smiled and waved, and soon left the room to give us some privacy.

Then almost immediately the room grew tense, just like in the weeks before she left. Victoria began to get agitated. She said some things, acting like her normal, stubborn self. It made me angry. We came all this way and here she was acting like a brat! She was twenty-one years old, yet she was saying that one of the reasons she left was because we didn't take care of her. We had told her she needed to start paying a couple of her bills, and she didn't like it. Then she said she left because we didn't feed her.

I went and sat on the other end of the couch, away from them. "Let's go back and leave her here!" I said, already annoyed.

"Don't be that way," my husband and son said to me.

"I can't help it. We came all this way and she wants to be her stubborn self. She doesn't want us here!" I said firmly.

The three of them continued to talk. They consoled her, calming her down, as she gave me the evil eye, as usual. I eventually came back to the bed and sat down. We were tired and wanted to go to the hotel that Sanjay had arranged for us, but Victoria said she wouldn't leave until Ranjit came.

"Are you ready for him and his family to come talk to us?" I asked, ready to get this over with so I could take my baby home. I wanted to take her and run. As far as I was concerned we could talk from our home in the U.S.! But Victoria had said if we spent time in the city with their family she would leave with us. And I fully intended on having a conversation with them as Pastor Leite and I had discussed.

Her dad then looked her squarely in the eye. He held his arms out wide and shouted, "Victoria! Look at me!

"*I'm in India!*

"*India, Victoria!*

"Something is wrong with this picture!" he exclaimed with hurt in his eyes.

She stared at him with a blank look, her jaw dropped.

The realization of what was happening was sinking in.

We didn't belong here.

We had never been out of the country. We rarely left our hometown in the U.S.

But here we were.

On the other side of the world.

"I'm supposed to be in Alabama!" her dad continued. "I hardly leave the house. This should tell you something!"

It would have been humorous if it hadn't been so serious.

"I came here, closed down the shop, to see you, and make sure you are okay. Because we don't know them. We don't know this place. Heck, we don't even speak the language, or know the customs. We don't know anything!"

Victoria began to soften. She knew this was huge for her dad to risk losing business, and losing workers, doing what he loves. She swallowed hard.

Brent was a very calm, soft, sweet person who rarely got upset or raised his voice. He was laid back and simple, but he needed to say this. He was overwhelmed, tired and stressed from the flight and all the logistics of the past week. We had practically been on planes and in airports for the last twenty-four hours straight. The sheer intensity of the situation was heavy.

And the destination wasn't some resort or spa. No. We could have all gone on a very nice vacation for what this was costing us. No, it wasn't a vacation getaway we were looking forward to.

It was uncertainty, apprehension, intimidation, danger, and downright fear we had to look forward to, and the real possibility that we may not be bringing her back.

That was what was at the end of this.

That was our reward.

Just *a possibility* of saving her.

Because here we were, having to work with a person who has her own volition, her own free will, her own choices to make, but has no idea what she is doing, and how dangerous it is. I didn't care how old she was. I didn't care that she was twenty-one. Grown men get in dangerous situations, and this was dangerous.

"Your turn," I quietly nudged my husband. Now that we had both gotten some things off our chests, maybe we could relax.

"So do you want to call Ranjit now?" I asked again.

"It's still early," she replied, "I can text him though."

She was right. It was only about 6:00 a.m. and still dark. We were on Mobile time. Everything was different here. Except for the temperature and climate, it was just like home: hot and humid. At least there was something we were used to.

She texted Ranjit and he replied that they would come when Dr. Mustafa called.

Sanjay said to me, "Why don't you go to the room in the back and get some rest from your flight for a while, then we'll call them."

I agreed. I didn't even know how tired I was. Yes, we should rest, especially prior to such an encounter as what was about to take place.

Sanjay led us through the kitchen and past a door where the shower, toilet, and washing machine were all together, to a room in the back of the house that had twin beds. Brent and Luke lied down together in one of the beds and I lied down in the other. Victoria came in and lied down beside me. We couldn't really sleep. We were too keyed up from what was going on. We dozed off a little, but Victoria wanted to talk. She was frustrated and upset again.

I remembered Sanjay saying how Ranjit and his sister would come over every day and sit on each side of her, talking in her ears all day.

She was now questioning me constantly about one thing or another and telling me all the things she didn't like or was upset about how we did or did not handle. I couldn't explain things, I couldn't think, all I could say was we did what we thought was best, we just wanted you to be safe.

I wished she would go to the hotel with us so we could rest and then we could talk. We could meet with Ranjit's family later after getting our bearings. I realized why Grant, Kelli, and Evelyn had wanted her to leave Dr. Mustafa's house and go to Ranjit's house so badly before we arrived. I bet they thought we would just take her and run without speaking to the parents. That's why Victoria didn't want to leave with us until Ranjit came. I bet she was told not to. Even though Ranjit had her luggage and I'm sure her passport, they weren't taking any chances that we might bail on them. They wanted to know where we were at all times, and if we left with Victoria, they didn't trust that we would return.

Around 10:00 a.m. the four of us decided it was time to call Ranjit. Sanjay made the call. We went back into the first room we were in, which I suspected was the living room, the one with the bed in it. Victoria got on the bed and Brent sat next to her. I sat on the couch to her left and Luke sat to my left. The rest of Sanjay's family came in and sat down with us, and we all waited for the Sharma family to arrive.

CHAPTER 21

THE MEETING

Soon Ranjit arrived with his mother and father, and with them was Esha, the high government official. I assumed she would facilitate the meeting.

Esha and the parents sat in chairs across from us and Ranjit sat next to Luke.

"We need to sort things out amongst each other," Esha said in an Indian accent.

"Tell us what your concerns are," she said looking at Brent and me, "and I would like Victoria and Ranjit to participate."

"I would like to know what their intentions are," Brent said, as everyone focused on Victoria and Ranjit.

Neither of them would speak. We looked at Victoria and waited for an answer, but she just looked at us as if she didn't know what to say.

"Don't be scared," Esha encouraged. "They just want to know what your intentions are."

Finally, Victoria spoke, "My intentions were just to meet him and his family."

Ranjit said the same, that he just wanted to meet her.

I questioned him, "What about marriage?" suspecting that was now his plan since he told me on the phone the night Victoria left, that he had to be married to come to the U.S.

"Whatever she wants; whenever she is ready," Ranjit said.

After that, the entire focus of the conversation was solely about marriage.

I finally spoke up and said, "You are Hindu, and we are Christian, and this is a problem for us."

"No, no problem, they both go to both church," Esha said, and she began talking about having both a Hindu wedding in the temple in India and a Christian wedding in the church in the U.S.

"No, because we do not serve the same God," I said.

"Yes, we do," Esha replied.

"Okay, then let's talk about God's character and we'll see if He's the same God."

"No, no we don't talk about that," she said, getting upset and wanting to change the subject. I had hit a nerve.

So, I said, "Look, either one of two things will happen. Either Ranjit will have to become a Christian or Victoria will have to become a Hindu; it's that simple. They need to be in agreement."

That's when Victoria interrupted the whole conversation and spoke up, "*I said I didn't come here to marry him, I only came here to meet them.*" It was unusual for her to be in a crowded room and cause all eyes to be put on her, but she wanted to make it clear that was not what she came for.

"Let's go to Ranjit's house so you can see it, hmm?" Esha announced, changing the subject. It was just as well. We were exhausted and ready to get to our hotel so we didn't push the conversation.

We went to the back room to get our luggage since we would be checking into our hotel after leaving Ranjit's home. I looked and felt like a wet dish rag, like a little mouse trembling in the corner. There was no way those people could've been afraid of us if they tried. It made me sick. I wished we would have been strong, but there had been no time to recoup from our travels, much less get a plan together. We simply planned to talk to them and show Victoria we were trying, but we had nothing specific in mind.

Why hadn't Brent and I looked *the parents* in the eye, and demanded to know *their* intentions? Why hadn't we put the responsibility *on them*? Questioned *them*? Maybe we didn't think of it because we were tired, or maybe because they didn't speak English. I'm sure Esha could've interpreted, but how would we know what was really being said?

Why hadn't we sought Frank to coach us on what *he* would do, and how *he* would have approached this? There had been no time with him having to back out at the last minute and the clock ticking; it was all we could do to get here, much less have a script planned out.

Sanjay walked to the room with us to get our luggage and he was crying. We didn't understand and looked at him, confused. He explained he was upset about how the meeting went. He seemed to think they were trying to use our daughter and that she would be forced to give up her faith.

The four of us rode in the back of a tiny car with Ranjit and his dad riding up front and Ranjit's mom riding with Esha. This was the first time we had been out in daylight. As we drove through the city, there was trash everywhere on the sides of the road and the stench was even worse. Ranjit's house wasn't very far and we soon arrived. The outside of the house looked nice. It had marble on the front. There was a gate and the name "Sharma" on a shiny, brown marble plaque with the house number next to it. We walked in through the gate and a little courtyard with plants and white rocks before going inside.

Once inside the house, there were the same walls with missing pieces of sheetrock. Marble, although beautiful, was so abundant there that it was like asphalt; it was everywhere, and sheetrock must have been rare.

Esha did all the talking and showed us around the house. It had two bedrooms and an office where Ranjit's dad, Zahir, worked from home as an accountant. Victoria told us he made about the same as a fast-food worker in the U.S.

As we stepped into one of the bedrooms, we were told it was Ranjit's and his sister, Tanvi's. I saw there was only one bed. I was told they shared a bed, and thought it was strange for siblings to share a bed, being as old as they were. Victoria told me Tanvi had gone out of town on a job and wouldn't be there all week, which I found interesting. We never met her and never saw her the entire time we were in India.

It was there that Esha asked me if it was now okay for Victoria to spend the night with them. They seemed nice, but the parents didn't speak English and I didn't know them, I had just met them. I didn't want my daughter out of my sight. What was the big deal, anyway? Why did she need to spend the night with them?

"What's the matter?" Esha asked, seeing the troubled look on my face.

"Where would she sleep?" I asked.

"She can sleep with the parents if you are concerned about that. I can promise you. Don't worry."

I didn't see how she would sleep with the parents, however I nodded, and they took us to the rooftop overlooking the neighborhood.

After showing us around, Ranjit's mom, Jahnavi, offered us a tray of Indian tea that tasted like coffee and little finger sandwiches with something orange inside that looked like pimento cheese, but on the sweet side. We each took one.

We then took pictures together before heading to check in at the hotel. I wanted these for documentation. Ranjit and his dad drove us to the hotel called Sun Stop where Sanjay had made arrangements for us.

After Mr. Sharma pulled the car to the curb, and he and Ranjit helped us with our bags, I wanted to take a picture of Victoria and Ranjit. To my surprise they just stood there, not even touching each other, and barely smiled. I had fully expected them to embrace with big grins, but they were mostly expressionless and certainly didn't look like two people in love.

The hotel was a hole-in-the-wall for sure. We checked in and they gave us an old-timey-looking skeleton key.

"Whoa, where's the treasure chest?" Luke asked as he inspected it.

Victoria went to Ranjit's house while the three of us got settled into our room. She would be coming back later. I knew if they did anything with her, everything we told them at customs would give the government information to look into it. We decided to get a second room for Luke to sleep in. The two rooms were next to each other and he came to our room for now.

We began to unpack a few things and take showers. As we looked around the room, all the wires were hanging out on the walls.

"This is a fire waiting to happen," Brent said looking at them. "Nothing is to code here."

"Well, that's probably because there are no codes here," I said, "This is a third-world country."

Looking out the window, I saw wires hanging everywhere outside as well. Not like normal power lines, but open, dangerous lines, hung and tangled around the buildings. There was trash everywhere. There was an unbelievable stench all over. No fresh air. No sewer system. Feces and urine ran into the streets. No toilet paper. No paper products were allowed because of the lack of a sewer system.

I looked in the bathroom. The room was one big shower with peach-colored tile and a toilet and sink in it. I ran to get away from the stench.

There were a couple of thin, white towels laying on the bed and little green packets on them with Indian writing. *How nice*, I thought, *They gave us mints*. I took one and unwrapped it with my teeth and started chewing it.

Oh no! How horrible! I began spitting.

"What is it?" Brent asked, both he and Luke looking at me inquisitively.

"It's soap!" I said, spitting bubbles, as they both got a good laugh.

"I'm glad you think it's funny. I'm here all week," I said grabbing a towel. *Unfortunately*, I thought, heading to the stench-filled bathroom to take a shower.

Soon, Pastor Isaiah arrived. He had been in the airport with Dr. Mustafa the night Victoria landed.

He was a short, little man with smooth, dark skin, and clean-cut, shiny, jet-black hair. He had a sweet, gentle demeanor as he greeted us, then told us we needed a SIM card for our phone, and that it wouldn't work without it. So, he and Brent left to get one.

Luke got in the shower and I opened my Bible to find comfort. *God, please show me, please tell me something,* I prayed. I opened to Psalms and my eyes immediately dropped down to a verse.

You have been astonished, but I will deliver your Beloved. (Psalm 60:3-5). I almost lost my breath as I began to shake and cry. *Oh God, thank you for giving this to me! You are going to save her out of this place!*

I couldn't believe how fast He answered that prayer and gave me a sure promise. I was so glad I had opened my Bible!

I then made a group text on *Whatsapp* to my parents and our friends, Keith and Anne Thompson, who were faithfully waiting back home for any word from us.

Shortly, Brent and Pastor Isaiah returned with the SIM card and put it in my phone. Now we had at least one phone that would work. Brent later told me that Pastor Isaiah held his hand while they were outside the hotel, telling him that it was dangerous to be out at night. They had gone to some back alley to buy the card and Brent felt like they were doing a drug deal. "It was weird," he said trying to put it out of his mind.

Grown men having to hold hands because the place is dangerous, I thought.

Soon, Victoria was dropped off with us without her luggage or passport. Pastor Isaiah prayed for her. After he prayed, Victoria said she felt "lighter." Pastor Isaiah said goodnight and, finally, the four of us could be alone.

CHAPTER 22

THE FLEECE

Alone in our hotel room, we all sat on the bed and talked for four hours. Victoria let it all out. Everything she was feeling, that was pent up inside. She talked about how mad she was that Ranjit was investigated and that it made him look bad.

As he listened to her, Luke's face was turning red and he was beginning to tear up. "You don't know how scared we were!" he cried.

"We care about you. Am I supposed to just let my sister go to some country to be with some guy we don't know? You didn't tell us. You didn't tell anybody, not even me! You could have talked to me about it, but you didn't," Luke continued.

"All of a sudden, you're in New Delhi, India, what were we supposed to think?

"You had two years to get to know him and his family.

"We didn't get that.

"We didn't even know Ranjit existed!

"We thought you were in a relationship with Vance!"

Luke never cried. Ever. He's quiet, smart, easygoing and loves to have fun. He was completely sobbing now. His eyes flooded with tears as he constantly wiped them with his sleeve.

This outburst from her brother did not faze her one bit. She stared at him with an angry expression, her brow furrowed, and as he poured his heart out, she was completely unmoved.

"I can't help how you feel!" she shouted.

We talked more and cried more. It was healing for us. She was beginning to feel better. She always kept her feelings bottled up. I was glad when she finally let us see inside because it was rare.

After a while, Brent said, "So, you like this guy, Ranch-it?" accidentally mispronouncing his name. Victoria laughed and so did we. After such intensity, we needed a laugh, even if it was at his expense.

After a break of laughter, it got serious again. Victoria said, "We need to pray."

I looked at Luke, and Luke looked at me. This was good. Very good. She grabbed my hand on her left and her dad's on her right.

As we all held hands, Victoria prayed that God would give her a sign, to let her know if she needed to leave or if she was safe here.

"What is the sign going to be?" I asked.

"Maybe if any of us thinks of anything, if God gives it to us, then we should say it," she said.

So, we all closed our eyes and asked God to give us something for Victoria. After a moment or two, Brent spoke up and said he had something.

"I'm seeing red…. So maybe if you cut yourself or bleed in some way…. If you see red on you… like blood…. that's the sign."

She seemed satisfied with that, so we went with it. It was like Gideon's fleece, and tonight we were putting ours out. In the Bible, the book of

Judges tells the story of Gideon's test in which Gideon places a sheep's fleece on the ground at night and asks God for a miraculous sign in the morning. We all agreed not to tell anyone what the sign was until after it happened, so as not to compromise the outcome.

We had gotten through to her! I grabbed my phone and texted the group back home:

WE'VE HAD A BREAKTHROUGH!!!

By now it was after 2:00 a.m. Victoria called Ranjit to come get her. He declined, saying it was too late, was too dangerous, and no one goes out after midnight. She seemed disappointed but said nothing.

"We have two rooms," I said to Victoria, "this one and one next door. If you and Luke want to sleep in there, Dad and I will sleep in here."

It had been a long day and the last four hours had been emotional and exhausting. I crawled into bed. Victoria crawled in beside me and laid her head on my chest. Luke crawled in on the other side of me and I wrapped my arms around them both. They remained there the entire night. It was getting cold in the room as the temperature dropped outside. We soon fell asleep.

Brent grabbed my phone and took a picture. He then sent it to my mom. She was probably wondering how things were going. This picture would tell all she needed to know.

. . . .

VOICES
BEHIND THE SCENES

Grant and Victoria:

Victoria: *My parents, brother, and I had family time last night. Please keep us in your thoughts and prayers.*

Grant: *I hope y'all can heal from this over time. You're starting to grow up. Remember, age is in the beholder's eye, how we view life. I really do hope this all works out for y'all.*

Victoria: *Me, too. I hope my parents leave here with a different perspective.*

Grant: *I think they already do. I think they are realizing you're an adult now.*

Victoria: *I don't just want them to realize I'm old enough. I want them to leave feeling better about everything. I hate seeing them like this. I hope their being here will make the family closer, and not break any ties.*

Grant: *I hope they can find peace with everything. If you need to talk about something, feel free. I hate I couldn't be there for you before all this, I just didn't realize how bad it was.*

I've been looking at Ranjit's Facebook page and there's nothing there about you. That doesn't seem right about him. As much as you've talked about him on yours, just seems weird.

Victoria: *We never posted about each other on Facebook, because we never met, and to post about your girlfriend/boyfriend you never met is kind of weird, and people would for sure laugh.*

⋏　　⋏　　⋏

Oliver and Victoria:

> Oliver: *I hope you were able to talk. I hope you can be heard…
> hang in there. Are you holding up okay?*
>
> Victoria: *Yes, the conversation went well last night. Today we
> are all going out together, him and his family, and my family.*
>
> Oliver: *Oh, darling, that's wonderful, but that's a lot of pressure
> right there. Just be yourself and try to enjoy it. You deserve a
> day out of quarantine!*
>
> *I know you have hundreds of people telling you what to do, your
> phone blowing up with their ideas of what you should do and
> what you should think. I ask you please to do what you set out
> to do. Explore. Spend time with Ranjit, meet his family properly.
> Enjoy India and get to know him and you. The rest….will sort
> out. And the irony of my giving you suggestions…not lost on me.*
>
> Victoria: *Oliver, you help me out a lot, and thank you for
> your guidance on how to deal with all this.*

ᚷ   ᚷ   ᚷ

Evelyn and Victoria:

> Evelyn: *How are you feeling? How are your parents? What
> are the plans?*
>
> Victoria: *I'm good. The conversation went well yesterday. I need to
> talk with Ranjit first before making final plans. Pray for God's will.*
>
> Evelyn: *Amen. I'm glad it went well!*

ᚷ   ᚷ   ᚷ

Austin (Victoria's school friend) and Victoria:

> Austin: *Are you okay?*
>
> Victoria: *My parents are here. They didn't have to come, but
> they did, and I feel so bad.*

WEDNESDAY, SEPTEMBER 26

CHAPTER 23

THE GIFT

The next morning, I awoke to see my mom's text, *I was just crying out to God to please let you hold your baby, then I picked up my phone, and see this*! referring to the picture of me cuddled with my babies.

Ranjit and his dad were coming to pick us up and take us to a different hotel. They said this one wasn't nice enough and the one they were taking us to was closer to their home and owned by relatives of theirs.

As we entered the new hotel room, we saw that it was, in fact, much nicer. It had a king-sized bed, a large-screen TV, a desk with a couple of chairs, and a window with a street view overlooking the front of the hotel. There were snacks and drinks on the table.

The bathroom was very nice, all made of brown marble, and the best part was it had toilet paper, and it didn't smell bad.

The three of us got settled in and Victoria went with Ranjit and his dad to their house until we were ready for them to come pick us up.

The plan was to spend the day with the family. We would go to the mall, have lunch, and end the day at the Golden Temple. The four of us would also be looking for "the sign" so we could leave.

I texted the group back home:

Me: *Last night was like being in a birthing room. Hard to describe, but beautiful, as we labored together for her!*

We have had zero contact with any of Brent's family since we left Dallas. They don't answer us. Please let them know we are trying to get in touch with them.

Mom: *I don't know what's going on with them.*

Me: *So, you haven't heard from them either? We should check on them. Maybe something happened to Granny.*

Keep praying because Victoria is with them now, and she could change back and we'll have to start all over, to get to where we are now.

Keith: *Did you see this? Please show it to Victoria. He sent me a message from someone on Facebook, which read:*

"I've been following the Victoria Harris story. The reason why this man cannot come to the U.S. is because he cannot get a visa to come here. Victoria is a tool in all of this. Punjabi boys prey on young, vulnerable American girls, lure them to India and marry them so they can obtain American visas. I know. I'm American and was a victim of the same thing. Please tell her to be careful. India is not a place for a young, white girl to be without any money or educative knowledge. Trust me on this. He doesn't love her. He loves the fact that she can get him a green card. Indian families do not approve of their children marrying outside of their culture."

Me: *I showed that to her already, and she said it's something she's been told before, and she has talked about it with him and his parents, and this is not that. But then she really started questioning if that was what they were planning.*

Anne: *Man, I wish I could be there to hug her, talk to her, and pray with her. There are so many negative comments on Facebook, it's disgusting. I had to stop looking, I was getting angry.*

Me: *I know, Anne. Don't think for one minute about the enemy. God is working. Stay positive.*

Mom: *The worst thing we can do is get pulled into that. It takes our focus from the truth. Then our hearts and minds dwell on it, instead of our blessings. God has done so many miracles, we must give Him thanks and praise.*

Keith: *I texted Grant and told him you wanted to know if everything is okay because you hadn't heard from them. Then he sent me this:*

"I'm not going to talk to you, I don't know you. This may look and sound bad, but I don't believe in a lot of what y'all have said. Please leave me alone."

I told him I apologize. I don't understand what he's talking about, but I'm weirded out about it. I apologize to you guys if I did something wrong.

I assured him he hadn't and told him I didn't understand it either.

Dad: *Take care of yourself. I need you to be strong. I couldn't make it without you.*

Keith: *My mom said you may want to start writing all this down. You may want to write a book.*

A book? I hadn't thought about that, but Keith was right. I needed to document everything.

Soon, Davison called and wanted to come by with Dr. Mustafa. Davison was the youth pastor at Pastor Isaiah's church where Dr. Mustafa's family attended. He had also been in the airport with Dr. Mustafa the night Victoria arrived.

Davison and Dr. Mustafa came and sat in the chairs by the window. Davison looked like the lead singer of the group *Alabama*. He was handsome with a full head of dark hair, a full black beard, and a lot of spunk.

Davison proceeded to tell us in an Indian accent, "Don't worry. He cannot come to U.S., and she cannot stay here because of the controversy. They have caused a scene, doing this the way they have done. Neither will she be allowed back in India after 'dis. Pastor Isaiah could not go to the U.S. They denied him within five minutes," he said holding up his palm, "and he has a brother who lives 'dere.'"

"We thought maybe they would have deported her back to the U.S. so we wouldn't have to come here," I said, sitting on the bed next to Brent and Luke.

"The government was going to deport her as soon as she landed here, but the Indian Church Conference told them not to. They said, 'Let the parents come!'" said Davison.

"What? Why?" I asked. I didn't understand why the church would do that and what authority did they have? Maybe there was a reason we needed to come here.

Dr. Mustafa then said something in Punjabi.

"The government told Dr. Mustafa if he let Victoria leave his home before the parents got here, they would deport her," Davison said.

Wow. God had it taken care of the whole time! If they had let her go to Ranjit's house, the way Grant, Kelli, and Evelyn wanted, she would have been sent home, and we wouldn't have even had to come. *Either way, she was in our hands!*

"You need to write a letter to Immigration. Dis' way you can take your 'dotter and leave."

"Okay, what do I tell them?" I asked.

"Tell 'dem, 'We need to take our 'dotter home. We cannot take decision here. All Victoria's family---her mom and dad, grandma and grandpa, brothers, aunts, uncles, cousins---everybody wants her back in U.S. 'Dey are waiting for her....'"

I got out a sheet of paper to write down what he was saying.

"Tell 'dem, 'We are depressed.'" As he said that, I stopped writing and looked up at him. I thought I was going to roll onto the floor. Depressed? That was the understatement of the century! I started laughing. I could barely hold it in. He looked at me strangely, as I'm sure he didn't understand what was so funny.

"Ohhh," I said holding my stomach, which was in stitches. Thank God for the medicine of laughter, "We're depressed alright."

I finished the letter, we visited a little longer, and they left.

It was almost 2:30 p.m. now. I texted Victoria, asking her what was taking so long.

>Ranjit answered, *We are almost ready, just waiting on Victoria, she is doing hairs...*

>*I believe it,* I texted back.

Soon Ranjit, his mom, and Victoria arrived in a taxi to pick us up. His dad would be meeting us at the mall. I felt we needed to get some Indian clothing so we could blend in. Everywhere we went, people stared. They seemed to be interested in "the Americans" with our blonde hair and fair skin. Except for Luke, with his brown hair and tan skin, he may have pulled it off.

Either the people there had heard about our situation or we were a rare thing to see, maybe both. They were the most hospitable people I'd ever met. It was their culture. Everyone held doors open for us, handed us things, and whatever we were doing they wanted to be right there next to us, helping us. They treated us like celebrities, and we felt rich.

"We could get used to this," Luke and I joked as we got in the taxi. As we drove to the mall, there was every type of transportation you can imagine on the road. Cars, trucks, SUVs, buses, mopeds, bicycles, horses with buggies, cows, tractors, cranes, bicycles with buggies, and pedestrians.

It was all there.

In one hodgepodge, in the middle of the street.

In addition to that, there were no lines on the road, no traffic signals, and no stop signs. No, they didn't use any of those things, they used horns to let you know they were coming! Everybody just went where and how they wanted.

It was utter chaos.

Every split-second we were coming face to face with another vehicle, but would swerve just in time, narrowly missing a head-on collision. Practically every vehicle in the town was dented.

It was so bizarre that Victoria and I didn't know what else to do but laugh. It was like being on a roller coaster. Swerve to the right, now swerve to the left, don't get hit!

Ranjit and his mom, obviously used to this, just looked at us confused, "Why are you laughing?" Ranjit asked with a serious look.

"Because we just keep cutting people off!" Victoria laughed as we swung around into another lane, and our driver laid on the horn.

"Cutting people?" he asked with a concerned look on his face. *Yes*, I thought, *be very afraid; we are laughing and talking about cutting people.*

Once we finally made it to the mall, and I got out of the vehicle, I was a nervous wreck. I didn't know how I could avoid getting back into a vehicle, but I never wanted to do that again, if I could help it.

We had to walk across the road to get to the mall. We grabbed each other's hands and waited for an opening in the traffic, and then decided to make a run for it, but as we did, Ranjit warned us, "No, no, no, no, don't run," he said as he walked us slowly across the busy highway, the myriad of vehicles somehow dodging us.

"What?" we asked, confused as we tried to do as he said. "Why did he say that?" I asked my husband, as he just shook his head.

We walked down the street passing mothers who were skin and bones, holding their tiny newborns, begging for food. When we got closer to the mall, we saw people holding mirrors under the cars as they walked by them in the parking lot. "What are they doing?" asked Victoria.

"They are looking for bombs," Brent told her.

Once inside, we were all frisked by guards standing at the entrance, which Victoria especially disliked.

After we were allowed in, we went to a clothing store and picked out several pieces. One store attendant got a bag for us, another held it while we shopped, while another took it from him, and put it on my shoulder when we were finished. We had about ten people attending to us at the check-out. I picked out several outfits; Victoria selected one while Brent and Luke each chose a dress shirt with square buttons and a belt, all of which rang up to only $200. As I began to pay, Ranjit argued that he should pay for Victoria's clothes, saying to her, "You are my responsibility now," as Brent and I frowned at each other.

Next, we went to get a bite to eat. As we entered the restaurant inside the mall, there was a birthday party going on in the back. We were placed at a long table and as we sat down, Victoria said to Ranjit, "I want to sit next to my mom." And she did, as he sat on the opposite side down from her.

We had delicious flatbread and some different types of sauces for dipping. There were some young men at the table next to us sipping short, skinny cans of soda. *No wonder everyone is so thin here.* We had water and were pretty full from the bread and sauces when they passed around a small plate with a few different things for us to try. As the plate came around to me, I grabbed what I thought was a green bean. I put it in my mouth, chewed, and swallowed. I soon realized it was a hot pepper. Within seconds, tears were squirting out of my eyes like sprinklers, my mouth on fire. They gave me some sugar pellets, but it didn't stop. I got up from the table to walk away and soon someone was handing me a vanilla ice cream cone, which almost instantly soothed the heat.

We decided to go ahead and leave. As we made our way down the escalator, Brent whispered to me, "I saw the sign."

"Where?" I asked, looking around.

"The first one. There were two parts. If the first one happened, the second one will, too.

"At that birthday party. There were red balloons. *I saw red balloons in the vision* last night. I just didn't say it because it didn't make sense to me. Why would God show me red balloons? I thought it needed to be something more spiritual. So, I just figured it meant blood. The blood of Jesus would get her out of here, and maybe she was supposed to cut herself or bleed somehow."

Wow. I was so excited! We could tell Victoria as soon as the second part happened.

We then made our way to The Golden Temple. I wanted Victoria to see their religion. I wanted her to see how they worshipped. She needed to know if this was what she truly wanted for her life. She needed to see how different it was from what we believed.

As we walked through the entryway towards the temple area, we passed by dogs curled up in the road. They were everywhere and we couldn't tell if they were alive or dead. As we walked through the narrow streets where people were selling goods from their little booths, a person was walking in front of us whose right foot was twisted so that they were walking on the top of their foot instead of the bottom. There were several people with the same disease walking around in the temple square.

There were children all around, and we were told to watch out for them because they would pickpocket. When we approached the temple area, we were instructed to cover our heads with orange scarves. We also had to remove our shoes and leave them at the entrance, to walk through water that was to cleanse our feet before walking on "holy" ground. We were supposed to have our legs covered. Luke was wearing shorts, but since he had come so far, they made an exception.

Upright, white tombs stood at the entrance and Ranjit stopped to pray to and kiss one. Everyone was walking in a big square around a courtyard to get to the magnificent Golden Temple which was surrounded by water. As eerie Indian music played, chanting could be heard beyond the temple and into the city. As we began to walk, Victoria grabbed her brother's hand and held onto it the entire time. She never walked beside Ranjit or held his hand.

We walked for some time and stopped to look down at the big, orange fish swimming in the water. It was getting dark and the lights around the temple came on. It was a beautiful sight. The light touching the temple caused the gold to shine like the sun in the dark. When we finally made it to the entrance of the temple, we were supposed to eat the bread at the door. I ate mine, but Victoria took one bite and dumped the sacred bread into Ranjit's hand. The look on his face was sheer terror as she nonchalantly walked off ahead of him.

We were so tired, we could hardly keep our eyes open, so we decided to forgo seeing inside the temple. I knew God knew our hearts. He knew whatever rituals we were taking part in meant nothing to us. These weren't real gods, and we were only there to serve a purpose. I hoped it was working. As we exited the temple area, we had to step over the water, not through it, as we were now entering back into "unholy" ground, and we picked up our shoes.

I fell asleep in the taxi on the way back to our hotel. As we got out and tipped the driver, Ranjit's taxi with his family showed up. He got out and the four of us stood with him in the parking lot.

I wanted to take Victoria by the hand and walk her inside, telling him we would see him tomorrow. I could have been firm about it and not given any room for anything else; just tell him that our daughter can see you during the day, but at night she stays with us.

Many times I wondered if I completely failed her in that moment. I should have been the strong mother, protecting my baby because I knew far better than she. She was young and innocent. I could have acted now, and apologized later, knowing it was for her good. She wasn't even against me but instead had been looking to me for guidance.

Holding my breath, I posed the question, "Do you want to go with him or stay with us?"

I let her make her choice. It would prove to be a devastating one. It was a decision I would regret many times over, but one I felt I had to make to show her I wasn't trying to control her life. I wasn't forcing her. I was giving her a gift. The gift of choice. I risked her safety and I risked losing her.

She hesitated.

"They only have one bed," Ranjit said, encouraging her to go with him.

"But it's a *big* bed," she countered, her voice soft and sweet, her innocent eyes looking up at him.

She looked longingly at me, but eventually said, "Mom, I think I need to go with him because of what we talked about last night." I knew she was referring to the sign. She hadn't seen it yet and thought maybe she would if she spent more time with them.

"Okay," I smiled, drowsily and said goodnight. That would be the last time we really ever saw her.

THURSDAY, SEPTEMBER 27, 2018

CHAPTER 24

POSTPONED

The next morning around 10:00 a.m., I woke up to Victoria texting me. My stomach felt queasy. She wanted some of the photos we had taken of us trying on clothes. I sent them over, told her I wasn't feeling well, and went back to sleep.

The next time I awoke someone was vomiting in the bathroom. I got up to look. Luke was hunched over the sink while Brent was on his knees bent over the toilet with his pants down. I began to feel like I was going to throw up and began to frantically look around the bathroom. *Where was I going to go?* Then the shower caught my eye. *Yes, I'll go in the shower!* I laid down on the cold tile shower floor, as I listened to them moaning.

Finally, we laid back down in bed and the three of us stayed there all day, each taking turns in the bathroom. We couldn't move without throwing up and it hurt our skin when the sheets moved across it. After Luke had thrown up for the eighth time, he said, "I'll stay sick, if it means getting her back. I can't go back to work knowing she's still here."

Victoria had texted me last night an hour after she left and asked how we were doing but we had already fallen asleep. Now I had texted her several times telling her we were sick and asking her to come to the hotel to help us, but hadn't heard back from her.

I received a text from the group. It was our friend, Keith Thompson.

Any answer on the fleece yet?

No, but she chose to spend the night with them. I think she knows it's her last night to see them and she's expecting the fleece to happen there. How this is going to go, I don't know. We don't want to leave without telling them. We don't want to hurt them; we just need to tell them she needs to go home.

I tried to take care of business back home. I needed to arrange for the employees to pick up their paychecks, our cell phone bill needed to be paid, and for some reason, my business checking was overdrawn. I wondered if I had accidentally paid my mortgage out of the wrong account, but there should have still been enough to cover it. I tried going to my online banking, but the site was down for maintenance.

I had to get this straightened out. I didn't want anything else bouncing. I certainly didn't want our phones turned off and Victoria's phone was on our account. The last thing I needed was to not be able to call anyone, plus the business phone needed to stay on back at the shop, and for some reason, I couldn't get in touch with the cell phone company either.

Mom was handling the paychecks for me and said they weren't delivered because I never sent the hours in. I know I sent them in the day we left. I had her re-send them, the paychecks were just going to have to be a day late. Nothing like trying to run a business from the other side of the world!

We still had not heard from Brent's family. Sanjay called to check on us and said he would bring some medicine later. It was Thursday. Our flight was scheduled to leave that night at 2:00 a.m. We planned on being out of work a week. We left on Saturday, but with the delay in Dallas and the time change, we had lost two days and arrived on

Tuesday morning. I was planning on Victoria coming and bringing her luggage so she could leave with us. I would have to get her a flight and change ours to match hers, but now we were deathly ill. There was no way we could possibly get on that plane.

Around 3:00 p.m., Sanjay and Dr. Mustafa came over with the medicine. Sanjay's friend, Felix, who worked for the airline, had also come with them. He told us he could take care of changing our flights. One hour and eight hundred dollars later, we had our new itinerary with a flight leaving Monday.

I had not heard from Victoria all day. Finally, later that night, she, Ranjit, and his dad showed up. She didn't bring her luggage or her passport with her. She said she hadn't seen the sign yet, so she wasn't leaving with us. Although we didn't need a sign, she did, and we were giving her a chance to see for herself. This way, it wouldn't be what we wanted, or what Ranjit wanted, but what God wanted. If we told her about the first sign, the real one with the red balloons, she wouldn't believe us because it wasn't told to her that first night, we reasoned. So we were waiting for the second one, the one Brent interpreted. We knew if the first one happened, the second one would, too. I told her to bring her luggage in case we saw the sign while she was with us, but she hadn't.

"They have what I had," she said, sitting at the foot of the bed near me, as she began to massage my feet and then Luke's legs with a technique she had learned at the health school.

"Why didn't you tell me these people were here?" Ranjit asked her, referring to Sanjay, his dad, and his friend, who were still with us. "Why didn't you tell me your family was sick?" He was being very firm with her as she looked up at him.

"You tell me, so I can deal with it," he scolded. "They shouldn't have come; I should have come." I didn't understand why he was making such a big deal out of wanting to be here when we were sick. It sounded like he wanted to be in control of the situation, not because he cared about us. Maybe *he* wanted to give us some medicine.

When Davison, the youth minister, and Pastor Isaiah showed up, there were eleven people in the hotel room. With so much commotion going on, it was making us feel worse. We were throwing up constantly. I told Victoria that we needed to rest and I asked her and everyone to leave.

Sanjay told me to call if we needed anything and reminded me to make sure we only asked for "sealed water" as they had told us when we first arrived in India because you don't want to drink the water there.

They all left a little before 9:00 p.m. and I rested for a few hours. Brent and Luke were sicker than I was. I had only thrown up a few times and was beginning to feel better. Around midnight, I decided to let everyone back home know what was going on. It was the middle of the day for them and after that night it would be another whole day before I could talk to them. I told them about Victoria not bringing her luggage, how I had to ask them to leave, and about our flight change.

> Me: *Brent said we may have to leave her here and trust God about not answering the fleece. But she doesn't need the fleece to be answered to make a choice if she hears God in her heart. The fleece was only training wheels because she was confused.*
>
> *If we get sick enough to need a blood transfusion, we know the fleece would happen, but we don't know if we should pray for that. I came here to make sure she is safe. I still don't know if she is, but that will be for her to find out. If I didn't try, I would have always wondered.*
>
> Keith: *Did Victoria say how she plans on coming home if she chooses to stay?*
>
> Me: *She said they would get her a ticket home.*

Mom: *That should have already been done. They didn't pay for her way back home, because they weren't planning on her coming home. What they did was not done in good faith. It did not show goodwill, to demonstrate to us they could be trusted.*

Me: *I still don't know how they got that one-way ticket. This is a terrible place to live. If this guy loved her, he wouldn't want her here. She almost got hit walking across the street yesterday and last night at the temple she looked disturbed. I can't believe she would still want to stay.*

Davison said they were going to deport her within five minutes of her arrival. Perhaps they are waiting to see what we do.

His family could be planning for her to stay here until he is of legal age to marry, which is about six months from now. They may be looking for permanent U.S. visas for the whole family, and she is their ticket.

If she stays here, we need to give her some phone numbers to people she can call if things get bad and Ranjit's family doesn't take her to the airport.

She told us she cleaned their dishes and washed their car. Felix said 'Dishes okay, car not okay. Man's job.' Once we get her home, I know she wouldn't want to come to our house right away. She needs somewhere peaceful, where she can be alone to think her own thoughts and rest from all this. I want to cook her a good meal, and read to her, and love on her. Mom, do you think she could stay at the house on Willow Creek Road?

Mom had a house in the countryside, down a quiet road that she had just finished renovating. It was spacious and had a big yard. Victoria liked it and I thought it would be the perfect place for her to recover

227

from everything; somewhere no one would bother her and she could relax for a while. I knew she probably wouldn't be able to return to work anytime soon. She needed healing and I wanted her to have space and time to do that. We all needed it.

Mom: *Yes, it's ready. I think that's a great idea. I don't want you to be concerned about me and Victoria. I realize she may see me as a threat and not want to be around me. I will work through that and accept it if I must. I just want you to be able to have a beautiful relationship with your daughter. You have been a blessing to me and I want that for you.*

Me: *She will be fine, Mom. It will all be fine. Just love on her when you see her.*

Keith: *Look at this article someone posted. You had very good reason to worry.*

"According to experts, India is the most dangerous country for women. It ranks the worst in cultural practices, sexual violence, and human trafficking, with New Delhi being the red-light district. Kidnappings, rape, and domestic abuse have increased. A judicial committee found that the inefficacy of the Indian government in prosecuting sex offenders has contributed to the frequency of violence against women."

Me: *Not a country I want to leave my daughter in. It seems they are not good at prosecuting. This gives me another reason to not trust any investigation. The police are bought and paid. I don't trust Esha or any of them. In this country, as little children, they are taught to pickpocket. From a young age, they do what they have to, to help the family survive, and when they are older, they learn greater things.*

Keith: *Did you see Victoria's post? Look how many comments are on it.*

I looked. There were 666. Interesting.

Me: When did she post that?

Keith: *Before you arrived there, I believe.*

Keith had commented under the post saying he didn't think Victoria had meant for it to be a hate-filled, free-for-all bashing of her parents, which it had now become, and posted the photo of me in bed with my arms around my babies.

Keith: *Victoria liked my comment, so that may say something.*

I had only skimmed over her post before. This was the first time I saw it, in its entirety.

It read:

I needed to create a post to stop all this madness. As most of you know, there are a lot of things being said about me on social media and on the news.

Don't believe all the sex trafficking gossip. That was never an issue but was completely made up by my family. I, as an adult, decided to meet a friend and his family. After talking to him for the past two years, we have created a strong bond of friendship. We accidentally found each other on Instagram. I'm embarrassed to say that because normally I would never talk to anyone online. I don't know why I did this time, but I did. When you talk to someone for that long, every single day, through a video chat, you really do get to know that person. You get to see their face, their personality, their mannerisms, their schedule, and their lifestyle. I felt very comfortable meeting him. He's given me plenty of proof that he is trustworthy. I've seen his house through video chat so many times I could draw the whole layout of his home. I've spoken to his parents and his sister, and I've even gotten to know some of his friends.

I left home without telling my parents about Ranjit or his family. Ranjit's dad purchased my plane tickets before I had the courage to tell my mom about him. So I was in a situation where if I told my mom about my travel plans, she could stop me from going, and the family's money would have been wasted. Or I could just write a long, detailed letter because I care enough to let my mom know I'll be fine and to let her know where I am. None of this mess would ever have existed if I had just told my parents about Ranjit and my travel plans.

So, because they were not informed, the only thing my family can think this might be is a sex trafficking ring. But it was not. This story is just about two young adults who fell in love and decided to meet. It would have been impossible for him to visit me in the U.S., so me coming here was the only option.

I never pursue a man. I came to him because it was the only way to meet. The Indian government makes it very difficult for them to get into the U.S.

The story my family spread on Facebook about it being a sex trafficking ring went all the way up to the President of India. By this time, I was trying to get on my last flight from the New Delhi airport to the Amritsar airport. I was stopped several times by the airline staff because of the lie my family told. My family did all this because they care a lot about my safety.

This lie caused some major problems for this innocent family. Ranjit was at risk of being sent to prison for intentions he did not have. His sister, who's a Punjabi actress, got several phone calls from her directors and producers asking why she is kidnapping. It put a lot of stress on him, his family, and me. I understand that my family is just concerned about my safety. Sadly, India has a reputation for things like this, but that doesn't mean that everyone in India are bad people. They did background checks on the family and Ranjit and I had to go through several inspections.

This put me on the news in both India and the U.S. At this point, I was emotionally shaken and angry, because I knew with all my heart I was not in any danger. At the Amritsar airport, I was forced to stay with a family connected to my church. My parents wouldn't allow me to stay with him until they came to India to meet him. My mom told me, if she feels he is safe for me, I can go to his house.

At this point, the police, the Embassy, the NGO, and others had already confirmed that he and his family were good people with nothing found during a background check. The family I was forced to stay with also knew Ranjit was safe for me, so he has been visiting me at their home every day this week, bringing me clothes to wear and food to eat.

Even after all my family has caused me, I've been waiting patiently for six days with absolutely nothing to do. Because the Indian government is involved in this, I can't leave the house regardless of my age.

On Friday, I got the opportunity to visit his home. It was the same home I had been seeing every day during our video chats for the last two years. It was an amazing feeling to finally be there. Then I had to go back to the other family and wait for my parents to get here.

Being a Christian in India is very different from being a Christian in America. In America, as we all know, you just choose whether you want to believe in Jesus or not. You don't get any benefits or financial aid. But in India, if you claim you are a Christian, the government gives you a lot of money. I can't speak for all, but most Christians in India are from lower class and uneducated. So, by them having me as their responsibility, they could very possibly be using me for financial benefit.

I told my mom it's funny how my family sent me to people I didn't know, and who are possibly liars, and made me not safe, when originally, I would have been in a safe place.

My only intention in flying to India was to meet Ranjit and his family. We had so many fun activities planned for when I got here. One lie from my family ruined it all. I felt like I needed to leave, not only to meet some friends but also because I was tired of being emotionally abused by my mom. At age twenty-one, I have the right to go and make myself happy. My family has humiliated me publicly by making statements that I'm mentally ill and don't know how to think for myself. They made me look like an idiot.

Anyone who has been in contact with me during all of this will tell you I have a good head on my shoulders. I'm not diagnosed with any mental illness, so for my family to say I have autism is not right. My only wish right now is for the truth to be out there. Then hopefully my vacation here in India can be enjoyed. I had no idea my trip here would end up on the news. I am completely emotionally destroyed by the lies that were told. Please help me get the truth out there.

I will agree, my intentions on coming here to India were good, but the way it was done was wrong on my part.

This post is what got me a 3:00 a.m. phone call from Los Angeles while we were in Dallas because she was saying unfavorable things about Sanjay's family who was keeping her for us, and about Christians in India receiving financial benefit from the government.

She was acting like Ranjit and his sister were doing her a favor by bringing her clothes every day. They were holding her luggage with all her documents and electronics, as a way to keep her from going anywhere. They should have given her luggage to her. But they were holding it, to hold her.

I texted the group:

> Me: *I don't understand Brent's family. His mother is always so concerned about us going anywhere, and now we are on the other side of the world, in a terrible country, and not a word from them. We've been trying to get in touch with them.*

> Anne: *I couldn't get in touch with them either. It's strange they aren't speaking to any of you, or us.*

> Mom: *She hasn't contacted me, so I've been calling to let her know what's going on.*

> Me: *If they don't want to know, they don't need to know. Grant and Kelli spoke condescendingly to us on the phone in Dallas. They were telling us how to parent and wanted us to let Victoria go. Now I don't know who to trust.*

> Mom: *I didn't care much for Evelyn. I always like everyone, but something about her didn't set right with me. I learned to like her and felt bad about my feelings.*

> Me: *I liked her, too but now I don't understand. It seems they all wanted to help, but all of them stopped talking to us when we didn't do what they wanted. They wanted Victoria to leave Dr. Mustafa's house and go to Ranjit's. We wanted to meet the family first to see if we felt they were safe, and we were only a day from arriving when they wanted Sanjay to let her go. We were not relying on anyone else's opinion of the family. No background check or report would be able to tell us that. There's such a thing as first-time offenders. She is our child. We're the ones who would have to live with the guilt if things went wrong. Not Grant, not Kelli, and not Evelyn.*

> Mom: *I wonder if my feelings about Evelyn have anything to do with what is happening now. Maybe my feelings were warranted.*

Me: *I guess they all got their feelings hurt.*

Mom: *It's one thing to get your feelings hurt and back off. But to turn to the enemy's side is a whole different thing.*

Me: *Well, none of them are helping now. Or asking questions. We are called to love even our enemies. And we are their family.*

Anne: *I pray for what seems to be division among some of the members of team 'Protect Victoria.' We were all working together for her and now we don't understand what's happened with some of the other members.*

Mom: *Jesus said Father forgive them for they know not what they do.*

Me: *That's the love of God. He loves the vilest one and He died for them. He doesn't see them as they are now, but what they can be. I pray that we can see through His eyes. I'm not angry at them, they are just weak and I feel sorrow for them.*

Mom: *I count them all as family. I love them, but I don't feel it right now.*

I showed them photos of us at the mall.

Me: *Shopping and having lunch with people who lured my daughter away from me. We were just trying to be polite. We should ask them if they will go to church with us since we went to the temple with them. We were too tired to go inside, but we did all the rituals with them. We didn't want to disrespect....or get shot, lol.*

I don't understand Victoria. She knows what we believe about being unequally yoked. How can two walk together if they are not in agreement? We have different values than they do and different beliefs. She will have to give up her religion or the marriage will be strained.

Mom: *Why on earth are we talking about marriage for goodness' sake?*

Me: *Because that's what they're planning. I wish I knew him better, what he was up to, and what he's really about. That takes a lot of time. Time we don't have.*

It was now about 8:00 in the morning.

Me: *I haven't heard from her. Not a good sign.*

Mom: *Back under the influence of 'Retch-ed.*

VOICES
BEHIND THE SCENES

Earlier that day…
Grant and Victoria:

> Grant: *Who in the world is this Oliver person? He's trying to make everything worse. I understand him hating Destiny, but he's attacking everyone.*
>
> Victoria: *I don't know who he is, but I think he likes drama. I know he's helped a lot, but I would ignore.*
>
> Grant: *It's hard when we're trying to fix everything. I've tried to talk to him, but he is determined to hurt all your family. He sent me this:*
>
> *"I hope your worried brother is having an awesome sightseeing day at the Golden Palace, paid for by the GoFundMe. I have nothing constructive to say to you, or your family. I feel racism and control are at the heart of all this."*
>
> Victoria: *I personally don't know him. I just know he wants to be involved. I never heard of him until all this happened.*
>
> Grant: *Looks like he's been coaching you for a while now. Just to let you know, I haven't been in contact with your family. They cut me out.*

人　　人　　人

> Sebastion to Victoria: *Your parents are so focused on making you live life the way they want you to. You have your own vision and path for your future. Don't let them "pray you away from that." It scares me you being there, but what scares me more, is you never living your life and enjoying it. Mobile is a dump.*

人　　人　　人

236

Oliver and Victoria:

>Oliver: *You having a good time with your folks?*
>
>Victoria: *Yes, but they don't trust the area and mom wants me home. I'm staying here though.*
>
>Oliver: *Good. I'm pleased to hear that. You must be the only person making those kinds of decisions. And you can go home easily enough. Look at what some pretty guy posted on Facebook:*
>
>*"I know Victoria's uncle, Seb Reinhardt. He's been hating Destiny and his mother, Priscilla, telling them he will get back at them; very vindictive person."*

Evelyn and Victoria:

>Evelyn: *I want you to know I am here for you always and forever, any time you need or want it. Everything we've talked about is true, and is from the bottom of my heart, with good intentions, and wanting to help you, because you deserve it. I love you as a mother or mentor, whichever you prefer, and would do everything in my power for you.*
>
>Victoria: *I'm so glad to have you. My parents are worried about the area. Mom clearly wants me home, but it's not happening. She's trying to prove something to everyone. I'm planning on staying here until Ranjit gets done with school. I'm not exactly sure where we will live, but for certain we want to live in the U.S. and he wants to go to college.*

Ranjit and Victoria:

Ranjit: *Your mom is calling. Answer her. We're going there in the evening.*

Victoria: *She wants me over there now.*

Ranjit: *Why now? To blackmail you? Tell her it's far and we have a lot of works' to do.*

Victoria: *It's their last day. They spent a lot of money to get here.*

Ranjit: *Ok, go back with them. I will drop you there. Pack your luggage.*

Victoria: *SHUT UP. THEY FLEW HERE TO SEE ME AND IT'S THEIR LAST DAY! MONEY THEY DON'T HAVE!*

Ranjit: *Okay, I will drop you there.*

Victoria: *THEY STILL CAME!*

人　　人　　人

Evelyn and Victoria:

Evelyn: *I hope your parents and Luke are feeling better, so sorry they got sick! When are they coming home?*

Victoria: *They are staying longer now, maybe 'til October 1ˢᵗ.*

Evelyn: *Your mom and grandma should really make a formal public apology to you, Ranjit and his family. Since she made all the lies public, the apology should be public too, and the right thing to do would be to do it before they leave. Ranjit's family deserves that and it would stop all the stuff people are saying on Facebook. Then you need to have some fun, see India, and enjoy Ranjit and his family!*

Victoria: *Mom said, "You're going against your parents, which even in India they know is wrong!" I'm so fed up!*

Evelyn: *She needs to go home. She's going to keep pushing you until you are sick of it, and just so she'll leave you alone, you'll go with her. Don't let her get to you. What she has done is illegal. Abuse, lying to federal authorities, lying to the court to get custody of you to be able to make decisions about your life, lying about your mental state, taking donations based on lies, that is stealing; asking the churches here for money to save their daughter, all illegal. And taking selfies all full of smiles, while in a supposed stressful situation. All fake. She hasn't earned your respect, or trust. Even parents must earn it from their children. You need to stick to your decision. Every time she says something, text back: "Apologize publicly to me, Ranjit, and his family."*

Just copy and paste. Every. Single. Time.

FRIDAY, SEPTEMBER 28, 2018

CHAPTER 25

"CLEAR THEIR NAME"

I told Mom I was getting a shower and would talk to her tomorrow which, for me, would be that night. We were feeling a little better. Our stomachs were still queasy, we couldn't eat anything, and we were weak, but the vomiting had stopped. It was now Friday. We stayed sick in bed all day again and rested.

I called Victoria several times throughout the day, asking when I was going to see her. All she would say was, "Clear their name," and would hang up. Each time she sounded groggy, like she had just woken up, but said she didn't remember falling asleep, and other times she was breathing hard.

That afternoon, Sanjay texted, *Mrs. Harris please do take your medicine now and have food at 10:00 p.m. I have given them instructions downstairs. If you need anything, call number 9.*

Sweet Sanjay. He was watching out for us.

I was still trying to get business taken care of from the day before. The phone bill was now past due, and I still didn't know why my checking account was negative but needed to fix that soon. Mom went in person to pay the phone bill and when I was finally able to get on the bank website, I found out why my account was overdrawn. It was payroll! I had completely forgotten about it. So I quickly transferred money over to cover it.

Finally, around 5:00 p.m., Victoria texted me.

Victoria: *Me, Ranjit, his sister, and his parents, all deserve a public apology.*

Me: *No! We deserve an apology. We will give an apology when you are back home!*

Victoria: *You promised.*

Me: *I said AFTER you are home in the U.S.*

I don't feel safe for you to stay with them, because they are not letting me see you. They are withholding you from us. This is wrong. Bring your luggage and stay with us the last few days we are here. That's the least you and they can do.

Several hours went by and I received no response.

Me: *Since you aren't answering me, I'm especially worried. I'm getting impatient with them. They're not doing right. Every time I talked to you today, you sounded funny on the phone. You stayed with them the last two nights, now you should be with us.*

Victoria: *They tried to send me there, but it's too late now. I'll see you tomorrow afternoon. I'm sorry. I really want to spend time with you.*

It was only 7:00 p.m. I tried calling, but she didn't answer.

Me: *It's not too late. We can come get you. We want you to spend the night with us and go to church with us tomorrow. Why aren't you answering me? This worries me.*

Several hours passed and still no answer.

I then put a post on *Facebook*. If anything happened to her, I wanted to document what was happening.

This is a parent's worst nightmare. We have sacrificed everything to help Victoria get back if things go wrong for her. If she wanted to come home, she might not be able to, being at the mercy of only two people who barely speak her language.

We have spent tons of money on passports, visas, airfare, and hotels just to get here, closed our business, and her brother risked losing his new job, being so sick we've been vomiting and in bed for two days.

We have gone countless hours without sleep, two days without food, and have had an insurmountable amount of stress. We do sometimes question going this far to help our daughter, but we are called to protect life when in our power to do so, whether it be our own or someone else's.

No matter how old you are, you are to honor your parents, even if you don't agree with them. Especially if you're still living under their roof and they are taking care of you. If she had been living on her own, it may have been different. But I'm still responsible for her. If she could do this, then she could've been living on her own, and not taking advantage of us, but the fact is, she is not able to, even at twenty-one.

That is why she did this. She wants someone to take care of her so she went somewhere where parents take care of their children forever.

If his family had booked her a return flight at least it would have shown goodwill.

As for the photos you've seen, the smiles are because, praise God, we've gotten to see her again. But don't let it fool you. We smile to keep from crying. It's horrible here and we just want to come home. We're in deep emotional, mental, financial, and physical pain. Our hearts are breaking. We want out of here asap.

We're trying to be patient with our daughter and his family. We would like her to come home with us so we can think and regroup because she isn't making sense and we are all confused and depressed. Making decisions while under duress is never a good idea.

Victoria is a totally different person with us as seen in the photos of her snuggling up to me in bed. But after she goes to his house, she comes back defiant and rebellious, acting hateful towards us. We believe there is mind control at play. This should be obvious, for how could one who never leaves home, go across the world? God will use all of this for His Glory, I firmly believe.

I thanked everyone for their help.

As for the few people making negative comments, all I can say is, "Father, forgive them for they know not what they do."

My uncle, a pastor, commented,

If you must leave there without her, are you prepared for that?

To which I responded, *Yes, I am fully prepared to leave without her.*

I had resolved in my mind that may be what happens. I didn't know how God would work it out. I just had to trust Him.

Later that night I texted the group:

Me: *They are asking for an apology.*

Mom: *For what? No apology for being afraid.*

Keith: *They would surely get no apology until my daughter was on a flight back to the states.*

Dad: *It sounds like it's time to get Victoria and leave. Things will only go south from here. Their government probably doesn't want any more complications. Them contemplating deportation bears that out.*

Mom: *Your dad is on pins and needles and won't rest until you're home. He said get her now and get out of there.*

Me: *It's insane to make these kinds of decisions while throwing up. We're leaving early Monday morning. Don't tell anyone, we don't know who to trust.*

Mom: So, *they hold your daughter hostage until we put out a public statement that we don't agree with.*

Keith: *The lesson in all of this is, if you don't want to be accused of being a human trafficker, don't lure someone's young daughter to the other side of the world.*

Mom: *Tell them no apology, but if they'll bring her to you, they won't be bothered with any more investigations. How are you feeling?*

Me: *I'm wearing out, and ready to come home. Sick of talking and getting nowhere.*

Keith: *This is one of the most trying situations I've ever seen a child put their parents through. I understand what you were trying to do going to the temple with her, and I know God doesn't see it as meaning anything. He knows your heart, but I'm afraid, they or their 'gods' may see it as giving them more power, emboldening them.*

Mom: *I'd like to get a hold of him. Let her bring him over here. I got some chores.*

With all her rental house renovations, she wasn't lying.

Me: *What if she had gotten stuck in Dallas like we did? We could've caught up to her!*

Mom: *All I can say is, God allowed this. For what reason, we don't know yet.*

Me: *There were a million ways this could have gone wrong for her.*

Mom: *How are Brent and Luke?*

It was now 2:00 a.m.

Me: *Luke is trying to sleep. Brent is upset and being negative. He says he never thought this was the way we would lose our business.*

He says we are somewhere we should have never been.

He's afraid of losing employees we just hired, worried about the bank account, about paying bills, and losing business. This is our best time of year, and we're missing it.

I told him we can't worry. It's in God's hands. He'll fix everything.

He's eating lunch at 2:00 a.m. I think we're still on Mobile time.

Two weeks before she left, we watched a movie about this, and I said right in front of her, "That would be my worst nightmare, to not know where my children are, and if they are okay," and she made no response. That was her cue to tell me and she didn't listen.

Keith: *To do what she's done, I'm sure she had to put up a wall. Here is a quote, I think your family needs to hear:*

"Uncomfortable grace takes us to places we never intended to go, so we'll arrive where God wants us to be."

Me: *This is so frustrating. We've been relying on these people for everything. They tell you one thing, and then have no commitment to time or keeping a schedule. Chris Cotton said we should be safe going out by ourselves, because people know about this. He said to stay in large groups, and we will be fine. They're just curious about Americans.*

We're going to figure out this Uber thing, and how to get around. About to take matters into our own hands!

Then Victoria texted me:

Victoria: *You have seen with your eyes that I'm not in danger in this house. I came only to visit, but now it's impossible for me to live in Mobile after what's happened. I had good discernment of the family before I came, and knew they weren't lying about who they are. I wouldn't have flown here if I had one spec of doubt. You hurt them a lot. Ranjit almost went to prison for being a "sex trafficker," and his parents wanted me to tell you about me coming, but I didn't and that's on me, but I wrote a long letter to you so there wouldn't be any confusion.*

Me: *They bought you a one-way ticket. That makes it extremely suspicious. We did what any good, loving parent would do. I'm not sorry for loving you and looking out for your safety!*

This country is known for violence against women. We don't know Ranjit and his family. We only know what they've done. They've taken you from your family, and it's wrong.

The fact they didn't give you a ticket home, shows they can't be trusted. I want you to come to church with us tomorrow.

Victoria: *You need to apologize to them. You now know it wasn't what you thought. You should be thankful I was right about this family, and you should be proud of me for judging them well enough, but still, you want to believe the worst. I'm not going to church tomorrow. It will be in a different language.*

Me: *They'll have an interpreter for us. You lied to your work and told them you were going to see a girlfriend you went to school with in the U.S. So, what were we supposed to think with all the lies?*

Victoria: *I didn't want them to worry and was going to clear everything with them once I got here. I didn't need anyone to stop me. I don't want to go to church. Why are you forcing me?*

Me: *In India, they believe it's wrong to go against the parents no matter how old they are. So they're even going against their own culture by withholding you from us. 're We want you to go to church with us because it is our faith. It bothers me that you don't want to go.*

Victoria: *There is nothing on their background check and I'll always be a Christian.*

Me: *The longer you stay away, you will never go back.*

Victoria: *I don't want to be with someone who makes me so sad and hasn't apologized.*

Me: *We will apologize once you are back home safe in the U.S. We cannot know that he is a good person when he will not let you go home with your family where you belong.*

Victoria: *I can go back whenever I want.*

Me: *He can always come to the U.S. as soon as he finishes school, or you can come back here. You can at least come back with us for now.*

Victoria: *I cannot trust you.*

Me: *What? Twenty-one years with me, and I've never lied to you. You have lied to us all your life. You're the one who snuck out of the house and went across the world to another country and lied to your job. But you can trust someone you just met online two years ago? All this has happened because of the way you did this!*

Victoria: *My letter explained everything.*

Me: *The detective said that letter is a prime example, that it's exactly like all the other letters from girls who are lured away from home and sex trafficked. Exactly like theirs! And it was typed out just like theirs. We have reason to believe the worst!*

You don't have to live at home, just come back to the U.S. Luke knows you're not going to be happy here, and that it's a dangerous place.

We should be able to see you every day. You should be staying the nights with us, and only see Ranjit in the daytime. We are leaving soon. But I guess you have chosen them to be your family now.

You don't want to come to church because they don't speak English? You are in a non-English speaking country, what do you expect? As for always being a Christian, you're going to want to be around people who believe the way you do, or you're going to want to believe and worship the way people around you do. You'll become like them, and you will give up your Christianity.

Can't you see how much you mean to us when we dropped everything to come here? And you say you can't trust us?

We must like being abused. Because we have nothing to gain from coming here but you, and everything to lose.

I never put anything on Facebook when you left. I was too busy trying to get to you. Grandma put the post out to get help, but Grant is the one who put Ranjit's name saying he was part of a sex trafficking ring. We did none of that. So, if anyone needs to apologize it should be Grant. Ask him.

It all boils down to you leaving without telling us, or none of this would have happened. You, and he, and his family did this, not us!

Look at what all I've been typing, and you won't respond. Just like at home.

I should have never helped you break up with Vance. You couldn't break up with him by yourself, in your own country, at home, with people who speak your language. Now when you get in an argument with Ranjit and you need help breaking up with him, who is going to help you?

Victoria: *That won't happen.*

Me: *We are your ticket out of here if you're truly visiting like you say you are. You may not be able to leave once we're gone, because they may not take you to the airport. You will be at their mercy.*

Why not leave now, while you have a chance?

You said you came to meet them, and you've done that.

Now let's go!

VOICES
BEHIND THE SCENES

Evelyn and Victoria:

> Victoria: *Mom said she will not give an apology until I'm home.*
>
> Evelyn: *That is wrong on every level! She lied about you and them and won't apologize! You need to post an update on Facebook and say how your mom is still abusing you emotionally, and how she refuses to apologize! That is disgraceful. She's trying to manipulate you into going home. Don't fall for it! Oliver got them to focus on him a lot, which was hilarious.*
>
> *Your mom knows how bad she looks now, and how embarrassed she'll be if she goes home without you after everyone has proved her lies.*
>
> *You deserve to be happy, and to be treated with respect and love. I'm working on getting Ranjit here and doing everything in my power to help you start a life together here in the USA, far away from Mobile!*
>
> Victoria: *I'm on the floor crying with relief because of your big heart!*
>
> Evelyn: *I love you like a daughter Victoria, and that means I will do anything for you. Always. You are stuck with me forever.*
>
> Victoria: *I love you, too. I've been researching how he can live in the U.S. All of this is new to me, and I don't know how we're going to do it.*
>
> Evelyn: *We'll help. Don't worry.*

Victoria: *Mom is giving me so much stress.*

Evelyn: *I know. I'm sorry. Is she pressuring you?*

Victoria: *I can't talk to her.*

Evelyn: *Has she been yelling and doing what she always does?*

Victoria: *Yes, she said this: I don't know that you're not in any danger. I only met them three days ago. We never said he was a trafficker, but that we feared he might be. The authorities wouldn't have investigated him only because we said so. They investigated because they themselves believed you were in danger. We didn't tell them anything. They told us!*

Evelyn: *That isn't true, she contacted the FBI and other authorities, even the Congressman from Alabama. She has done so much damage that people here in my college are talking about you!*

Victoria: *Really? Uggggghhhh!*

Evelyn: *You are an adult, and do not need to go back and live with your parents. If you do, your mom will have you locked up at home or in a psych ward just to prove she was right. Your mother is not being Christian-like, or a decent human being by not apologizing, after all she has done!*

Victoria: *She wants me to go to church with them and bring my luggage.*

Evelyn: *Say no! You do not need to do anything she says! With your luggage? Does she think you are stupid? That is so they can hold you.*

Victoria: *She has wasted my time and hurt so many.*

Evelyn: *And calling you autistic and mentally ill. That was low.*

Victoria: *She says I need to stay with them until they leave. I'm not stupid.*

Evelyn: *But she thinks you are. She has lost control over you and it's driving her nuts. You don't have to go. Just say no, don't give excuses just say, "No mother, you no longer control me. I'm an adult and will do what I want with my life!"*

You are an individual, different from her, special, unique, and amazing! Now she has lost you. It's her own fault! If you do what your mother wants, even going to church with her, or anything she tells you, you are taking a step back into her web.

You need to be very careful from now on. You are now a free adult woman. Think hard, and make decisions that are to your benefit, and for your happiness.

Do not stay with them in the hotel. You don't know what your mother is planning. Tomorrow you should go out with Ranjit and his family sightseeing. Do your own thing.

The lies and abuse must stop. No more yelling and disrespecting you and Ranjit's family. Either she treats you properly or she can forget about you.

She's trying to get revenge on people and using you to do it, for her own agenda. You're not a puppet or a toy she can throw around and hurt or love when she feels like it. You're a person, a human being. She's being vindictive and cruel, only thinking about herself.

As your mother, she should be loving and respecting you. Maybe later you can fix your relationship, but for now you need to draw a line.Sorry for giving so much advice, but the way she treats you makes me so upset.

Victoria: *Don't say sorry, you're helping a lot.*

Evelyn: *She should be happy I was right about this family. You can send me screenshots of your mom's conversation and I'll help you deal with her if you'd like.*

Victoria: *She said this, 'We didn't contact any FBI in India. We don't have that kind of authority outside of the U.S. It's not possible for us to make their government investigate. They did that on their own. You are being fed lies.*

'You need to listen to me. You're listening to him and his parents. Remember your and Luke's Bible teacher? She's from India and said it will be difficult for you here. There's a reason she went to America. Sanjay was born in India, but he and his brothers moved away to have better lives.'

Evelyn: *She is lying. What about going to court to get custody over you? She has contacts in the FBI and talked to police through her sister-in-law. She even contacted the State Department. I have it all in my conversations with her. Here's an article: 10 Signs of a Narcissistic Parent.*

Victoria: So, you *have proof.*

Evelyn: *Yes, but even though we have proof, you still need to show her you're in control. Live your life on your own terms, not hers. Can you imagine what your life would be like if you came back to live with them? If it was bad before, imagine after all this. I'm still upset about them not feeding you. You never deny food to your child, no matter how old they are. In our family and culture, we believe our children are our responsibility forever. We decided to have them. It was not their choice, and they are ours. We love them unconditionally and will always be there for them.*

Victoria: *That's exactly right. She didn't care if I ate. She said I work and I have money to feed myself.*

Evelyn: *Tomorrow, get up and go out with Ranjit before 8:00 a.m., so when they arrive you're not there and they can't do anything about it. It will show them you have taken control of your life.*

Do you have a ticket to go home if you want to?

Victoria: *Ranjit said they will take me back whenever I want.*

Evelyn: *So, what the heck is she talking about? She's trying hard to guilt trip you into leaving. Look at what someone posted to your mother:*

"You are close to Jesus, and Satan is trying to destroy you. This is the biggest test of your faith so far. We have believers all over praying for special strength and wisdom. Do you have a pastor there who can reason with his family?" Then your mom answered, "We do. They are going to talk to them tomorrow."

Evelyn: *Someone is going to talk to you and Ranjit's family. Just so you are prepared.*

Victoria: *Great.*

Evelyn: *Keep yourself focused on your future, not on what she is trying to do to you. Here are some websites on getting a fiancé or student visa for Ranjit. I'll be calling you tonight so we can chat.*

SATURDAY, SEPTEMBER 29, 2018

CHAPTER 26

SHIFTING

The next morning, we tried to order something from the restaurant downstairs. We thought French fries might be safe and we could keep it down, but everything in this country was spicy, even those.

We decided to move to another hotel. We didn't want to be in the one Ranjit's family had chosen for us any longer and we didn't want them to know where we were. They were keeping our daughter from us and making demands for us to clear their name. Every time I asked her when I could see her, I kept getting that same response.

I had no authority to clear anyone's name. No one from the government had cleared them of anything, as far as I knew. No one had informed me that he hadn't been involved in something criminal. No one had reassured me of anything. If he was cleared, why didn't he have the government inform me of that?

Being here made us feel like we were six years old. We didn't know where we were, we couldn't drive, we couldn't speak the language, and we didn't know how things were done. I had never felt so helpless. "Try to find a map," Dad had told us, but we hadn't had a chance. We had only been here four days and two of them were spent sick in bed. We hadn't heard from Victoria today, didn't see her all day yesterday, and barely the day before that. We came all this way to get ignored.

By moving, they would no longer be in control of us. She wouldn't know if we left without her. Would she care? Would she call and try to find us? Would the family be wondering or afraid of what we may be out doing? It was their turn to need answers.

We got dressed and called an Uber. We were going to find another hotel, but first we were going to church.

As we stood by the door of our hotel room, about to leave, Luke said this was the ultimate mission trip. "It's a trip. We're on a mission. And we're here to save at least one person."

We checked out of the hotel and had the Uber driver drop us off at church. As we entered and set our luggage in the back pew, we said hello to Davison and Pastor Isaiah and met some of the members.

There was a lady with a large tumor on her face, who spoke to us, "That boy is not good. They worship idols and try to marry girls to go to the U.S. Hindus are known for that." She was very sweet, gentle, and kind.

Then she said, "Your daughter will go home with you. Don't worry. Don't cry. She won't stay here. This will be easy for God." I wanted to believe her. I hugged her, thanked her, and told her I would be praying for her, then made my way to sit in the pew with Brent and Luke.

The little church had a dirt floor with astroturf on top. There were two rows of pews on top of that with an aisle down the middle. Some young men sang a few songs and when it was time to hear the message, we were told to turn to the Book of Judges. The message for the day was on Gideon's Fleece. Brent, Luke, and I all looked at each other as we sat in the pew. We hadn't told anyone about our night in the hotel room or about the sign, the "fleece," we had asked for.

Smiling from ear to ear, we all knew that God had His hand on us. God was good. This day in church brought us strength. After the sermon,

Pastor Isaiah showed us the room he and his family lived in underneath the church. It was like a cement bunker: dark and damp with no electricity. I couldn't imagine anyone living there. These people were truly some of the humblest.

"Did you get 'shifted' to another hotel?" Davison asked. (I had called him earlier that morning to see if he could pick us up.)

"Not, yet. We need to find one," I said.

"Come on, I'll show you. There's one around the corner," He got on his motorcycle and told Luke to hop on while Brent and I rode in the "auto," which was like a golf cart used as a taxi. The hotel was just on the other side of the street.

As we approached the hotel, the stench was the absolute worst yet. Davison escorted us inside. We booked our stay and carried our luggage upstairs.

It was a large room with two king-sized beds on each wall, facing each other. When I peered inside the bathroom, the smell was unbearable. We decided we would only go in there to use the toilet, and only if we absolutely had to.

Davison told Brent he would pick up some "sealed" water for us.

"How much?" Brent asked, taking out his wallet. "A hundred."

Brent had a look of pain on his face.

"Rupees, Brent," I said.

Davison laughed, "Yeah, a hundred American dollars would be bad."

"Oh, yeah, yeah, here you go," Brent said giving him some cash.

"That's only a dollar or so," I laughed, but I don't think he wanted to spend another cent.

When he returned with the water, Davison talked about a plan for the next day, Sunday.

"We will go to Immigration, and 'den we'll see if we can get the whole church to meet us at Ranjit's house." He was quite a character, a fighter with a zealous heart, and probably a little ADHD. I liked him. He always had me laughing, without which I don't think I would have survived.

"Don't take tension. We will get your 'dotter. He doesn't want to see me. He's afraid from me," Davison said. I smiled. Whatever we were lacking, Davison was making up for it.

Our plans were to try to talk to her. And get her to come stay with us in our hotel. We'd had only one day with her and as soon as we let her go with Ranjit for one night, we weren't allowed to see her again. We had been cordial and polite as we didn't want to upset them.

"Get some rest. I'll see you in the morning." After Davison left, the three of us went to the restaurant downstairs, across from the hotel. Maybe we could finally get something that agreed with us. As we walked inside, there was a gold statue of Krishna, a Hindu god. It was a clean and fairly nice place. As we sat down, there were two small bowls on the table. One with little green herbs and one with multi-colored sugar pellets, both to soothe the pallet after eating spicy food. When we finished eating, we paid thirteen dollars for the three of us and asked for a box to take the leftovers home. They brought us a plastic shopping bag which we weren't quite sure what to do with. Apparently, we were to dump the plates of food all together into the bag.

That night Victoria texted me.

Where are y'all? We were going to pay for your hotel, but you left without telling us.

I found it ironic she was upset that we left without a word.

I sent her the address, Tomorrow Ranjit needs to bring you here.

Just then, I received a text from Sanjay and his friend Felix. I told them of our plans the next day to talk to Victoria and take her back home with us. Felix said, *If you try to take her, you may lose her.*

That's a chance I am willing to take. Even if she never speaks to me again, at least I'll know she's in the U.S. and that she's alive and safe, and I meant it. I didn't care which state she chose, even if it was all the way to the Northwest corner of Washington, just having her back in our country would feel like having her in our backyard compared to this, and I would be so grateful.

Plan A wasn't working, and this was Plan B.

VOICES
BEHIND THE SCENES

Earlier that day...
Evelyn and Victoria:

Victoria: *I think mom left the hotel and is staying with someone else. She won't answer my texts.*

Evelyn: *She has another strategy, to make you worry that something has happened to her and feel guilty for standing up for yourself. Ignore her. When she sees that her manipulation isn't working, she will text you again, and if she doesn't, it's her loss. You have tried to make things right with her, but she doesn't want to make things right, she only wants to control you. Have you spoken to Luke or your dad? Why do you think she is staying with someone else?*

Victoria: *I haven't, and I think because the hotel is expensive.*

Evelyn: *Didn't they go to church? I thought Ranjit's family was paying for the hotel.*

Victoria: *I think so and they went to stay at a church member's house. She was supposed to let us know they were leaving so they wouldn't have to pay full price for the hotel, but they left without informing us.*

Evelyn: *This is all part of her plan.*

Victoria: *Ranjit's family is being nice to my parents, but mom is stabbing them in the back.*

Evelyn: *Yes, she is. She doesn't care about their feelings, or yours. Only herself, and how she looks. Did she make a big deal when you didn't go to church?*

Victoria: *She never came.*

Evelyn: *Just relax, sweetie, she is doing this to make you feel guilty and worry, and to be able to say his family lied and didn't pay for their hotel. What else did she say?*

Victoria: *She said, 'For clarification, this is what I posted: We were told by a local news channel that Gulf Shores has become a hot spot for trafficking. It has raised awareness about this problem in our area at a time when we weren't aware. Watch out for your loved ones. We are not sure if the person our daughter is with is doing this, but given the circumstances and area, we were not willing to take any chances. We will be happy to clear his name if we find out otherwise after we return to the States with our daughter.'*

She just won't talk to me today.

Evelyn: *That about Gulf Shores is crap, the only news is this: Son of restaurant owner indicted on child sex trafficking charges.*

She is making it sound like Ranjit's family could be part of it. This guy is a white American.

Victoria: *Wow.*

Evelyn: *Did you see her post on Facebook, I told you about yesterday?*

Victoria: *I can't find it. I looked everywhere.*

Evelyn: *Here it is: 'She left the day before her father's birthday. In the letter, she said 'Happy Birthday, Dad!' As if it was going to be a happy birthday. There is a lack of empathy, to feel what others feel, or care.'*

And this: 'She is in a dangerous area only thirty minutes from the Pakistan border and with only two people who barely speak English. The police don't even speak English.'

Victoria: *This makes me so angry. Ranjit and Tanvi know English well. I'm not in any danger.*

Evelyn: *Now you and I need to be smart, since your mother isn't. She is trying to provoke you.*

Victoria: *They need to leave me alone.*

Evelyn: *Victoria, this is evil. She is trying to look good because she realizes she is coming back without you. She admitted she didn't take care of you without realizing it when she said, 'She came here for Ranjit's family to take care of her.'*

I apologize on behalf of mothers everywhere. Most of us are responsible, caring, and honest, not like her. That post is a pity party. She's looking for sympathy.

Victoria: *I just remembered something. In my letter, I told mom I wanted a career of my own, and she still says all that stuff about me wanting to be taken care of.*

Evelyn: *I read that. She will always do that. What you have done is not a mistake, it is the best thing you have done in life so far! I'm so proud of you. Now that you have opened your wings, keep flying. I'll be here to guide you.*

Here's another article, 'Seven Arguments that Only Toxic Moms Have with Their Kids.' And a scripture for your parents, 'Fathers do not exasperate your children, instead bring them up in the training and instruction of the Lord.' This is said directly after 'Honor your mother and father' so they go hand in hand. They are not treating you right. They do not deserve your respect, and have not earned it. Has she contacted you?

Victoria: *She ordered me to come to the new hotel they are staying in.*

Evelyn: *She spends the day ignoring you, writing crap about you and Ranjit on Facebook, now orders you to go stay with them, and expects you to just say, 'Yes, Mommy Dearest.'*

Look what she replied to someone:

> *Commentor- I have two daughters, and this scares me to death. I thought after this age, they would be more mature, but now I'm not so sure.*

> *Mom- I hope this raises awareness. I thought teenagerhood would be bad. I practically breezed through that just to end up with this.*

> *Her visa is for ten years. A little more than a visit don't you think?*

Don't let people project their fears onto you. She is belittling you publicly. Just more things to apologize for!

SUNDAY, SEPTEMBER 30, 2018

CHAPTER 27

"WE'RE LEAVING HERE WITHOUT YOU"

The next morning we awoke at 4:30 a.m. and spent time praying and studying to know what to say to Victoria. I called her asking when they were bringing her. Ranjit said he would later, then later said he couldn't. She sounded groggy again and I asked if she knew how many nights she had spent with us, and she couldn't answer. Then the phone went dead. I made several attempts to call both of them with no response.

It was getting close to noon and Davison still hadn't arrived. He, like everyone else, was never on a schedule or in a hurry to do anything. If you were told a time, it may be three hours later. Forget appointments, things change, and they don't update you on it.

I sat on the bed. "How far are we from home, anyway?" I wondered out loud. I grabbed my phone and did a search, "7,986 miles."

Luke, who was as long-suffering as molasses in winter, was getting impatient. Finally, Davison called with fire in his voice, telling us what he had been up to.

"He never does anything when you want him to, but he gets it done," Luke smiled, happy to hear from him.

"Sounds like someone else we know," I smiled, "God."

As Davison arrived, he told me something else to write in the immigration letter.

"Just tell 'dem, 'We are not in the mood,'" to which I had to smile and chuckle again.

It was showtime. We were about to see what we were made of.

I texted the family group:

> *We're not going to be able to talk to you much from this point forward.*

Mom: *You need to block Sebastion asap. He's gone crazy.*

Keith: *Not by might, nor by power, but by My Spirit, says the Lord of Hosts to the Harrises.*

We took these pictures right before going to Ranjit's house
to capture what we were feeling, which showed in our expressions

Davison accompanied us to the restaurant downstairs to eat before going to Ranjit's house. We had gotten spiritual strength the day before and that morning, but were starving by then and needed physical strength for the encounter ahead. As we were seated, President Trump was on TV.

"You like 'dis guy?" Davison asked. I'm pretty sure the waiter asked us the same thing the previous night.

"He's okay," Brent said.

"Yeah?" he asked, ticking his head to one side. It's their culture, sort of like when we nod our heads, and I found it quite entertaining because he did it so fast, it kept me laughing.

"We don't want to leave her here," Brent told him.

"Not seeing her for two days has set us back a lot," Luke said, "Now that they are in her head again, if it took four hours the other night, it will take a lot longer now."

"First off," said Davison, "You are not going to leave her here. Nobody can stop her from leaving with you if you are hard."

"We need to get hard. This is the first time we've been forceful. We've been nice," I said.

"We've tried to let her make her own decisions, and she's shown us she can't," Brent added.

"Not good ones," I agreed. "Like hanging up on your parents. You don't do that, especially when you sound drugged."

"We can't go all the way around the world, and her do this," Brent said.

"They could be giving her something to put her in the alfa state, and then feeding her information," Luke said.

"They don't even have to drug her," Brent said. "They are telling her things in such a way that has caused her to not trust us and she sounds totally foreign to us. He and his sister could be doing something behind their parent's back."

"Because you're not staying with 'dem, they could be doing any 'ting," Davison said.

"Evelyn said they wanted us to stay with them. We should have," I said.

"You don't go sleep in the enemy's house," Brent told me.

"I wanted to," I said. "But then we might have been under their control."

"*We* could have been drugged; they could have slipped something into our drink or put something over our nose while we were sleeping," said Brent.

"Yeah, you're right," I said, "Then we'd all be in trouble."

"You don't go into the enemy's territory," Brent said. "We got a hotel room because she was pushing against Dr. Mustafa and you, the church people." He looked at Davison, "So we tried to find neutral ground, but neutral ground is over... It's time for full-on battle."

"They think we don't know anything and think they had us in their pocket," I said, "That's why they put us in that hotel, so the people who own it could watch us. They are relatives of theirs."

"Yes, they have kept you 'dere so they can keep an eye on you," Davison said, "They must be getting every report about who is coming and going. Plus, the cameras are 'dere, they can see."

"Yes," I said, "And the owner was chit-chatting with us when we were paying at the front desk before we left."

"What he was saying?" Davison asked.

"Can I get some more ketchup?" Brent asked the waiter.

"Oh, just chit chat. We didn't tell them where we were going," I said.

"He did ask though," Luke said.

"He was being very nice. He wasn't being pushy," Brent said.

"He was getting information, *Brent*. Of course, he was being nice." I said.

"He was working for 'dem," Davison said.

"Exactly. Remember when Ranjit's family introduced us to them when we checked in?" I asked. "They took them aside and spoke in their own language for a while. I'm sure it was about making sure our sheets were changed daily," I said sarcastically.

"I made mistake. I didn't come to visit Dr. Mustafa house," said Davison.

"Why is that a mistake?" I asked.

"I didn't visit. It's happened before on me. I didn't come. I didn't see anything. That problem has been solved before on me. My mistake."

"It's okay," I laughed, "We didn't even know about you."

"I still don't understand why they didn't deport her," Brent said. "Victoria is doing something that is totally out of her character. She can articulate and make it sound good, but…"

"I 'tink someone is writing for her on 'da phone," Davison said, tapping his index finger on the table.

"I think so, too" Luke said. "It doesn't even sound like her."

"So dat'… parents will hate her," said Davison, as the waiter refilled our glasses with water.

"Make *us* hate her?" Brent asked. "There's nothing she can do to make us hate her."

"Somebody's not letting her pick 'da phone, Davison said, "Maybe they must be giving her some medicines, make her sleep, lose consciousness."

"No matter what time of day we call, she sounds like she just woke up," I said. "I'm surprised they even let her answer the phone sounding like that. Why not wait until she sounds better? Maybe it takes a while to wear off."

"We're worried about her now," said Brent, "They shouldn't be keeping her from us. How do y'all eat so much faster than me?"

"We're hungry," I said as Luke laughed. Finally, we were getting food.

Davison got a call and stepped away from the table. After a few minutes, he returned. "Dr. Mustafa said Ranjit's dad called him. He said your family is rich; they saw it at the mall and that the girl is not willing to go. The church members also say they are praying for you and to let them know if you need any 'ting."

"They are wondering where we are and what we're up to," I said.

"Dr. Mustafa is talking to Ranjit's dad?" Brent asked worried. "We don't want anyone against us while we are trying to get our daughter back."

"That's God's problem. We don't have to worry about it," I said, "Dr. Mustafa is not against us."

"We know our daughter's going to be a handful when we get there. Trust me. Or we wouldn't be in India," Brent said.

"I didn't have their number," said Davison. "Otherwise, I would have given 'dem lots of bad words. 'Dey must be telling her to say such things to mom, dad, and brother, so 'dat 'dey can get vindicated, and you'll leave her behind, and go," Davison said.

"That's what I wanted to do the first hour we got here. I was so irritated," I said.

"The boy is totally underage," Davison said. "He is twenty-plus, not yet twenty-one. You don't want her to get married in India."

"Meet and marry are two different things," I said.

"Two different 'tings. Visit means," Davison said, "you stayed here, you saw things, you ate food, and then you left. You don't get married."

"She has been staying the night with him," I said.

"Night is not good," said Davison. "Pastor Isaiah said she should not be staying with 'dat boy so much, and not at night. She should be with parents and see him only a little because 'dey stay inside her head."

"Ranjit told her, 'You are my responsibility now,'" I said.

"He was saying 'dat word? Why he say 'dat word? You should have said, 'Who are *you*?'" said Davison.

"When we were at the mall buying clothes, Ranjit wanted to buy her outfit. And we didn't want him to."

"You said, 'Who are *you*?'" said Davison, "Dis girl is ours. Who are you to say 'dis word?' Be hard now. Don't be soft now."

"That was when we were trying to be nice. We're not being nice anymore," I said.

"When the police question you, they are not soft; 'dey are hard," Davison said, "We are behind you. I told you last night, you start the 'ting and we'll come behind you."

"We'll have you as backup," I said, nodding.

"Like you got a heater to start 'da car, you just need to give us 'da heat, then we'll do every 'ting," Davison said. He was feisty.

"We're ready for that," said Brent. "We don't know what the parents may know. I'm ready to take her. This is my daughter; she is coming with me. I'm sick of this. I'm tired of playing around," he said as he wiped his hands and threw the napkin on the table.

"Thank you, Brent Harris," I said, "You're getting it now! Get on it! Ain't that right, Luke?" I was glad to see him taking control.

"You didn't pay her ticket to come. 'Dey did. That's the main question you must answer. You didn't send her to meet 'dis boy," Davison said.

"No, we didn't," I stated emphatically.

"And she didn't have a turn-around ticket," Brent said, "One and only."

"One round, one side," Davison said. "You know when you travel, you need to have both sides. "Dat's bad, 'dat means they have a bad idea. But we're strong as a team," Davison said.

"Amen," I said, "Let it be!"

I sat back to let my food digest. It was about to be a rough ride, in more than one way.

"You don't put milk in your tea?" Davison asked.

"No, we don't put milk in it," I said.

"Just try one matcha. It will help you digest your food," he said leaning back in his chair.

"Yes, we've had some. It's good. Tastes like coffee to us, because of the milk."

"Victoria doesn't watch TV," Brent said, "She's never watched anything like this. She doesn't know the news. We watch the world news. We know things can happen."

"When I get home, and I'm free, I watch 'da news," Davison said, "You know what's going on in 'da world. Sometimes it helps."

Davison took pictures of us before we headed out.

"Please don't blink. I charge you hundred a piece," he smiled. "Did you throw your food?" he asked as we walked towards the door.

"No, we still have it in the bag. We just couldn't eat anymore. Too spicy."

"I thought he meant throw up," said Luke.

"No, throw away," I laughed.

"No ants in your bed last night? I was worried," Davison asked, as he held the door for us.

⅄ ⅄ ⅄

The sun was shining brightly as we left the restaurant. Davison got us an "auto," and gave the guy the address. "He knows where it is," Davison said, "I'll call you later."

I thought he was going with us. Change of plans again. I guess we were on our own.

As we stood outside in the dirt alley in front of our hotel, the smell was so strong! At first, you thought you were smelling good food, like something fried at a carnival, a mustardy smell, then the smell turned to feces, then strong urine that burned your nose. I began to feel sick and started to gag. I felt like I would vomit and I couldn't breathe.

Sewers in the streets, trash littered everywhere, hazardous power lines hanging out, dilapidated buildings, emaciated people, people with terrible diseases, crime, no traffic lights, no stop signs, no lines on the road, animals and people defecating in the street. There was no order anywhere. Just chaos and filth.

This is what it would be like if the devil ran the world, I thought. I felt sorry for the people who lived there and wished they could have a better life. This is not where I wanted my daughter. Or anyone.

The taxi driver took us to Ranjit's house. It was about a forty-five-minute drive. As we rode, we pulled our shirts up over our mouths because of the smell. Then we discovered something. We could breathe! We could get fresh air inside our shirts and it worked amazingly well.

The address took us to an empty lot between two houses. I remembered Evelyn telling me the address didn't exist. The taxi driver asked for their names. We told him and he said he knows. He drove a couple streets over and stopped a short distance from the house.

As we got out of the taxi, he said he would wait for us. We opened the gate to the courtyard and knocked on the door. Ranjit opened it.

"I want to see my daughter," I said. He stepped back. Victoria was sitting on the couch behind him with an angry look. The three of us stepped inside. I got on my knees beside her, pleading for her to come to the hotel.

"We've had one day with you; we want you to spend time with us. We came all this way, and it's our last night here."

"How can I go with someone who said horrible things about me on *Facebook*?" she shouted.

"What things?" not sure what she was talking about.

Ranjit's mother brought a tray and offered me a glass of water. "No, thank you," I waved her away. Davison warned me not to take any drink from them and I wouldn't have this time anyway.

Victoria kept rubbing her stomach.

"What's wrong?" I asked. "Do you have a stomachache?" I thought maybe it was from a drug.

"Yes, all of you here is bothering me."

Ranjit was keeping quiet over in the corner. I'm sure he had already done his damage, getting her riled up against us, now he only had to let her finish us off.

Brent and Luke wanted to go. They wanted to leave her.

"You need to come with us, Victoria!" I begged.

"No, I don't."

"Yes, you do!" I kept repeating. "We're afraid if we leave, we'll never see you again. We don't know what will happen if we leave you here. We haven't been able to see you the last two days!"

"Why are you making me? I don't have to if I don't want to!"

"Destiny! Let's go!" Brent said as he and Luke walked out the door, "We're leaving her here!"

I didn't want to go. I didn't want to leave her. Seeing I was getting nowhere, I stood up and backed out of the doorway, my face pleading with her. *We needed help.*

We went outside into the street in front of the house, and that's when Luke started shouting. "You love this family, more than you love us!" he screamed at the top of his lungs. "You traded our family for this family!"

Tears were streaming down his cheeks, "We're leaving here without you! We'll never see you again!"

I felt bad for him, but I couldn't believe how "done" he and Brent were with her. They were adamant about leaving her there. *In India.*

What had gotten into them? We were coming here to take her to the hotel and they didn't even try or put up a fight! It was like they had given up the minute we walked through the door. We were there all of five minutes.

I felt that nightmarish feeling come over me again. A helplessness. They were losing it, and I was losing them. They wanted nothing to do with her.

Ranjit's mother came out and shouted something at us.

"She's going to call the police. Get in!" the taxi driver said.

As we road back to the hotel, I called Ranjit. "Why are you doing this?" I asked. "Why are you keeping our daughter from us?"

"I'm not keeping her from you. She is free to go."

"Right," I said. "You made her not want to come with us. What have you told her?"

He told his mother, "She thinks I washed her brain."

"You said it, not me. You drugged her."

He laughed.

"You don't take people from their family. You took her from her country, the only thing she knows. We came here and you have kept her from us! You are not good people!" I shouted over the noise of the engine and the city.

Seeing the conversation was pointless, I hung up.

* *

VOICES
BEHIND THE SCENES

Sebastion and Victoria:

Victoria: *Mom is trying to make me feel guilty because they closed the shop and Luke risked his new job to come see me, and they are in debt. They are saying I replaced my family, which I haven't. I came here to visit. Mom won't even clear his and his family's name until I'm home.*

Sebastion: *Yup, manipulation at its finest. Don't let her make you feel guilty. They chose to close the shop. That's their choice and their problem, not yours.*

They had a chance to do this the easy way and not get all these people involved. I begged them to send me over there and let me handle this without all the chaos. I'm sorry you and Ranjit are having to go through this. You should be going on first dates and learning new things about each other.

Victoria: *I just want all this to go away. It wasn't necessary.*

Sebastion: *I feel like you and I are the only normal ones in this family. The GoFundMe was the last straw for me. They called Sophie and me fools because we asked for help to pay our bills. I think Destiny has lost her way… and her mind. I'm in therapy right now from all I've been through with our family. I just want you to know you're not crazy. You're doing what's right by you, and that's all that matters.*

Victoria: *Looks like they deleted me from Facebook. Jokes on them because I deleted them from my life.*

ᚤ   ᚤ   ᚤ

279

Evelyn and Victoria:

Evelyn: *Anything happen with your mother? I see she deleted some of her posts. I guess she couldn't handle the comments.*

Victoria: *Yes, they came to the house and she was telling me to come to the hotel. I said I wanted to see them, but I don't want to go with someone who has talked so bad about me on Facebook. They were yelling in the street because they wanted to see me and spend time with me. I told her she needs to delete that crap, and so I guess she's deleted some of it.*

Evelyn: *Yelling in the street? That's awful and embarrassing!*

Victoria: *I understand they wanted to see me, and I wanted to see them, too.*

Evelyn: *Your mom still needs to apologize, and you need to keep insisting. I know you want to see them, but your mom has done so much to you, and even though she deleted that stuff, a lot of people have seen it, mostly people from Mobile.*

Victoria: *She won't apologize because she thinks they aren't safe, even after all this, and Luke thinks they aren't trustworthy. I told them I'm fine here and can leave when I want.*

Evelyn: *Look at this comment on Facebook from someone named Sebastion, 'Most of these comments are ridiculous, Victoria is her own person. And to top it off you start a GoFundMe asking for handouts.' He is awesome! Is he your uncle? Is he helping you?*

* *

CHAPTER 28

"NO MAN ON THIS EARTH CAN HELP YOU"

It was still Sunday. After leaving Ranjit's house, we drove back to the hotel and called Davison. "The church people have been praying for you!" he said and asked us to come to the church next door. So that's what they were doing. They were back at the church praying. I thought they were coming to help.

The sun was going down as we sat in the church courtyard in folding chairs. The lush, green shrubs all around us gave a little hedge from the chaos in the streets. Davison, Pastor Isaiah, Sanjay, and Felix were there with about ten young men from the youth group. Their ministry was doing social work in the community.

As Davison spoke with the young men, I assumed he was explaining our situation to them and they were coming up with a plan to help us. Every once in a while one of them would ask a question or tell us something in English.

They wanted to talk to a lawyer. We showed them the immigration letter, but they dismissed it. Maybe the office was closed. As the hour dragged on, the situation was beginning to feel hopeless. Our flight was leaving the next day. As they talked among themselves, we noticed how fresh the air was. There was no odor in the courtyard of the church.

It must have been from all the luscious green trees surrounding us, giving off their oxygen. It was like being in a different place, with just the hedges separating us.

Then we all decided to pray, and as we finished, one of the boys noticed a man walking in the distance, passing by the church. "It's my uncle! He can help us!" he said as he ran over and grabbed him. The white-haired man, with black-rimmed glasses, was wearing a crisp, white button-down shirt, gray slacks, and black dress shoes. He was a politician. He came and sat with us, and again, they spoke among themselves in their language.

After another thirty minutes of discussion, the older gentleman turned to me, his white hair contrasting brilliantly against his tanned skin. Putting his elbow on the arm of the red folding chair, his dark eyes looking squarely and deeply into mine through those black-rimmed glasses, he leaned in further towards me and said slowly and decidedly,

"There is no man on this earth that can help you."

This time my heart did *not* skip a beat.

This time it did *not* sink ten meters down.

This time it was being pumped full of what felt like adrenaline.

Power.

Excitement.

Hope. not despair.

No.

What he had just said was *music to my ears.*

If no *man* could do it, that could only mean I had one option left.

Holding his gaze, and without missing a beat, I said,

"Well, that's good. Because God can!"

God was going to *have* to do it!

As soon as I said that, the old, white-haired man stood up and said he knew someone. It was as if on cue. As if all he had been waiting for were those words. As if he didn't even mean the other words he had just spoken to me.

It was just about dark as we all got into vehicles and drove to the Minister of State's office. As we rode in the back seat, I got a text from the group. It was Keith.

> *And they rose up in the <u>twilight</u> to go to the camp of the Syrians... The Syrians heard the noise of chariots, horses, and a great host... and they said, '<u>The King of Israel has hired</u> against us, the king of the Hittites, and of the Egyptians to come upon us' ... and <u>they fled from their houses.</u>*

I thanked God again for His promises to us. Right on time. As the sun was going down. We were on our way.

> Anne Thompson: *God has not taken your family this far to abandon you now. He is still answering prayers, and he is still blessing. There's a lot of people praying for you.*

As we pulled up to the old, white, cement block building, surrounded now by the night sky, I noticed news vehicles parked there. They were in the middle of a press conference. We made our way inside as Davison and the young men walked alongside us. The room was small and plain, with white walls. There were several rows of foldable, tan metal chairs. In front of the chairs, the Minister of State sat behind a brown desk, with the country's flag pinned to the wall behind him. The news crew was there beside him.

All seventeen of us walked in and sat down, and Davison and the young men began to speak to the Minister of State. He was a heavy-set man with a head full of black hair and a red dot on his forehead. We didn't understand what any of them were saying. As the Minister of State conversed with the church people, there was only one word we understood, and the Minister of State said it four times.

That word was, "*Blackmail.*"

Finally, the Minister of State looked at me, and with the camera rolling asked, "What would you like us to do for you?"

My eyes were burning from the tears mingled with mascara as they rolled down my face and I could hardly see from the bright light that was shining.

Looking into the camera, my lips shaped like I had sucked a lemon, I cried, "I want to take my daughter home!" as my whole being trembled with the embodiment of the last two weeks. Everything was coming down to that one sentence, at that moment.

Then he spoke the most precious words to me, "Your daughter will go home with you tonight!"

They changed our flights to leave in a few hours, telling me, "We don't know what will happen tomorrow."

We were told they were sending the military over to Ranjit's house and they wanted Luke to go with them. As Luke left, Davison told us that Ranjit's family had taken Victoria out of the city the last three days and that's why we hadn't been able to see her.

The room was in an uproar as they fussed over us, arguing about whether to serve us Indian or English tea, then escorted Brent and me into the Minister of State's back room. On the way, we passed by a long dining table where some staff members were having a bite to eat. There were two tall, majestic, winged-back chairs trimmed in thick gold against the wall at the head of it, fit for a king and queen. We turned left into the Minister's room. It was spacious. There were purple couches with thick silver trim and purple and white marble tables. We sat on one of the long couches on the back wall while we waited for them to bring Victoria to us.

They served us the milky, peach-colored tea as we had before, cookies, and the same little finger sandwiches with the orange filling. The Minister of State would not allow us to thank him, telling us it was his duty.

Davison and Pastor Isaiah had come to the back room with us. The Minister of State also came and sat on the smaller couch next to me, crossing his legs with his slippers on.

Then everyone came into the room and an astonishing thing happened. The young men from the church, along with Pastor Isaiah and Davison, the Minister of State, his staff, and even the news crew, all got down on their knees. As we held hands, Pastor Isaiah led us in a prayer for Victoria.

Meanwhile, at Ranjit's house, ten military guards with machine guns surrounded the house while Luke watched from the military vehicle. A large guard stood at the door in front of Victoria and told her to get her passport.

"We have orders from MLA," he stated in Punjabi.

Then my shy, introverted daughter looked up at the guard looming over her, giving her orders, and shouted, "I'm not going! I don't believe you! You're lying! Where is your proof?"

Soon Victoria and Ranjit were put into the back of the military vehicle with Luke while Ranjit's parents were put into another vehicle.

Victoria was frantically texting on her phone. Ranjit said, "This has happened to my family before," as they drove to the military station.

A text came through on my phone. It was from Victoria:

> *I am safe here. I came here on my own. If you do this, I am not your daughter! You are stopping me from living my life. YOU are the problem! Let me make my own decisions. You are ruining myyy lifeeeee!*
>
> *YOU CAN'T DO THIS TO ME!*
>
> *RANJIT WASN'T WHAT YOU THOUGHT.*
>
> *I CAME HERE TO SEE HIM.*
>
> *YOU DON'T CARE ABOUT WHAT I WANT. YOU ONLY CARE ABOUT WHAT DESTINY WANTS.*
>
> *It's because of you this is happening.*
>
> *I will never forgive you!*

Soon Luke was in the room with us. He told us what transpired. "They all got arrested," he said. "The parents and Ranjit."

"Wow," I said. "His mother tells you she is going to call the police and hours later, you bring the military with you, and they put them in jail! If this was a movie, that was the best part!"

Soon, they brought Victoria to the room and everyone left to give us some time alone. Her dad and I stood up and wrapped our arms around her tightly telling her how much we loved her as we cried. She hated us. She was livid.

Then, we sat on the couch with her. As her dad began to speak, she reached for his throat but stopped short of touching him.

"What is your name? Tell me your name." I asked horrified by her actions.

"I don't have a demon," she said.

"Then what is this?" her dad asked. "Because our daughter doesn't do this."

"I came here to see my friends and you ruined it!" Victoria cried. As I sat beside her, I noticed her toenails were ice blue.

"They are not your friends," her dad spoke softly to her.

Victoria was telling us to shut up. "Yes, they are!" she moaned and my heart ached for her.

"He ruined it, and you ruined it," I said.

"The way you left..." her dad began.

"Stop talking to me!" she shouted.

"We are going to have you drug tested," I told her.

"I haven't been drugged."

"Then why, when I called, you sounded like you just woke up and couldn't remember falling asleep? Where have you been the last three days?"

"They could have easily slipped something in your drink," Luke said.

"They told us they took you out of the city," I continued.

"Shut. Up." She told me. "They are crazy. Y'all are crazy."

"That's the government, Victoria. The Indian government. Look at this room. Do you see things like this outside this building? These are government people," I said.

"I should be able to make my own decisions. I came here on my own."

"You were still living in our home. They are being investigated right now. Because it is warranted."

"He's twenty years old. What could he have possibly done?" Victoria asked.

"He got a girl to go across the world," Brent told her, "You could go to California and back twice for how far this is. And there's a first time for everything, so it doesn't matter if he hasn't done it before."

"Please stop talking to me. I'm done!" she cried.

"You were out of the city with him today, and the last two days, while we were puking our guts up. You didn't call to check on us. We've made a lot of friends since we've been here and with the government. Who have you met?" Her dad asked.

She said nothing.

"It's a beautiful room isn't it, Victoria? When you were little, you loved purple," I said getting up to take pictures. "Remember, baby girl?"

She began to cry, telling me to shut up. I wanted to hold her so badly.

"Look what you did! You are ruining my life!"

"You didn't tell us you were leaving and you left from our home, not your own home, living on your own," I tried to reason.

"I didn't tell you because I knew you wouldn't let me. You are so freaking scary to talk to!" she shouted. "Even if I had been living on my own, you would have done this!"

"You don't scream at people you are afraid of. And it would have been very different if you were living on your own."

"You won't let me do anything!" she shouted.

"You can do anything you want, except leave the country. If you go somewhere, you need to tell somebody. That's all we're asking. You were planning on coming back home to live," her dad said.

Hearing all the shouting, someone popped their head in the door, and in a soothing voice said, "Calm down, calm down. Smiiiilllllle."

"I don't want to smile." She used to say that as a little girl when I tried to take her picture.

"If you were me, and your parents stopped you at twenty-one years old from going to see a boy who had a perfectly fine family, you would be pretty ticked off, too!"

"You know why we came? Because you are twenty-one, but you can't take care of yourself, or you wouldn't still be living in our home," I said.

"You weren't taking care of me at all!"

"You were living in our house. If you're twenty-one, we shouldn't have to feed you, clothe you, and buy your toiletries," Brent said.

"You saw they are nice people!"

"We were with them *one* day! They don't even speak English!" I said.

"You shopped, ate lunch, and took pictures," she said.

"We were being *nice*! What were we supposed to do? If we just came, grabbed you, and left, you wouldn't be happy with that. You would say we didn't give Ranjit a chance. You said you wanted us to spend time with them in the city, and then you would leave." I reminded her.

She then got up and went to the bathroom. "I hope she doesn't try to do anything to herself in there," I said.

"If she bleeds, that'll be the sign I told her," said Brent.

"You don't think she would do you?" Luke asked, concerned. "I prayed with her while we were with the guards."

"We don't know what she might do," Brent said.

"Is everything okay?" a man asked stepping inside the door.

"No, it's going to take time," Brent said, "He's been grooming her for two years. It's going to take more than fifteen minutes to get her back."

"You knew she was coming here?" the man asked.

"We had no clue; she just disappeared," Brent said.

"Oh, my God!" he replied.

Just then Victoria re-entered the room, and soon we were leaving. The Minister of State gave me his business card adding his personal cell phone to it and told me if I ever needed anything to call him. As we turned into the hallway, a guard gave something to Brent and he slid it into his pocket.

Felix, again, changed our flights, adding one for Victoria and adding to our tab, but it would all be worth it. We celebrated and took pictures with the young men eating round, orange pastries as they put orange scarves around our necks. We took photos with the guards and the Minister of State, and to my surprise, one of the guards told me he was a Christian and his family lived in Texas. It made me feel already a teensy bit closer to home.

I thanked the young men from church who had helped us and told them I wished it was one of them she had been coming to see. They were so happy. It was ending well and they had helped.

Sanjay and Dr. Mustafa, along with Felix, drove Victoria and Luke to the airport. They were going to wait for us there.

Brent, Luke, and I agreed not to let Brent's family know when we were coming back. Since we had not heard from them, we didn't know if we could trust them. We had the feeling we needed to be cautious. I texted Mom, telling her we were on our way home, but to not tell anyone.

Once Brent and I got to the hotel to check out, we only owed sixteen rupees but were short a few.

"I'm going to need an ATM machine," I said, and Davison offered to take me to find one.

"I'll stay here," Brent told the hotel attendant as he nodded.

We walked out of the hotel and I got on the back of Davison's motorcycle.

"Is it okay to sit like this?" I asked him as I straddled the motorcycle. I was not about to sit on it sideways like I saw all the women in dresses doing.

"'Is' okay," he said, as we took off, and I heard a girl say, "She's doing it wrong."

It was close to midnight. We went from store to store to find an ATM and nothing was open. It was like a ghost town except for the few crowds of people walking downtown. We passed a few dark alleys where women were walking all dressed up. As Davison weaved through the crowd, my thighs came centimeters away from brushing against people and cars.

"Don't take tension," he told me, as I held on tight. We got on the interstate and finally took an exit where I was able to get cash. We rode back to the hotel, I paid our bill, and went upstairs to grab our bags. That is where Brent and I said our goodbyes to Davison. We were going to miss him. He was a firecracker; you had to slow him down or he could be confusing, not always thinking things through, but he was animated, full of ideas, and always came with excitement. Contagious and delightful.

We couldn't stop smiling around him and he would get confused as to why we were laughing, which made us laugh and smile even more. He had made our time in India bearable.

Standing in the hotel room, we put our arms around each other as we cried and prayed together. We hugged and thanked him knowing we probably would never see him again.

As we took a taxi to the airport, a text came through my phone. It was Sebastion. *You're a psychopath,* he texted me. I immediately blocked him. The last thing I needed was to be terrorized by him.

The others were waiting for us at the airport with Victoria and Luke. We took pictures with them as we all celebrated, except for Victoria, who was miserable. I felt so bad for her. I told Sanjay that Victoria's things were left at Ranjit's house and asked if he could get them and send them to us. He said he would try as we said our goodbyes.

We were finally going home.

VOICES
BEHIND THE SCENES

Earlier that day…

Evelyn and Victoria:

Victoria: *Yes, that's Mom's half-brother.*

Evelyn: *Have you had a chance to talk to Ranjit about what we discussed last night? I saw your uncle said you guys can go stay with him, is that something you want to do?*

Victoria: *I'm leaning more towards Pastor Mark. Mom is calling.*

Evelyn: *Do you want to answer?*

Victoria: *Ranjit said there's no way he'll be able to pay the first year of college. That's what you must do on a student visa, I think you said.*

Evelyn: *Yes, you must prove that he can cover his first year, but we can do it through a cheaper college. I know you want to decide together with Ranjit, but as an independent woman, it would be a good thing for you to do what you want. If the only other option is the fiancé visa, then you need to come back home as soon as possible and start working, and making a life so you can bring him over here.*

One thing I thought of this morning that I haven't told you; when you travel, never leave your passport lying around or give it to anyone. That is your safety. Your passport should always be with you. If you lose it or it gets stolen, then you are stranded in a foreign country where getting anything is complicated, and without a ticket back home, even more complicated.

If anything happens, or something goes wrong you would be in a bad situation. So please keep your passport in a safe place with you. I had mine stolen once while in a foreign country and I was alone. It was a huge mess.

Victoria: *That's scary. You've been through some stuff.*

Evelyn: *You have no idea. It was terrifying. I have only told you a tiny bit. Maybe you should get an open-ended ticket, where you can leave at any time. Then you can tell your parents, 'Here is proof they have good intentions.'*

You are coming back anyway. We can change it if the time comes and you are not ready to leave. I found a flight that leaves within a month, at a really good price. I think you should buy it. Can we get this done tonight? I can do the booking online; I've done it tons of times.

As I said, in any foreign country, it is so important to be able to leave whenever you want because if there is war, or the government decides they do not want foreigners in their country anymore, or there is a military take-over, there are so many things that can happen, and it isn't your country. You need to be able to leave anytime you want or need to.

Victoria: *Is it refundable?*

Evelyn: *If you buy the insurance. The first step in taking charge of your life is making decisions with dates and sticking with them. When you are financially dependent on other people, you are automatically letting them be in control of your decisions and your life, so you need to decide and execute. What type of visa do you have?*

Victoria: *A ten-year tourist visa... I'm thinking about it...*

Evelyn: *Can I call you? My fingers hurt from typing…Let me know what's going on… Victoria, I'm worried…*

Victoria: *My parents sent police here to take me to them.*

Evelyn: *Victoria, the police can't do that. They can't force you to go to your parents, can they? No, they can't. You're an adult. You're twenty-one years old and you're living out of your home. You're independent and they can't force you to do that. You don't even know if it's really the police. What if it's people who want to kidnap you?*

This is exactly what your mother wants. Make so many problems for Ranjit's family that they want you to leave. If I were you, I would take a flight out of India and leave them there, come home, get your stuff, and your car while they are not here, and move far away. Make your life, make money to go back and forth to visit Ranjit until he can come here…

What is going on? I am dying here! Victoria? Hello?

If you must go to your parents, please erase our messages!

Grant: *You need to contact the US Embassy.*
Tel: 91-11--5555-5555.

Oliver: *I just heard the news. It sounds too awful for words. Your parents are evil. I'm sorry you had to go through this.*

Sebastion: *When you get back to America, I'll come pick you up. You don't have to live with them. I'm talking to a friend of yours named Evelyn. She's going to help us.*

Screenshot of the actual text message Evelyn sent to Victoria.
I added this one as proof that I have all the texts.

MONDAY, OCTOBER 1, 2018

CHAPTER 29

BETRAYED

In the airport, Victoria followed me around like a little duckling almost stepping on my heels. She didn't take her eyes off me. On the plane to Qatar, she sat next to Luke and slept the whole time, missing her meal.

Once in the Qatar airport, as we waited in the lobby, she wanted to talk. I was trying to follow logic, but she wasn't. She was upset and I had to move away from her because I couldn't take it. I was tired and stressed; I needed a break.

On the fourteen-hour flight from Qatar to Dallas, Victoria again slept the entire time, never eating or speaking. She and Luke sat behind Brent and me. As I sat on the plane, I wished there was somewhere we could go instead of straight home. We needed time to talk as a family. We hadn't had a chance to decompress. Maybe we could change our flights again while in Dallas, go to Mexico, to a real vacation on an island somewhere. We needed to de-stress and relax. But I knew Luke and Brent needed to get back to work. Victoria and I could go, but we had already spent so much. I fell asleep. I was too tired to put thought into it. I wish I hadn't been.

This is a selfie we took on the 14-hour flight home

When I awoke, I remembered how Frank had not come and Chris Cotton's friend, Phillip, who was supposed to meet us when we arrived, wasn't there. How Fern with the human trafficking agency, and Laura Cotton, Chris' wife, had offered to come with us, but I hadn't accepted. How we thought the church was going to accompany us to Ranjit's house, but they didn't. How the boy from church's uncle had told me, "No man on this earth can help you."

All our earthly support had been cut off.

We were weak, so God could show himself strong on our behalf.

I texted the group back home: *The government told us Esha had been on Ranjit's side. I knew not to trust her. This was a traumatic experience for all of us. If it wasn't for the inevitable humor that naturally comes from being in a foreign country and being able to laugh, we wouldn't have survived. I wouldn't have been able to keep my focus, would've been out of control, engulfed in the environment surrounding me. Praise God for the medicine of laughter. To be able to smile while your stomach is churning with the reality and uncertainty that what you wish for, what you hope for, may not happen, even by God, your loving Father not allowing it, and surrendering your will to His.*

Knowing it's possibly not part of the divine plan, and then being willing to let go. That is why He sometimes waits until the very end, to test us and make us stronger. For a mother, losing a child is the most unnatural thing in the world.

That poor, little church with the dirt floor, and Davison and Pastor Isaiah, along with a good group of nice, young men helped "Bring Victoria Home" and we plan to begin sending money to that little church to help it grow and let it become a place for God's truth to shine in the pit of the Hell that it is in.

I think I know why none of Brent's family were talking to us. Victoria was on the phone with Grant when she was in the military vehicle, so they must have been talking to her the whole time. That's where they were getting their information from, her and Ranjit.

I knew they were sleeping and would not get my message until morning, but I wanted them to hear from me and know we were on our way home.

As we arrived in Dallas, we were the last ones off the plane, and as we walked up the steps, a lady in a police uniform was waiting for us at the top of the stairs.

Oh, God no. They weren't going to take her from us, were they? How did they even know we were on that flight? How did they know who we were? Did Ranjit's family have some kind of pull?

Once we made it to the top of the stairs, the policewoman told us she was detaining us. She had some questions to ask us. As we followed her, Victoria told me she started her cycle and needed a feminine pad. I asked the policewoman and she said she could get one. I began praising God, knowing what that meant. She wasn't pregnant!

The police officer asked Victoria and me to come to her office and for Brent and Luke to have a seat in the lobby. While Victoria was in the restroom, the officer asked me what happened while we were in India.

Who told them? How did they know who we were? I thought. I explained everything to her as she nodded. Victoria came out as I was saying, "They all got arrested."

"You had them arrested? Oh God, those sweet people!" Victoria said.

The female officer then asked Victoria questions. I believe she sensed Victoria's naivety. The police officer ended by saying, "If he is doing anything nefarious, we don't want him coming to this country." With that, she let us go.

Once we made it to the lobby, I was secretly hoping we would get another overnight layover so we could talk about everything, but I was also afraid of her trying to leave us. I just wanted to get home. My heart couldn't take anymore. Victoria didn't have her phone. They had taken it from her at the military station, but I wasn't putting anything past her. The guard in India had given Brent her passport and he was holding onto it.

I watched Brent talking to someone on the phone, and then I realized something. Victoria's driver's license, birth certificate, and debit card were at Ranjit's house. Someone could use her card.

"We need to move money from your bank account to mine until we can cancel your debit card because it's at Ranjit's house and anyone could use it."

"They wouldn't do that," she said.

"Anyone could get it." I used my phone to transfer the money over while she watched. If anyone used her card, being that all our accounts were linked, they could possibly get to any of our checking accounts.

Earlier, I had told her, 'You don't need a sign, Victoria. The sign is us. We are here and we're taking you home."

"God needs to tell me," she said.

"He *is* telling you *through us*, your parents. Scripture says to honor your parents. You haven't done that in the past, but right now you need to do that because we are here, we care about you, and we have your best interest at heart. You need to trust us."

But she didn't. Victoria had never trusted anybody. Ever.

I walked towards Brent as he was getting off the phone with his *mother...* and *then* his brother.

"Who were you talking to?" I asked.

"I let both Mom and Grant know we are coming."

"*What? How could you?!* We agreed not to tell anybody." I was fuming. I couldn't believe he had done this. How could he be so naïve? He was too trusting.

"I also told my mom she's part of the reason Victoria left," Brent said.

I wish I had looked at my phone. If I had known what lay ahead, I would have changed our flights right then, no matter what the cost, but because of being distracted with the bank accounts and Brent's phone call, it wasn't until we had already landed in Mobile and were sitting on the plane waiting to exit that I saw Mom's text.

I'm at the airport and Evelyn is here. Sebastion is getting a group together to meet you here to protest you bringing Victoria back and saying it was against her will.

I didn't think much of it. *There goes Sebastion and his plans again. Nobody is going to do that. None of his friends even know us. They wouldn't get involved. I wonder what Evelyn is doing there.*

I texted back, *How did they know we were coming? We weren't supposed to be back until tomorrow.*

They're guessing is my guess, Mom texted back. *You need to go straight to your dad's truck with Victoria when you arrive. He will be waiting outside. We'll take her to the country house where she can have some solitude away from you for a while, and we can work on healing from all this.*

Walking to the gate inside the airport, Brent and Luke were far ahead of Victoria and me. Our whole family was out front waiting for us. Mom, Dad, Isabel, Brent's parents, and our friend, Keith Thompson. They were all there to see Victoria. Mickie from *Channel 15 News* had wanted to meet us there when we came back, but I had told her not to. I didn't want to overwhelm Victoria, embarrass, or upset her. She had been through a lot. We would all be tired and I told Mickie we would do something later.

Brent and Luke went through the gate, and as Victoria and I approached I told her, "Come to the bathroom." Then we side-stepped into the ladies' room just inside the gate.

"Now, listen to me, Victoria. Evelyn is out there. What we are going to do is go straight to Grandad's truck and to Grandma's house." If I had known what was waiting for me around the corner, I would have never exited that gate.

"*No!*" Victoria said and walked out of the bathroom. I thought it strange. As far as I knew, she hadn't spoken to Evelyn the whole time we had been there, and she didn't know Evelyn very well. But she was angry with us, so I guess anybody would do, and she saw Evelyn as her escape route.

As she walked through the gate, her family hugged her, crying, so happy to see her make it home alive and safe.

Then Evelyn looked at me and said, "Can I speak to Victoria privately?"

"Sure," I said in disgust, holding out my hands, very suspicious of what was going on. Evelyn had called the airport ahead of time and told them to have the security guards ready for us. I don't know what she told them, but they didn't like us at all and they were standing around us and our daughter.

Evelyn took Victoria aside and whispered something in her ear. The airport security guard then asked us to give Victoria's passport to her. Brent slowly removed it from his pocket and handed it over. Then Victoria turned and followed Evelyn towards the escalator.

"Why are you taking my daughter from me?" I asked, tears starting to well up and a huge lump forming in my throat.

"Well, it seems you won't let her talk to anyone but you!" Evelyn said.

"I just let you talk to her alone!" I said, baffled.

She turned and stepped on the escalator with Victoria right behind.

"*Victoria,*" I said breathlessly, watching her go downstairs. She never looked back, even once.

I caught eyes with Carlos, Evelyn's husband who had come with her, and looked at him as if to say, '*You! How could you do this to me?*'

He only looked back for a moment, then left with a sorrowful expression. He didn't speak much English. He was from another country and didn't "wear the pants," so he likely wouldn't have said anything anyway. He probably didn't know what his wife was up to and I bet he didn't know she had a man in another country who was her best friend, Troy, the private investigator.

I had no idea what a smart, evil genius this woman was. She didn't need to be working with children. She didn't need to be anywhere near children, and she needed to remove her name from the membership of our church. She was no Christian. Not at all.

After Evelyn and Victoria left, we, andas I stood with my mom, I could see one of the security guards through my peripheral vision. He was keeping an eye on us. My dad and Isabel went outside to wait for us in the truck.

As Mom and I stood there talking, we looked and several feet away from us, Brent fell to his knees, crying in agony in the middle of the airport. I had only seen him cry once when we were dating. His mom and dad, and our friend Keith, were standing next to him. His mom was bent over placing her hand on his back and she was crying too.

"I can't," he cried. "I can't take it," he sobbed. I watched as his dad and Keith put each of their arms under each of his to hold him up, his legs limp, as the tips of his blue tennis shoes dragged the floor. They carried him out and put him in my dad's truck. It was the most awful thing I'd ever seen. I knew what he had sacrificed to get her. I knew how miserable he was, and all he had been through, just to get here and have her taken from us!

I had a pit in the bottom of my stomach. Mom and I cried watching the scene. *I hoped the security guard saw that. They didn't know what they had helped do.* This was *not* a man taking his daughter to hurt her, he was *saving* her.

Luke and I got in the back seat of Dad's truck next to Brent and I called Evelyn. I left a voicemail telling her if she cared anything about Victoria to get her a drug test and a gynecological exam. I knew she had started her cycle, but I wasn't taking any chances. She could be pregnant. The blood could have come from intercourse. As far as I knew, she was a virgin, and I also wanted to make sure she hadn't been raped, because I was sure she had been drugged.

Then it hit me. "She was bleeding! That was the other sign!" I whispered to Brent and Luke as we rode in the back seat. "Both signs came true! The real one and the one you interpreted incorrectly! That's why her stomach was hurting at Ranjit's house! If we only had known, we could have told her!"

Heartbroken, everyone came back to our house before saying goodnight. We recounted the awfulness of what just transpired.

"Sebastion did this to them!" Brent's mother, Jeannie, said.

"And Grant too!" my mom said.

"Grant?"

"Yes, Grant."

My mom stayed with us that night. The next day I didn't wake up until 3:00 p.m. My aunt and uncle brought us food. Dad and Isabel also came and brought a bottle of scuppernong juice from Mississippi. It was comforting and tasty! I was so thankful to have food we could eat.

"When y'all came off that plane, you looked like refugees," Mom said. She was right, I weighed 106 pounds and Brent was 135. "That Evelyn. I hugged and chatted with her in the airport while we were waiting for you. I had no idea what she was about to do!" Brent said he had hugged her, too. That thought was unbearable.

Soon, everyone left while Mom stayed. We were all still tired and my head felt groggy.

Our family had just left when Evelyn's vehicle showed up with two police cars outside our home. Her husband, Carlos, and Victoria were with her. Evelyn called Brent's phone and said they came to get Victoria's belongings and her car that was parked out front.

"She can't come in this house," Brent said, watching them through the window, seeing Evelyn holding the phone to her ear. They were standing outside the locked front gate with the police… the gate around our home and business, the one in which we kept customer vehicles secure. "And that car is in our name. You have a policeman standing right there. He can run the tag."

Victoria got on the phone, "I can come in my own house."

"You left this house, remember? Everything in this house is mine. I bought it all."

They were not going to bully us in our own home. Evelyn was not coming inside and I couldn't be sure that if I opened that gate, she wouldn't try. And I was sure she wouldn't let Victoria come inside without her.

My nerves lit up, tingling, as my skin itched and I felt myself coming out of it. I called Dad, explaining what was happening, "I am going to the office to double-check the title on her car."

I couldn't remember if it was in both our names and hers, or only ours. I opened the filing cabinet and found the it. Her name was not on the title. "Only our names are on it. So they have no reason at all to be here," I told Dad.

Evelyn and Carlos thought they were going to take our daughter and then come here with police, making demands on us, less than twenty-four hours of disembarking an international flight?

"You took me from India with nothing but the clothes on my back," Victoria told her dad on the phone.

"I will bring you some clothes in a little while," Brent told her, still staring out the window. They hung up and we watched them drive away, the police following. Brent would meet Carlos later, to hand over some of Victoria's clothes until we could figure out what to do.

Brent called Pastor Leite, who said he would come over and talk with us.

As I stood in the kitchen with Mom and Brent, and we ranted about it all, I looked over and noticed Luke standing against the counter. He would be leaving soon. I needed to be spending time with my child who *was* here, *who* hadn't left, who had stood by my side, who *did* love me, instead of letting the one who hadn't take all my attention. I walked over and hugged him, telling him how much I loved him and thanking him for being with us.

I was so mad and depressed; I couldn't see straight. I went to Luke's room where the sun shone brightly through four windows and lie on the bed, one he hadn't been in, in a long time. Brent came, laid beside me, and held me while Luke was in the bathroom. I was hurting so bad; I wanted to die and I screamed it at the top of my lungs, along with some other things I should have never said. I lost my religion at that moment, all the while knowing my son was in the next room and he could probably hear it all. He came out of the bathroom with a sad look on his face and walked out of the room. He had never heard his mother say such awful words, and I was immediately sorry I said them.

There was a knock at the door. It was Pastor Leite. I came into the living room and sat on the brown leather chaise as Brent let him in. I was wearing a white turtleneck and blue jeans I had thrown on. The only thing on my face was redness from the tears, hurt, and anger, and my blonde hair was all in disarray, hanging in my face. Pastor Leite sat down in the recliner in front of me. Mom and Brent sat on each side of me on the chaise and I kept my head down.

It was my first time meeting Pastor Leite. He spoke gently to me. After about an hour of him speaking, I finally looked up at him, wiping the tears away and the hair out of my face. He had dark, receding hair, and dark eyes behind black-rimmed glasses.

"How could she do this to us? She's a member of our church. She was supposed to be a friend," I cried.

"And we will be having a discussion about it at the next board meeting," he assured me softly. (Evelyn and her family would never return to our church.) "Now, about giving your daughter her things," he continued, "You want her to have them, right?"

"Yes, I want her to have them. I want her to have what she needs to leave Evelyn's house and go on with her life," I cried softly.

"My advice to you is that things must be done in order. You can't just hand them over, then she'll say you didn't give this or that. It needs to be recorded by a lawyer so she can never say you didn't give everything back.

"Also, for your grandchildren, your posterity. If she ever has any children, you don't want her saying the reason she never brings them to see you is because you kept anything from her, so you'll have the recorded proof that you did all she asked."

He was thinking ahead. "It's about protecting your honor and your heritage." We visited a while longer, and as he was about to leave, we walked him to the door.

He stopped in the foyer and turned to me, holding his hands a ruler's length apart, his fingers together, and said, "Before God put this on you, He measured it. Then He looked at you, and said to Himself, 'Yep, it's just right. She can handle this,' because He knew He could trust you with it."

I closed my eyes, pushing the tears out, as they rolled down. *No, I thought, at first. How could He trust me with this?* Then it was like a warm blanket covered me. I was comforted to know that before He allowed this to happen, God had considered the impact it would have on me. Then He had carefully let it rest upon me, knowing the whole time He was going to be right there walking beside me and, at times carrying me. And the fact that He could trust me with it meant that He could trust *me* to *trust Him* and that He was going to help me get through it.

As we stood together, Pastor Leite looked at me again and said, "You know when you bake a turkey, you need a long, slow roast. You don't want to take the turkey out when it's raw, or half-baked. You want to take it out when it's fully done. It takes time. You must be patient, and wait until the turkey is ready, then it will be delicious for you to enjoy," he smiled as he turned to go.

I hugged him, telling him it was nice to meet him. Pastor Leite would prove to play an instrumental part in the aftermath of all this. I could not have made it through everything I was about to face without him.

"Likewise," he winked as he stepped outside and closed the door.

After he left, my mom read us a text she had sent to Evelyn, and Evelyn's response. Both parts of the conversation made me want to vomit. Mom told her what she did in the airport last night was a gut-wrenching experience for Victoria's family, and Evelyn told her that we should be grateful to her for taking Victoria and taking care of her.

"Why did you go into the wasp's nest?" I moaned to Mom. Why did she have to go and bring out all the poisonous stings from Evelyn? I didn't need it. It was obvious Evelyn didn't care anything about us.

"I was just trying to plead with her," my mom replied.

"Plead with Satan? He doesn't care!" We needed to leave Evelyn alone if she was going to be an agent of the devil.

"You know what?" Mom asked. "You and Evelyn talked about Victoria staying with her when this was all over. You would have been fine with Victoria staying there if she didn't want to be with you right now, but that wasn't good enough for Evelyn. She had to take her *by force*."

She was right.

Brent gathered some of Victoria's clothes to take to Carlos. When he returned, I asked him how it went.

"It went fine. I gave him her things and told him what he was doing was wrong. He said he wanted no part of it, and I know he doesn't. I trust Carlos."

"You *trust* him? *How can you say that?* He took our daughter from us! He isn't standing up and being the man of his house. He's letting Evelyn run him. He says he doesn't want to be a part of it? Well, *he is!* *He's right in the middle of it!*" We were in our bedroom and I began punching Brent with my fist on his shoulder as hard as I could while crying. I didn't know that our friend, Keith, had accompanied Brent to meet Carlos and had come back to the house with him. He was watching us from the dining room table, through the white French doors leading to our bedroom. I caught a glimpse of him.

Mom had placed three valium pills on my bedside table, telling me to take only a piece of one at a time. I told her I didn't want it. I didn't take medicine. At that moment, seeing the pills on the table and wanting out of my misery, I grabbed all of them, swallowed, and got in bed.

I awoke fourteen hours later, still just as mad as I'd been when I went to sleep. The house was quiet. I got up, took a hot shower, and put on some clothes. I thought about Victoria's phone that they had taken from her. *If only I knew what all had transpired while we were there, it may shed light on things.* I had many questions.

Then I remembered something. At one point, when the kids were in high school, I had put an app on their phones so I could monitor what they were doing. Most kids were just starting to have cell phones, and we only allowed our kids to get them once they started driving. I had been cautious about cell phones especially when the internet became accessible. I hadn't looked at the app in years. I didn't think I needed to and had forgotten all about it. Until now.

All I had to do was pull up my cell phone account. The service on her phone was in my name. I got out my laptop as I sat on the bed. I went to the website and logged in. I then synced with the app installed on my computer. In just a few minutes, I should be able to see every contact, every phone call, every photo, and every text.

I downloaded everything from her phone to my computer, up until the time we left India. The next several hours would reveal what was behind her rebellion towards us. It would reveal why everything we were doing was being undone and who was working against us.

I wanted to take this apart piece by piece. I read all of Sebastion's, Grant's, and Ranjit's conversations with her. I saw where Grant admitted he hadn't been speaking to us, but said it was *us* who had cut *him* out. I saw where Sebastion said Evelyn was going to help him.

I then moved on to Evelyn. What I found there horrified and appalled me, but I was also shocked and comforted by Victoria's comments to both Evelyn and Ranjit about wanting to see us, even when it looked like she didn't. That day at Ranjit's house, when she was so hostile towards us, after we left she had immediately texted Evelyn saying she really wanted to see us! My heart was warmed. My little girl *did* want us, she just couldn't reach us with all the interference. Evelyn had discouraged her, calling us evil!

My mouth dropped open when I saw Evelyn say she would do everything in her power to get Ranjit to this country, and how dangerous it was to be in a country alone because anything could happen. *Exactly.* And when she told Victoria if she had a return flight it might make me feel better about Ranjit's family. *Duh.* It's like, in that moment, Evelyn had suddenly woke up out of a slumber and realized what was going on. It seemed she began to think like an adult.

Everything she said to my child was keeping her from the people who cared about her most and who could protect her: her family. Evelyn put my child in direct danger, undermining everything we were doing. Now I knew why it had been so hard to reach Victoria. Now I knew why everything we were doing was being undone. I wanted to go to her house and strangle the life out of her with my bare hands. I had suspected it was all Ranjit, but Evelyn was doing his job for him perfectly, and she was doing it well, but she wasn't doing it alone.

I saw where those three words were coming from that I kept getting from Victoria anytime I asked when we could see her. The words, "Clear their name," Victoria kept feeding me were all instigated by Evelyn, telling her to ask us for a public apology and to not leave until we did, knowing we would never do that. I thought it was quite interesting that the very thing Evelyn was doing to get Victoria to stay was likely the very thing that got her sent out of the country because it had made it look like we were being blackmailed. And I believe we were.

By whom, exactly? How much of it Ranjit was involved in, or how much it was Evelyn's doing, I didn't know. Evelyn having Victoria tell me to apologize or "clear their name" all while Victoria wasn't coming to see me made it look to the Indian government like we were being blackmailed. Since this was all public and they didn't need any trouble with the U.S., they sent her home. They just needed to wait to see what the parents wanted and get it officially on camera, that was my surmising anyway.

I saw text messages from some Oliver guy. Seeing that he was Evelyn's best friend told me all I needed to know. He was her sidekick and up to no good. This guy didn't even know our family. We were complete strangers, yet he was telling my daughter how evil we were and to not listen to us. I barely paid attention to his Luciferian, blunt, and brutal conversations.

Then came the humdinger of it all. The truth. From Victoria herself. Victoria had texted Tanvi, Ranjit's sister, the day she was preparing to leave us:

This is my first time traveling with carry-on only.........................

I'm crazy.

I'm insane.

But I'll do anything to meet y'all!

There it was.

She knew.

She knew better.

When Tanvi had not heard from Victoria, she began to get worried.

Tanvi: *If you don't come, our parents will scold us and we'll never be able to trust anyone again. Why would we give you all our information, tell you everything about us? See, you can trust us!*

Tanvi had shown her hand. Why did she feel the need to convince Victoria they could be trusted? This made it even more compelling that what we feared was the truth.

Ranjit had used the word *blackmail* in a text to Victoria in reference to us being the blackmailers. It was the word the Minister of State had used four times. I learned a long time ago that when someone accuses you of something, it's because they themselves are doing it. It's a tactic to deflect what they are doing to you, to distract from themselves.

After seeing it all, I closed my laptop and went into the living room to find my husband and Luke in the recliners, talking.

"I have it all," I announced standing in front of them. Brent and Luke looked at me wide- eyed. Mom came into the room, brushing her teeth. "What?" she asked, her mouth full of toothpaste.

"I have it all. It was Evelyn. The whole time it was Evelyn. I downloaded everything from Victoria's phone to my computer."

"How in the world did you do that?" Brent asked.

"Remember that app we used back when the kids were in high school? Well, it just paid huge dividends."

I went on to tell them everything I had found. They were as shocked, and angry as I was, especially Mom.

"She's a mother herself. She should know better. How could she do this? Unbelievable."

"That woman should be in jail," Brent said. He was about to take Luke to the airport. I know he hated to see that place again. I hugged Luke and told him to be careful and call me when he made it home, as they left.

"You should post all that on *Facebook*. People need to beware of her. Put it in the newspaper, or a sign in her front yard, and all over town that says, "Evelyn Da Cruz – Don't let her near your children," with her picture on it.

I had already thought of all those things, and much more I wanted to do to her. Our brothers had betrayed us, talking to the enemy and his victim, our daughter, while not talking to us, and what Evelyn had been doing behind our backs beat all we'd ever seen.

"It will all come out one day, Mom, but for now I must wait. There is a perfect time for everything."

Now I had answers. Now things made sense. God brought to my mind the phone app. He wanted me to see what had been going on behind the scenes.

PART III

THE AFTERMATH

OCTOBER 2018 - MARCH 2024

CHAPTER 30

LETTING GO

The next day, I received a letter from Victoria's attorney demanding we give her all her possessions, including her car, and money that was taken out of her bank account. It also stated that we were to have no contact with her. My mom also received a similar no-contact letter.

Although it broke my heart, and my spirit, I knew Evelyn was the mastermind behind it all. I had seen her text messages. Victoria would never hire a lawyer. She couldn't talk to the bank or the postman. People intimidated her and a lawyer would surely be no different. I e-mailed Victoria and told her I wanted to give her things to her, and included all our family's phone numbers since she didn't have her phone.

I decided to find an attorney to help transfer her possessions and record it, as Pastor Leite had advised. When I opened my laptop to begin searching, a *Facebook* message popped up on my screen. To my surprise, it was Ranjit. I was confused as to why he would be messaging me, and then to my amazement, I saw Victoria answer him. *What is going on?* I thought. Then I remembered she had been logged in on my computer before she left and it looked as if she still was. But how was it possible that she could be logged in on both my computer and wherever she was messaging him from? I figured I was supposed to see this, at least until I couldn't.

I made an appointment with the attorney. It was going to be $500 to give her things to her. What a shame. I was sure Victoria would be paying the same. If Evelyn thought she was helping her, she wasn't. She was not guiding Victoria in what was best for her. I would see the attorney the next day and set a time to make the transaction.

When I met with him, I told him we wanted to see our daughter and talk to her. This was the last bit of leverage we had. We didn't have to give these things to her, but if we were going to, the very least she could do was talk to us *without* Evelyn present.

I told him I would like her to get counseling with us, as I told him the entire story. We had just been through a traumatic experience and we were all hurting. We needed some type of intervention, someone to help put the pieces back together, even if we got counseling separately. The attorney didn't know her, I did, and I knew if we didn't get help or stay connected in some way, we would never get her back. Her mind was slipping away from us, along with her heart.

We could have argued she owed us money for not coming back peacefully when she said she would, causing us to spend hundreds extra on changing our flights. That alone was half her bank account. Or that she owed us the entire trip. But we didn't want to do that to her. We wanted her to have her money. We didn't need it. We just wanted something to bargain with, so she would talk to us. And we would give her things to her because we *wanted* to, not because some attorney *told us* to.

But I knew how stubborn she was. She would forego all her money and possessions to not have to talk to us, and then for the rest of her life say we took her money and she would never want to see us again. I chose not to risk it for her own sake. I didn't want her blaming not having her assets as the reason for things not working out for her, and I didn't want anything holding her back from getting away from Evelyn and making a life for herself.

We could have taken our time to think everything through. We didn't have to rush.

"Just let her go," the lawyer said, and I eventually gave up.

"We're going to have to hope that Victoria sees the error she has made," Dad told me. "After you settle everything with her; she, Evelyn, and Carlos will have to start dealing with the reality that they are now on their own and the problems they have created are solely theirs to solve."

Jeannie stopped by one afternoon and sat at the dining room table with Brent, Mom, and me. It was the first chance we had to talk since we returned. I wanted to know why we had not heard from her while we were in India. She said she couldn't figure out the app, even though she had created a group on it and added me to it, and she hadn't been in touch with my mom or Anne at home, either. andIt was as if she was being informed some other way and didn't need or want to talk to us.

I had a good mind to never speak to her again. If she wasn't concerned about us being in a foreign country, in my book that meant she wanted us to die. She had given Brent some excuse about being too upset to want to know. I wasn't buying that. Then she said something that made my stomach turn.

"How does Victoria know we will even accept her if she does come back?"

My face became hot. I was stunned. Too shocked by her words, Brent and Mom continued talking as if nothing had been said. None of us felt that way, and even if we had, it wouldn't be her place to say it. I now had even more reason to distance myself from her.

If, or when Victoria did come back, no matter what she had done, I would be waiting with open arms. How dare she say that about her grandchild. Maybe because Victoria was a part of me, she was indifferent to her. She never acted like she cared much for her.

She hadn't raised girls. Jeannie had raised boys and she treated Victoria like one, on one occasion buying her a blue Spider-Man wallet.

She favored the boys more, whether she realized it or not. The previous year at Christmas, as all the other grandchildren were opening gifts, Jeannie told our children she would take them shopping for their gifts so she could spend some time with them, which I thought was wonderful.

The first week of January, she took the boys, but she never took Victoria. Victoria kept asking about it, and Jeannie kept telling her she would, but always had some excuse. In September, nine months later, she still hadn't taken her. Soon it would be Christmas again. Victoria told me it didn't make her feel valued or loved. I was heartbroken for her. She had been patient with her grandmother. It wasn't about the gifts; it was about promises not being fulfilled. She wasn't there for Victoria's first birthday and she wouldn't have been there for her graduation if I hadn't put my foot down.

I had to hold myself back from telling Jeannie she was ruining her relationship with her granddaughter by breaking her trust, but I felt that Victoria needed to stand up for herself and I didn't want to get in the way of that. Victoria never said anything. I told God I didn't know how He was going to fix this, and then Victoria was gone.

I thought surely Jeannie would be sending Victoria some kind of apology letter by now with a Christmas card and money telling her to take that shopping trip, but to my knowledge she never did. Sitting at the dining room table that day, my distrust in my mother-in-law was growing.

A few nights later at her house, she told us she called Grant as soon as she came home from the airport that night. She told him about Victoria leaving with Evelyn and about Brent breaking down, and his dad helping carry him out.

Jeannie asked him, "Did you have anything to do with that?"

"Somewhat," was Grant's reply.

"Then you have no idea what you have done to your brother. Even if he never forgives you, and I don't blame him if he doesn't, *you* will never get over it."

"I don't have to listen to this bull crap!" he said.

"No, you don't," she said and hung up.

For once in our lives, she had stood up for us, and I was grateful for what she had done.

She had won me back!

So, Sebastion, Grant, and Evelyn had all conspired to take Victoria from us at the airport. Sebastion had marketed the plan on *Facebook*, Evelyn had executed it, but Grant had the one crucial piece of information to make it all work: the time we would be returning. In the Dallas airport, while Brent was telling Grant we were on our way home, Grant was about to use it against us in the worst kind of way.

Victoria was going to be on the news. We gathered around the television to watch as she spoke from Evelyn's living room about how things had played out.

"I didn't want them to save me," she said.

Mickie from *Channel 15 News* had contacted me once we returned, as had a few other local news outlets, to do a report. I had e-mailed her our side of the story but never heard back from her.

The Washington Post also contacted me. I gave a phone interview and written report of my side of the story. Pastor Leite told me, "Whatever you say, say it as if you are telling your daughter. Always remember she will be listening." I never forgot that bit of advice. *The Washington Post* had also contacted Victoria and Ranjit to get their side, but right before the story was to be published, suddenly it was dropped like a hotcake and I never heard from them again, just like Mickie. I found it particularly odd, as if someone had told them, *"Don't touch it."* Frustrated, I decided God wanted this story to come out *how* and *when* he wanted it.

That day I saw a girl on a talk show who *almost* did the exact thing Victoria had done. Her name was Mackenzie Baldwin. She was outgoing and had lots of friends. So, I knew right then, it didn't matter that Victoria didn't have friends or wasn't popular in school. Here was a girl who had those things and still got pulled into the trap. It didn't matter that our daughter didn't have a close relationship with us, because this girl had that; especially with her father, and it *still* happened. I knew then, this could happen to *anybody.* The book she and her dad wrote is titled, *Almost Gone.* The difference in their story and ours was her parents were able to discover her plans and stopped her before she left. They kept saying they didn't know what would have happened if she had actually gone.

But we did.

Our daughter wasn't almost gone.

She *did* go.

Where Mackenzie Baldwin's story ended, is where ours began.

ㅅ   ㅅ   ㅅ

The day came when it was time for us to transfer Victoria's possessions through the attorney's office. Brent got her car ready. He put her tires on the new rims she had bought at the car show and had been sitting in the shed. He checked all the fluids, aired the tires, and changed the oil. He didn't want anything happening to her if she were to get on the interstate.

We packed everything in her room and bathroom, leaving only her furniture and bedding. We always told her she would get those things when she left home with our blessing. We stuffed everything into her car, along with cards and letters from each of us telling her how much we loved her. It was the last form of communication we had. I gave her a check for $200 in case she needed it, but she would never cash it. I had the title to the car and a cashier's check for the amount I had transferred from her bank account at the Dallas airport.

We headed out that solemn day, and as we went up the elevator to the attorney's office and sat down, he told us she had requested not to see us. She just wanted to pick up her things and go.

This picture was taken as we found out Victoria refused to see us

"She should at least have to look at us," I said.

He just acted as if it was my call, but I knew what he would say. *I'm just supposed to just let it go. Let it all go.* The last things I have of her, and never see her again. Not even make her look me in the eye as she takes them from my hands.

"Fine," I said. We gave him the title to the car, the keys, the cashier's check, and signed everything. They asked for her phone and I told him I would bring it, if I ever received it from India. It had only been ten days since we had arrived back in the country. He relayed to us a reminder from her lawyer that texting her was not allowed, as it was a form of contact. She didn't have a restraining order and had no reason to get one, so it wasn't legally binding, but they were insisting we don't.

We were told to wait in a room nearby while she signed and picked up the papers, and then we could come back in to pick up our copies. When she arrived, we could hear them in the next room as they finished everything up. We waited for them to leave before we ventured out of the room. I could have caught her on her way out, but I didn't. I gave her, her privacy. It would have hurt too much anyway.

CHAPTER 31

THE FRENZY

Iregretted ever having put anything on social media. I had been keeping people who were concerned informed, but my enemies had used everything I said against me, to pry me away from my daughter. *Facebook* had become the arena where an audience of two sides were watching as everything played out.

My brother was on a rampage to destroy us. He and Evelyn had created a *Facebook* page called "FREE VICTORIA HARRIS" with Oliver and Victoria as administrators and Grant and Kelli as members. It was essentially put in place to "Free Victoria from her parents and send her back to India," and they set up a *GoFundMe* to raise funds.

Sebastion had put out a post while we were en route home stating that upon our arrival to Mobile, we would be committing Victoria to a mental institution and he was calling on everyone to show up at the airport.

> *Victoria is in more danger at home than she ever was in India. She thinks she has no choice but to go with her parents. Victoria and Ranjit have so much support, they just need to see it. I won't stop until my niece is physically and mentally free from these people.'*

It was a private group, but I could see it through Victoria's account on my computer. Most of the members were young and rebellious and strangers to our family, while some were adults and parents themselves. Some were distant family of ours, and some were children of our friends from church.

None of them knew our family well and they were ill-informed. It was evident from the news feed, the page intended to harm us.

Previously, Victoria had Ranjit and his family, Evelyn and Oliver, our brothers, and their wives all influencing her, but now she had a whole new support system of 851 people encouraging her to leave her family and further this relationship. With almost one thousand people's voices in her head daily, she didn't have a chance to think for herself.

We had brought her back physically, but it was going to take another divine intervention to bring her back to us mentally. Our family needed healing from this traumatic experience. We needed to debrief and decompress.

But no one was talking about restoring our family.

No one.

Victoria was posting on *Facebook* and telling news outlets we stole money from her bank account, stole her car, clothes, and possessions, had her arrested, and that she was now jobless and homeless. "They mentally and emotionally abused me, my entire life," she told them as one news article stated, ending with: *The future is sad for this family.*

Free Victoria Harris pagewas companySebastion had a day scheduled encouraging people to show up and picket at our place of business, saying, *"They messed with Victoria's money, now let's mess with theirs."* Total strangers were posting awful reviews on our business page and rating us, causing me to temporarily remove both my business and personal pages.

Pastor Leite asked to join the page to observe. To our amazement, Victoria accepted his request. I knew they were combing through the list of members, but they never seemed to see Pastor Leite, even though Sebastion had posted his name and phone number as the one leading "this insane brigade," and I was Victoria, so they would never see me.

They were having trouble getting their *GoFundMe* account approved and were trying to report and attack ours, saying it was fraudulent, that we took Victoria against her will, so we shouldn't be given money to help. It ended up costing us $18,000 including missing two weeks of work, and we received $7,000 in donations, while their donation account ended up collecting enough to pay Victoria's attorney.

Sebastion began distancing himself from us, calling our mother by her first name, just as Victoria had done to me.

The only people brainwashing Victoria are her parents by not letting her grow up, and feeding her religious BS. Victoria has suffered mental abuse from this family just like I have.

I was "raised" by Destiny's mother, and she is just like her, hiding behind a Bible because she has no backbone to lean on. They both called me crying and asking what to do, but instead of taking my advice and letting me go with Victoria to make sure it was safe, they brought in church people to make her feel guilty about what she's doing.

Her parents were praying over her constantly, and they have disrupted this poor Sharma family's life. Sex trafficking would never have been a concern if anyone had researched the family like I did. They have Facebook pages and everything. Completely normal family! These people are not strangers, they are people just like you and me. I bet one hundred percent it's because their skin is darker and their religion is different. We were able to get Victoria out of her parents' hands at the airport and she is safe at the home of a close friend.

He ended with:

They are no longer my family. I hope Priscilla removes "Reinhardt" from her name. I'm dead to them.

Sophie, his fiancé, told us, *Don't ever contact our family. I choose not to have a relationship with you*, and posted, *Brent, Destiny, and Priscilla are a bunch of losers.*

The page had become a group of piranhas.

One day while reading the page, I walked into the bathroom while Brent was taking a shower. "Honey, apparently, we're the "*Deadly Duo who takes down foreign governments.'* I wish I had known that, or we wouldn't be washing cars for a living!" I told him.

We were called "soulless spawns of Satan who didn't deserve children, and should be punished."

The group page was teeming with accusations against us:

Victoria said, '*My parents lied when they said they brought me home safely. That implies I was in danger, when I wasn't. Ranjit's now getting threats in his country.'*

People were commenting:

'*It's the saddest thing, this sweet girl and this poor family being demolished by this demon of a "Christian" mother. How horrible for her to cause people to be suspicious of Ranjit and his family in their own community and beyond. You have a legal case against your parents.'*

'*No parent should try to control their grown children. Good for you for leaving your family. Surround yourself with loving people who truly care about your well-being. Now that you've left them, you'll have a life filled with peace, happiness, and love.'*

'You should keep a journal of all the bad things your parents have done to you. Write it down while you are angry and clear-headed, so that on dark days when you start to have doubts, go back and read it, and you will be reminded of what has been done to you, and that you are doing the right thing, no matter how others make you feel.'

'You're allowed to be angry, selfish, and unforgiving to those who have hurt you. You don't owe anyone an explanation for taking care of you.'

'Victoria should get evaluated to prove her parents wrong and that she isn't autistic.'

'What her parents did was childish.'

'Her parents didn't incur any cost, Ranjit's family paid for everything.'

Victoria was thanking everyone for their love and compassion for her and Ranjit and saying their prayers and donations were saving her life because she wouldn't have gotten her belongings back without them, and that she was going back to India.

'Fate will bring you back. Trust me," Esha told her.

People were telling her it was a great story and she needed to share it. Others were saying it would end up being a movie.

I do wish the truth was out there, she replied.

Anytime someone tried to talk sense into the situation, they were silenced, ridiculed, or blocked. People got into their own arguments, putting down each other's country and their president.

'Her 21 trips around the sun does not make her an adult.'

'No idiot wants their daughter in a third-world country.'

'She didn't act like an adult by not telling her parents. If her family didn't care they wouldn't have gone to the lengths they did. Something's not right. She's a beautiful girl, why would she have to go to another country to find love? Just makes no sense.'

'If he loves her so much, why does he have zero info about her on his page?'

'Internet relationship is a joke.'

Some members were from "sleuth groups" and some ran "missing persons groups." Since they were doing more to hurt than to help, maybe they were helping missing persons get and stay away from their families.

Evelyn posted a meme of a glass of wine being raised, *'Here's to all my girlfriends who will help me cause trouble in the nursing home.'*

Victoria posted, When we came back from India, my mom was going to take me home, but eventually, she was going to have me committed for life. My parents believe my friend who took me from the airport is the new brainwasher when everything I do is my own decision. I decided to go with Evelyn, just like I decided to go to India. My mom said, 'You were taken from us a second time,' when the only people who have truly taken me are my parents. They didn't let me choose, they kidnapped me, and my friend at the airport rescued me.

She may have been making her own decisions, but those decisions were based on lies. Just like the ones planted in her mind by Ranjit to make her believe she was being abused, causing her to leave in the first place.

They posted news footage of me in the Minister of State's Office pleading to take my daughter home. It had nearly one million views. Evelyn posted a furious emoji under it with the words *'Oscar winning performance.'* I showed it to Claudia because she and Evelyn were friends. *How can she be so cruel?* I texted.

334

ਅਮਰੀਕਾ ਦੀ
ਰੀ ਨੇ ਪੰਜਾਬੀਆਂ
ਨੂੰ ਪਾਈ ਭਾਜੜ

unjabspectrum.news
Mobile woman ████████████ eturns from India
US-based woman, who had landed here a fortnight ago to...

👍 9   29 Co███nts

👍 Like   💬 █t

Oscar winning performance 😞

A screenshot of the actual post where my sorrow
was called an "Oscar winning performance"

335

I'm sorry, I know that must've hurt, was all she wrote and I never heard from her again. Maybe she felt guilty for getting me in touch with Evelyn. It was because of Claudia we had made contact with Dr. Mustafa's family in India and had a safe place for Victoria to go. I didn't understand how she and Evelyn could remain friends.

On my page, people were commenting:

'Thank you for spreading the awareness about trafficking. It's not something we have ever really thought about, but obviously something we need to.'

'I just finished my English paper on this topic. It's happening more and more recently and is dangerous and getting out of hand. Talking to someone online for two years, then leaving in the middle of the night to go to another country, sounds like she signed up for sex trafficking,' someone commented under a news article.

'A girl was kidnapped and murdered by a guy that had a machine gun on his profile just like his does.'

'I still tell my parents where I'm going, and I'm 71 years old.'

From Singapore: Two percent love white girl, and ninety-eight percent love green card.

Johnny: Let him come over here. He'll wish he never did.

High school friends: You have a tribe behind you, Destiny, and we do mean TRIBE!

Me: He asked if he could call me mom.

Commentor: Tell him he can call you plaintiff.

Then people from the *Free Victoria Harris* page began commenting on my page. They called themselves *Team Victoria and Ranjit,* while Anne had called us *Team Protect Victoria.*

'*She obviously loves her parents,*' commented one of my friends.

Oliver: *She certainly does not! On any level!*

People were asking Oliver what his relationship to Victoria is.

Oliver: *Who I am to someone is between that person and me, and not anyone's business.*

'*Won't God handle it? If you trust the Lord, leave your daughter alone, and keep your nose out of it,*' someone from their page mocked.

'*A mother's love doesn't stop once their child turns eighteen. You are doing exactly what any loving parent would do,*' replied someone from my page.

'*She was raised as good as it gets.*'

'*Let her learn her lesson, even if it blows up in her face. She is being misled by her world, not just Ranjit. Social media is a very powerful outlet,*' commented someone to my page.

Pastor Leite: *Love is to suffer for others' decisions.*

Oliver: *She may be making the best of the worst decision of her life.*

One you helped her make! I wanted to scream through my laptop.

You let your son go to Australia, but you won't let Victoria go anywhere? How come he gets treated differently? Someone commented.

Eddie Upchurch: *The devil presents himself in so many nice forms to tempt the world... Do not fall for this devil. If his intentions were honorable, he'd be in America. Bring her home.*

Keith Thompson: *If, when she left home, her parents had said, 'She's twenty-one, she can do what she wants', and she ended up in the sex trade or dead, these same people expressing vehement hate would be the very same people saying the Harrises hated their daughter and stood idly by, doing nothing to protect her.*

Keith was right, we were condemned either way.

Pastor Leite had messaged me when we returned, *I'm so proud of you. You guys are worriers!* I had to smile; his English was a little off. I knew he meant *warriors* and he was our mentor, and our biggest cheerleader.

They posted the photo of Victoria and Ranjit in the New Delhi airport the day we left Mobile. Underneath was Evelyn's comment, '*So cute!!!*' with heart eyes.

When had she said this? Why hadn't I seen it?

Mom reminded me what her friend had said, "You will come under attack this very night.' That was the night you landed in Dallas and Victoria made that post."

She was right. From that point on, our family turned against us. Some people turned from prayers for us, to hate. Once people saw her post explaining her side, they got all wrapped up in this "love story that beats all odds," instead of seeing it for what it really was, which only put her in more danger. With her saying we abused her, none of these people tried to talk to us, they only listened to and encouraged her. They did not know what they were being driven by. I said, '*Father forgive them, for they know not what they do*' but they mocked that, too.

338

Victoria commented, referring to her post, *it's sickening to read hate comments from people who don't know you. I'm not even against my family, I was just telling my side. I will always love them. I just hope this gets a better ending.*

᛭   ᛭   ᛭

At night, I read the private messages.

Sebastion and Victoria:

Sebastion: *Ranjit is amazing and his parents seem so nice.*

Victoria: *They seem very loving. Evelyn is helping me figure out where to live, where to go to school, and what career to pursue.*

Austin and Victoria:

Austin: *You should read the notes your parents sent you.*

Victoria: *My friend is taking me to another lawyer tomorrow about suing my parents. I would read the notes if it didn't say, 'To My Beautiful Butterfly' I don't want to read them. I'm afraid it will be more gaslighting.*

Austin: *What's that?*

Victoria: *It's a form of manipulation, where you are made to feel crazy and guilty. They play with your emotions to make you believe what they want.*

Victoria: *Ok, I went ahead and read the notes. They WERE lying and manipulating me, and I hated reading them.*

One beautiful thing I can say about long distance relationships is, they weed out fake people because they can't touch you physically, but they still make the effort to talk to you regularly and keep the friendship going strong. It's more meaningful, and that's true love.

My mom, at age sixteen, went and got herself pregnant, and she's worried the same thing will happen to me. But I'm not her. I'm my own person and I could never get that close to someone before marriage.

The worst part is my parents made it public. I can't even go to the store to buy underwear because I'm embarrassed someone will notice me. They made my face well-known to predators. So many guys are messaging me now.

Austin: *It was dumb of them to say it was human trafficking when your letter clearly explained everything.*

Victoria: *Human trafficking never entered my mind. I thought they would read it, contact me, and see I was okay. They didn't even mention the letter. They just told the news I was autistic and that it was trafficking. It broke my heart. I spent time on that letter, putting my soul into it. I explained everything clearly and was very apologetic, but they didn't listen.*

Of all the things I had been reading, this penetrated my heart. A lump formed in my throat and the pit of my stomach ached. I didn't want her to hurt. I didn't want her heart broken. She sincerely believed her letter was supposed to make it all better, but it had just confirmed our fears even more. All I wanted was to hold her.

Victoria: *The church made this whole thing possible. They helped pull me out of the country.*

Austin: *Where are you now?*

Victoria: *A woman who used to be friends with my mom was helping me, and telling me what would happen if I didn't go with her, and other people were saying the same thing, that I would never see the light of day again, and that my parents would try to get guardianship over me. So I'm staying with my friend who took me from the airport.*

340

I was happy she had read our letters. And she was right, everyone's prayers made it all possible.

People were messaging her from all over. A woman in Virginia was sitting at her daughter's gymnastics class when an article came across her phone with the *Free Victoria Harris* group page linked to it; she had been following the story ever since, and someone in the UK had seen it on the news.

I kept reading…

An Indian woman warned her:

India is a poor country with few jobs. If you aren't smart enough to get a job, you look for other means to earn some handsome money. Thousands of Indian boys and girls make friends from some rich country and manipulate them in the name of love.

If that country is America, that's a lottery ticket. It's the easiest way to go abroad and settle. This is a tactic to be rich.

Think about it; you met on social media. No one can love you more than your mother. I got concerned after watching her cry.

Victoria: *You are wrong, and my mother is fake crying. He never wanted to come to America. The world doesn't know the true story. You can't talk about someone you don't know. I know him better than his parents. I am highly aware of how Indians lie about love to get into America and to say that's his intentions is insulting. I researched the country for two years and know a lot about Indian people. I'm not naïve, it's true love. It's one hundred percent wrong what my parents did.*

Others were warning her:

'*This is what Punjabi boys do. They are known for this. It happened to me.*'

'Ranjit will never enter the U.S. He can't get tourist visa. He's a criminal. I know him from my childhood.'

'*Do not believe Ranjit. He has many girlfriends. He make you foolish.*'

Then I saw a message to Victoria from Jackson (a guy friend of hers from church). Jackson was the only young person that was standing up for us parents and telling her the hard truth.

Jackson: *At the end of this fantasy world, I hope you really do realize what good parents you have to actually care enough about you to drop everything and come see you, and try to teach you about God and to have good morals. It's a shame that you choose some dude on some app over them, it's ridiculous and you're wrong to treat them like this. Most parents, especially in a world so cruel, don't give two craps about you. But you're going to have to learn the hard way about how bad it is in a world like this, because when this little fantasy world ends, you're gonna be all alone in a country with no money or education and family will be all you have. Then I'm gonna just pray for you, that you come to your senses.*

Strangers were offering her to come live with them. I didn't know if we would know where she was, or if we would ever see her again. I was hoping she would decide to go with someone we knew. Somewhere safe. It looked as if she was deciding between Sebastion and Grant, so we were relieved.

Her "gym family" was behind her and she still had a job, but was too embarrassed to live in Mobile anymore. I couldn't go back to the gym, either. It would be too painful since it's where this horror began.

I continued to read the *Free Victoria Harris* news feed:

'Hopefully, your parents will admit how horribly they handled their fear.'

Victoria: *I don't want to hate them. We are all human, and not perfect. I just hope they didn't cause permanent damage where I won't get to see that beautiful family again.*

Victoria's Bible study teacher: *I was ninety-nine percent sure it was an awesome Bollywood-style love story, and one-percent skeptic and scared.*

Victoria: *This is not about human trafficking or about parents loving their kid, it's about control.*

Oliver: *It was impossible for you to talk to them, Victoria. You had no option but the one you chose.*

Victoria: *My "parents" left me on the street to die.*

Reading that, I sat up in bed. *We were bringing you home!* I wanted to scream, but my eyes dropped down to a comment:

'Much love to you, Ranjit, his family, your amazing uncles, and your family friend.'

Next, I came to Ranjit and Victoria's conversation. I grabbed some water and continued reading.

Ranjit: *I hate your parents and that black pastor, M F*er. Can I kill him? I want to kill him with a shotgun but unfortunately, I can't. My reputation is ruined. People here are making fun of it and they will keep doing it unless we get married.*

Victoria: *What has been done to us is criminal.*

Ranjit: *Yes, they just took you. They should have let both the families talk to each other, then let you decide, but they just sent you back.*

I cringed, burrowing my shoulders deeper into the pillow. *Really. Both families should have talked to each other before taking her? Hmph.*

Victoria: *I don't think you realize I'm suffering for you. I could go back home to my parents, but I have nothing because I love you.*

I mused, *So, if she went back home to her parents, she would not be suffering, and she would have everything?*

Ranjit: *You are my drug. You don't answer when I call.*

Victoria: *I was cleaning Evelyn's kitchen and watching the kids.*

Ranjit: *I hate you. If you don't answer, I will never come there, but I will always be here to annoy you.*

Victoria: *I don't want to see your face yelling at me. Please don't hurt me.*

Ranjit: *Have a great night talking to strangers.*

Victoria: *I do not have friends! It's just me, you, and Tanvi. I have been ignoring thousands of people for you.*

Ranjit had her login info and was telling people to leave her alone.

Ranjit: *I told you to stay away from Facebook. People can wash your brain.*

Victoria: *Really? Brainwashing? Lol.*

Ranjit: *Yes.*

Victoria: *Evelyn is asking me to come to dinner.*

Ranjit: *She told me, 'Victoria won't eat meat.' I said, 'She Miss Nutritionist Victoria Harris. Give her, her green drink, see if she wants that. Lol!'*

She didn't care that he was making fun of her, but then again, they had derogatory pet names for each other. He called her "Vamp-toria" and "Vomit-toria" and she called him "Rank-it."

Victoria: *My mom wasted your money. I want to repay your dad.*

Ranjit: *Dad reputation is ruined.*

They began to talk about getting married and deciding if it would happen in India or the U.S. They shared photos of Indian wedding attire and made plans for their life together.

Ranjit: *I will ask Dad for money to buy your ring. He always asking me to work with him, but I say my back hurts, now he say he will do by himself. I've been playing video games with Uncle Seb. He likes guns like I do. He said he will come here.*

Victoria: *He'll never make it past security. Your face was on our news today. My secret love was on the news!!!*

Ranjit: *I'm your mom, I'm your dad, I'm your pet. I'm everything. Trust in me, and God, and Seb and Evelyn, and my family. Forget others.*

He then sent her two photos that made my mouth drop open.

In one, she was unconscious with his arm around her head in a football hold. The other one was a meme that said, '*Your Hole is Our Goal.*'

Unbelievable. I shook my head. He drugged her. And he had the money shot to prove it. He was parading it in front of her, his prize he had caught. And that word "*our*" goal. This was a group endeavor. Sounded like a traffic ring to me. I guess he thought she wouldn't care, and I guess he was right. She didn't say a word.

The meme Ranjit sent

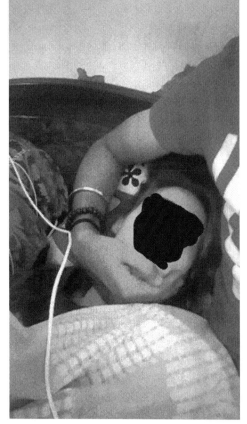

A photo Ranjit sent to Victoria
which shows her unconscious

Just then my phone dinged. I sat up in bed. New messages were coming through her phone to the app.

Ranjit: *Tor? Your phone is working.*

Evelyn: *Victoria? Hello?*

Sebastion: *How's snooping through your daughter's phone?*

Oliver: *Victoria, I see you're there. Has your vile mother given your money back?*

Then he quoted a verse of scripture.

"If anyone does not provide for his relatives, and especially for members of his household, he has denied the faith and is worse than an unbeliever."

I was confused. Should we leave her alone? Or provide for her?

Oliver: *Just realized this is Destiny reading this. That's awesome. Another item stolen by her family.*

You must be choking. The police are coming. They have a recording of plotting the mental institution. They will arrest you. They'll take you off in handcuffs and you'll lose everything.

The recording shows conspiracy to commit fraud and to commit your daughter. According to the law, a minimum two years in prison, not counting wasting police time, and filing false court documents. I felt sorry for you for two seconds, then I remembered what you did to Victoria and now I am waiting. Patiently. They are coming for you.

Every time your business door opens, you will be thinking,

'Is it today? Will they take me today?'

I was pretty sure that's what he and Evelyn would be thinking.

Hmph, I thought. *Evelyn and her friends from other countries. She sure had a lot of them. Troy Garfield, Oliver .... then it dawned on me.*

Wait.

Could it be?

You've got to be kidding me!

Was Oliver actually Troy Garfield, the private investigator? The one I almost gave $15,000 to find my daughter? Who had actually been telling my daughter to *stay* in India and not listen to us? Yes. It had to be. As I thought about it, a lot of things made sense. I was almost played. It felt eerie when he never contacted me again or asked where the money was. He and Evelyn were probably in on it together and were going to share the money while they continued to keep Victoria in India. God had protected me.

One morning as I sat down for breakfast, someone from Singapore said he wanted to help and told me if I gave him money he could make my daughter come back and leave Ranjit. I told him to not speak of that anymore with me.

"That's voodoo. I don't do that. My daughter needs to be with me because she wants to." That's probably exactly what Ranjit had done. Paid some witch doctor to spellbind her to him. Even Davison said such things. I felt bad for him. It seemed ingrained in their culture. You become like the environment that surrounds you. He knew better than that, but he was getting desperate for us. He hated how things turned out. We were so optimistic when we left India.

Keith sent a message from an American woman who had been married to an Indian man and had lived in the same area as Ranjit.

I was drawn to your story. Indians do not marry outside their culture or even their caste. If they do, the family will publicly disown them as my husband's father did. Victoria has caused major embarrassment for their family. Trust me, Ranjit's intentions are not good nor are his family's. Ask yourself, why no Indian women are in support of this relationship.

It's every Punjabi boy's dream to come to America. He will never be able to get a visa to come here because of the controversy between him and Victoria. All of this has been recorded by his local police department. Believe me. The embassy will deny his visa even if he marries Victoria.

This confirmed what Davison told us that first day and what the policewoman who detained us in Dallas had said. The police must have a record of it and didn't want him coming to the U.S. It calmed my fears of him making it to this country.

Ranjit's page had a meme that read,

> *Stop caring what others think, stop taking caution in your actions, listen to what you want.*

And that's just what he had done.

The day came when I could no longer see Victoria's *Facebook*, and I was glad. I had seen all I needed to see.

CHAPTER 32

INTERFERENCE

Victoria stayed in Evelyn's house the month of October. Evelyn helped her close the bank account she had with me and opened one at another bank.

Going to India turned our world upside down. It had been a feat to accomplish, frightening, uncertain, and a drain on our income and emotions, but we made it out alive, with Victoria, and it had only taken a week. God had come through for us, but the pain of the aftershock would reverberate for years.

A lie had been fabricated to turn our daughter against us and make her not come home. We had no plans of putting her in a psych ward. No one can force a person into one, adults must admit themselves. Our daughter didn't know this, but the ones who told her that did. Grant knew it; he had told us in Dallas, although at the time we didn't understand why he was bringing it up. As far as I knew, mental institutions didn't even exist anymore. We wouldn't have spent $18,000 to bring her back just to put her in a mental institution. We could have just left her in India.

In the weeks to come, Grant and Kelli persistently spoke to Brent's parents about what they thought was going on. Kelli insisted the title to the car was in Victoria's name. Brent's dad kept telling them, "Destiny and Brent went to India, not you," and told him he believed Luke and was not discussing it.

Why had they all helped us in the beginning? It wasn't out of love and concern for us. Something was happening and they wanted to be a part of it, to show off their smarts and connections, to be heroes. We were their little project, and they were willing to invest their time in it. They had gotten so involved that it became personal to them when it never should have been. We appreciated the help, but boundaries were crossed and our role as parents wasn't respected. They all turned on us when we didn't do things their way.

They hadn't had a relationship with Victoria or with our boys in the past, but all of a sudden, they became interested in her? No. They were using Victoria to hurt us.

After telling him the whole story, the lawyer asked me why I thought they had done this. "I don't know. There were just little things…" I began to say, as he interrupted and said, "Oh, you would be surprised at what people do to each other, over *little* things."

Evelyn and her friend, Oliver, had mommy issues. They saw themselves in Victoria and were living their lives through her to get back at their own mothers. A clue to what they are is always in what they say about you. They mirror or cast onto you a portrait of themselves. Evelyn said I was using Victoria for my own agenda, to get revenge on someone, and Oliver had told Victoria, *I lost my whole family because of a woman just like your mother.*

Sebastion, Grant, and Kelli wanted revenge because of past rifts between us. Evelyn and Oliver wanted revenge on their family, and we were taking the brunt of it all.

They had interfered in our relationship with our child, a young adult, whose brain had not fully matured, who they did not know, nor understand, a child who was not their own. What Ranjit had started, they were perpetuating: hate and irrational fear and distrust of the two people who were put in place by God to love and protect her.

A verse came to my mind, *If anyone causes one of these little ones to stumble, it would be better for them to have a millstone tied around their neck and be thrown into the depths of the sea.* (Matthew 18:6)

I desperately wanted to tell them that if anything happened to our daughter, her blood would be on their hands. I was concerned she might get hurt or pregnant if she went back to India, and this is what they were helping her do. In scripture "meddlers" and "busybodies" are on the list with "murderers." Now I knew why. They had murdered us. Sebastion and Grant had too much time on their hands. If they had been paying attention to their own families, they wouldn't have time to put their noses in ours.

I thought about the text messages with Victoria, and the airport, and the fact my daughter was gone.

I felt like a crime had been committed, but I didn't know what to do about it. It was like infidelity. When a woman takes another woman's husband. There's nothing you can do about it, and it destroys families.

If someone had come into my home and stolen my television, I could call the police and have it returned, but something much more valuable had been taken from me, my precious daughter, and yet I had no recourse. She was gone; I had no way to contact her and I knew the influence she was under was so strong, it would take a million miracles to bring her back. But I had to count all the miracles that had already happened.

The closest thing I could find to what I was experiencing was "Alienation of Affection," "Predator Alienation," and "Undue Influence." The state of New Jersey was lobbying for it, but it hadn't become law.

God became so close to me in my pain, I decided I would rather walk through the valley of the shadow of death holding His hand, than to walk anywhere without Him.

I had prayed a dangerous prayer. I'd been praying for it for fifteen years.

Lord, please use me for whatever you want, for as long as you want.

But this wasn't the answer I was expecting. I hadn't meant *this*! Not pain! I meant helping people! Through a ministry!

Still, I had prayed it, and I needed to trust Him.

He *had* started using us. Eight years before Victoria left, we had turned our lives completely over to God. We went into a deeper relationship with Him than ever before. We had a newfound faith and love for Him, and we were ready to share it with the world.

Our whole family was dedicated. We were ready. Brent and the boys were all good at sharing their faith through speaking and Bible study, and Victoria and I were learning practical skills in the kitchen and had a desire to teach healthy living principles. We had a family business, now we wanted a family ministry.

What in the world were we about to do that made the enemy hate us so much, that he had to stop us with *this*?

This is just a small interruption, a thought came.

Yes, God was going to use this. Someway. Somehow. I just needed to wait for His timing.

CHAPTER 33

POWERFUL INFLUENCE

November 1st, Sebastion flew down and drove with Victoria to his home out West. She was going to live with him and Sophie and wait for Ranjit to come.

What our family had done to us stood against all reason. They were treating us like the criminals and Ranjit and his family like the victims. Some kind of power had overtaken them. The same power that made Victoria leave her home. It happened the minute we left the country and were headed to our daughter. From the moment we landed in India, everything we did was undermined from that point forward. They all stopped talking to us and were only listening to Victoria and Ranjit. We were there on the ground, yet they believed they had all the information they needed to make intelligent decisions about our daughter's life.

I was trying to pinpoint where this turn, this change, in our family had taken place, what had caused it, and why it was so severe. I looked over the post Victoria made the night we were in Dallas, the night Mom's friend said we would be attacked. Victoria had stated we abused her. What caused her to say that? Where had it come from? When we arrived in India, she had told us she left because we didn't feed or take care of her.

I looked back through the conversations I had with her the month before she left. We had fun at the gym together at 4:00 a.m. only five days before, and I was always asking her what I could pick up at the store, from a restaurant, or what I could make for dinner. Even while she was writing the letter she left us, she was eating the Subway sandwich I had bought her. When I had asked if she wanted me to pick up lunch, she looked up at me, with sad eyes, and in a pitiful voice said, "Yes, I would like food." I had thought it strange.

I remembered what Kelli said about Ranjit's parents saying we had an abusive household, *It's not clear how much of this Victoria portrayed to them, or how much it was skewed by Ranjit.*

Skewed by Ranjit? It was *planted* by him.

What else could he have made her do? What if she hadn't left that night? What if, instead of leaving, she had hurt us as we slept in bed? Because she really wanted to go, and didn't want us to stop her? Could he have made her believe it was so bad at home that she had to keep us from stopping her and there was only one way to do it? Grant said she was going to kill herself if she didn't go. Or was it something else?

I began to believe God had protected us by her leaving. The thing that brought us so much pain could have actually been our protection. We never know how God is acting on our behalf because we don't know the whole story. We don't know what is really going on, so we must trust the all-knowing God who cares for us. That realization helped me see this pain we were going through, was keeping us from something much worse.

I began looking for clues as to where this change had come from. As I skimmed through her photos on the app, what I found shocked me. Two photos caught my attention. In the first one, Victoria was wearing a cute, turquoise top, a silver tiara, and a sweet, pure, innocent smile, looking like a princess. I scrolled to the next photo. She was wearing the same top, but the tiara was gone and so was the smile. Instead, there was a demonic face staring at the camera. Her face was painted black and red. Her nose was black, but it wasn't her nose. It was bigger like a cat's paw. Her cheeks were black, her entire eyelids were black up to her eyebrows, under her eyes were black with gray veins trailing them, and thick red eyeliner traced the top and bottom rims of her eyes. The rest of her face was gray with black stitching over her mouth. She must have used a "filter" on her phone to make the image overlay her face. Seeing it made me jump. I gasped as I covered my mouth. We didn't even celebrate Halloween, and as far as I knew, she had never looked at anything scary or gory.

If that wasn't enough, I scrolled past that photo, to a video clip, that would put the pieces together. It was a man in a suit, in mid-sentence, "If we don't restrain those thoughts, we are brought under the influence of evil angels, and we *invite their presence and control.*"

Why had she clipped this part of the video and saved it?

I scrolled past. There was a screenshot of her post the night we landed in Dallas, the night we would "come under attack," the post that turned our family against us.

 She had circled in red, "666 comments."

She knew.

She knew what was happening.

CHAPTER 34

OSTRACIZED

One day in December, as Brent and I had lunch, he got a call from his mother saying his brothers didn't want us coming to our annual family Christmas. Grant didn't want to see us and Derrick said his wife, Tabby didn't want me there. His mom was crying. Christmas was her favorite time of year and she loved cooking, decorating, and having all her family together. Brent sadly hung up the phone as he told me. "She and your dad are allowing this," I said.

In January, I texted Grant. I couldn't understand what we had done to make them hate us so much and wanted to do my part to make things right.

I'm sorry if I did anything to hurt you. Please forgive me. I don't know what I've done to deserve this. You were always like a little brother to me. Preston said you're holding onto some things. Let's talk about it. Remember what you told me about Tabby, that we needed to make it work because family means so much to you.

Don't ever contact me or my kids, came the reply.

Don't contact *his* kids? What a hypocrite.

I had still been sending his kids birthday and Christmas cards with gifts. We didn't want the kids to forget us or think we had forgotten them. I messaged Kelli, telling her we loved them and the kids, but she ignored it. I sent her a birthday card with a gift, thinking if I couldn't

359

get through to Grant, maybe I could to her. She was a mother; she should understand, but they just wouldn't talk to me.

I messaged Tabby, my other sister-in-law, and told her the same thing, but she never replied. "I don't know what else to do," I told my mother-in-law, Jeannie. I wanted her to know if there was a rift between any of us, it wasn't going to be because of me. Jeannie only said she hoped it would get resolved.

Sebastion had stopped all contact with Mom and Sophie was sending her hateful messages. They were still demanding we send a letter of apology to Ranjit's family. They must have needed it to get him into the country.

I had to keep my mind busy, so I got lost in my work. God was blessing us. Every time someone hurt us, we would receive a ton of business. I was thinking about Victoria every day, hoping and praying she would text or send me a letter, anything. She had all her family blocked on social media and from her phone so no one could contact her. I had been sending her e-mails, but wasn't sure if she was receiving them. On February 20th around 3:00 p.m., as I sat at the dining room table working on my computer, Brent walked into the house with two large, brown bags, and set them on the table.

"This is from Victoria."

"What?" I gasped and began to cry. He didn't seem happy about it.

"What is it?" I asked.

"A delivery girl from *Grub Hub* dropped it off, saying, 'This is from Victoria for her parents.' I told her I haven't spoken to my daughter in a long time. I didn't want to accept it. It may not be from her. It may be poisoned. Evelyn may have sent it, saying it was from Victoria. Maybe Evelyn wants to kill us."

He had a point. Evelyn could be up to something. I opened the bag. It was from *McAllister's,* our local deli, a whole spread. Two large vegetarian entrees, a bread bowl with soup, two large, sweet teas, and two large slices of chocolate cake. I looked at the receipt. It read: "Victoria" and the total was forty-two dollars. She had splurged on us! She wasn't normally generous with her money, and it meant the world to me. And she had called us "her parents"! We were still her parents!

I was so excited! She was coming back! She was sorry! After months of silence, this was what I had been praying for. I was jumping around, shouting, hugging Brent, and praising the Lord. It was just like her to use food. "It's her love language," I explained to my friends as I told them the good news.

I texted her, flooding her with thank you's, love you's, hearts and kisses, then snapped a photo of her dad and me and sent it. I just knew this was the beginning of restarting our relationship. Crying, I waited for her to respond. I knew she would be expecting to hear from me. She didn't respond that day….…..or the next day…...…..or the next.

It took a whole week for me to realize she wasn't going to respond, and then it appeared I had been blocked. It became a mystery to me and I was never sure it had been her.

Later, we would find out "I sent it because I felt guilty about everything, but I immediately regretted it."

In April, Sebastion and Sophie married. Mom and I weren't invited to the wedding. It crushed us, and deep down I know it crushed Sebastion, too. The wedding was in Florida, and Grant and Victoria met there, sharing a hotel room.

Brent and I met his parents for lunch one day and as we sat at the table Jeannie, his mother said, "Victoria destroyed this family." Shock grabbed me by the throat. I wanted to reach across the table at her.

Victoria? What an ignorant thing to say. She was a young girl in love, who made a foolish mistake, and Brent and I had brought our daughter back safely. If we had been allowed to bring her home, we would have all healed by now and this would be over. But because our family interfered by collaborating to take her from us at the airport, our whole family was still hurting.

Grant destroyed this family. He had no reason to get involved, but he already hated us, and Victoria going to India had brought it out.

"I want to know what Grant is doing at my brother's wedding," I simply replied.

They say the aftershock is worse than the earthquake. Victoria going to India may have shaken our world, but it was nothing compared to what our family had done to us.

And yet, we were the ones who had been excluded.

By our whole family.

They had abandoned us in our time of greatest need and were continuing to cause our daughter to hate and distrust us. We were being treated like monsters. Like we had committed some hideous crime.

"Victoria has told them so many bad things about both of you," Jeannie told me one day, referring to Grant and Kelli.

"And they chose to believe it, because they *wanted* to believe it," I had responded. Victoria had also told Grant and Kelli she wanted to mend the relationship with her parents, but neither of them were encouraging her in that.

After three years, Grant and Kelli had finally worn Brent's parents down. They had completely turned against us.

"We don't know who to believe," his mom told Brent while he and I sat in a hotel room. We were on our way back from a family trip, and while passing through Grant's town, we stopped so Brent could try to talk to his brother. He had called his mom to ask her to contact Grant so they could meet. "Grant never wants to see you again, and I can't give you his number," she told him.

"*You don't know who to believe?* I went to the other side of the world, risked my business and my life, to get my daughter, and make sure she was safe, and you don't know who to believe?" I could hear him on the phone in the other room sobbing, just like he had in the airport. Her words killed us that day, the same way our brother's actions had. It hurt, but we understood they weren't going against us, they were going against our Savior. This was spiritual warfare. I was reminded of the words, "*I will fight those, who fight you, and I will save your children.*" (Isaiah 49:25)

Pastor Leite was preaching one morning about Adam and Eve when they trespassed against God; how they ran and hid. They were afraid because they had done wrong and were guilty. God came looking for them, to reconcile the relationship, but they didn't want to see God's face. Maybe we weren't being ostracized at all, maybe they just couldn't face us.

CHAPTER 35

DISHONORED

If I had been wrong about Ranjit, and he really loved our daughter, I expected him to reach out to us, wanting a relationship with our family. He never did, and when I tried to contact him, I was blocked. He was not encouraging our daughter in a relationship with her family, nor did he want one.

I thought about the ten-year visa. Why did she need one for that long if she was only visiting for two months? Why not get the 60-day? Having a ten-year visa meant this was long-term. This was more than just "to meet."

I'd been thinking about the two plans. Sex trafficking or marriage? I still believed marrying her to live in the U.S. was only Plan B because Plan A was thwarted. Then a thought struck me. If the plan had been to marry her and live in the U.S., she wouldn't need a ten-year visa to India. It ruled that plan out. There was a reason they had met her in New Delhi. To make a transaction with someone. Someone who needed her to stay in India for a long time. To *work* her.

Immediately following Sebastion's wedding in April, Victoria returned to India, only seven months after we brought her back; and she and Ranjit were married mid-June 2019. She sold her car to make the trip. Someone sent me the wedding photos. That's how I found out. She was dressed in red and gold with beaded jewelry hanging down on her forehead in true Indian fashion and a tunnel of bracelets engulfed her arm.

"You know what's next?" Brent's parents kept saying. I knew they were alluding to Victoria getting pregnant by Ranjit. "I've prayed against that," I told them confidently.

I wasn't sure if it was official, but if Ranjit was trying to use it for a marriage visa, then I'm sure it needed to be. By this time, I had become severely anemic, and I discovered she had gotten married on the day I received my first iron infusion, and the next day I went into the ER due to hemorrhaging. I didn't find out about the marriage until November when Victoria returned to the U.S. six months later. But my body knew. It had responded by bleeding with sorrow.

Ranjit and Victoria had admitted they were wrong, by the way she left our home, but instead of making it right, they continued to move forward by getting married in the *exact same way*: without our knowledge. Our precious jewel, meant to be *given* in marriage to the very best, had instead been ripped from our lives. They dishonored us then, and they were dishonoring us now, but according to Sebastion, Victoria returned from a much-deserved vacation, that was so rudely interrupted a year ago.

CHAPTER 36

UNDERMINED

Brent and I were grieving, but we were doing it differently. Now I understand why some marriages end in divorce when parents lose a child. Before, I couldn't understand how people could split up when they needed each other most. Brent wanted to forget about it and move on with life. I wanted to grieve and do something about it. Mom wanted to analyze everything and talk about it every day, and I couldn't handle that. We were like a gradient with Brent on one end and my mom on the other, and I needed to be somewhere in between. We couldn't understand each other's pain process. It came in waves and it was ripping us apart. I felt like I was losing them as we grappled with the trauma in different ways.

It was called "complicated," or "ambiguous" grief. As if grief alone wasn't enough, ours was complicated. It had now been four years and we had not received a single word or even a text from Victoria. She was alive, but it felt like she was dead. And it was her choice not to be here. She had rejected us. Even when you've dealt with grief as healthfully as you know how, holding onto your faith, once a tidal wave has hit you, it's almost impossible to not have some detrimental effects. It's the nature of suffering. Even when you feel emotionally stable, there are always things running in the background, in the subconscious. Your body knows something's off. *My world is not right.* Somebody's missing... at every birthday, every holiday, every vacation, in every photo.

We hadn't gotten out of this completely unscathed. Back in January 2019, a few months after we arrived from India, my cycle had gotten thrown off and disappeared for four months. Following that, I bled for forty days straight and became severely anemic, qualifying for blood transfusions. I wasn't only losing blood; I wasn't making enough red blood cells. The same month, my mother-in-law, Jeannie, was diagnosed with congestive heart failure and her kidneys were functioning at 40 percent. She and I couldn't visit with or help each other because we were both struggling. Because of my low blood count, I had lost my appetite; nothing satisfied me anymore. I couldn't think, I had no drive and was numb. This continued for four years.

Brent was suffering from low blood pressure, his chest hurt, and he had several heat strokes along with dehydration and digestive problems. After working for many years in the heat, it was as if his body couldn't cool itself anymore. Because of the grief and health issues, our sex life was gone, and I knew we could grow apart.

We were too young for all this. We were supposed to be in our prime, having weddings, and grandbabies, growing our family with big family vacations. Instead, we were having a mid-life crisis, menopause, and empty-nest syndrome in the worst way, along with these health issues. I believed our boys were holding back on dating because they didn't want to get married and start families with ours being broken. Seeing others' lives move forward, enjoying these things, saddened me, but God gave me the strength to not envy. I decided to be happy for others and enjoy those things through them, that I wasn't currently receiving in my own life.

Now I understood what it meant when God said mothers would have pain in childbirth. I always thought with modern medicine and pain medication, we had escaped that sentencing. Now I realized it wasn't just about the act of giving birth that caused mothers pain. Every month we were reminded as we dealt with our cycle, and even more so as our children leave home, and we must come to terms with "changing jobs or retiring" from something we've done for so long. It's not an easy task. Then having to watch them go through their own pain in this life, there is no epidural for that.

I wished I could say I had perfect faith through it all, but I didn't. Our role as parents, as well as our health and our family, had all been undermined. I found it hard to pray for Victoria as much as I wanted to. I felt happier when I didn't think about it. But I learned to think about her long enough to pray for her. It was easier if I looked at the situation as if it was someone else's, not mine. It was the only way I could talk about it and I prayed as if I were praying for someone else.

I learned about long-suffering, it's patience that lasts not just moments, but decades. I learned about forgiveness, it doesn't happen just once, it happens over and over; it's a resolve to *continue in forgiveness*. I had to forgive them. Because if it would be hard for them to forgive themselves, they didn't need me standing in the way.

I learned what a sinful human being I am, still in need of God's grace. My carnal nature showed itself several times in ways I never dreamt possible. I never knew those things could exist inside of me. One day I realized, *This is what murders are made of. This is how they happen.* So, I learned to pray for my enemies. I got better and better at it. Our brothers needed to be happy I had a religion, the one they had rejected. I didn't necessarily want them to hurt, I just wanted them to know how they had hurt me, and you can't know what that feels like without experiencing it.

God is bigger than my humanness and He kept picking me up out of that pit I kept falling into time and time again. He gave me a desire to show love to my enemies through my actions. He helped me do for them, what

I wished they had done for me, instead of what they *did do* to me. It was He in me, showing them His love. I could never love like that.

I could have ended up dead, in prison, lost my marriage, or lost our business. But God was there through it all. There were times of refreshing along the way. He hid me in the cleft of the rock when I wanted to run away and hide and reminded me there was nowhere to hide but in Him. He told me to come stand beside Him on the mountaintop so I could get a good view. I needed to see things the way He saw them. When I was down in the middle of my problems, they looked big. But from the mountaintop, they looked small and had their proper place. So, I spent a lot of time telling Him everything, even if the dishes didn't get done.

There were many things that helped me heal, both practical and spiritual. I read books by people with stories similar to mine. I needed to know that other people had gone through something like me and came out on the other side. I needed to know I was not alone. I read instructional books on the subject of estrangement and joined online groups. I received counseling to help process my emotions.

I wanted an RV so we could get away and have a change of scenery, which the counselor said was a good sign. So, we bought one. We got really good at vacations and tried new things. I had the privilege of traveling to several places I had always dreamt of visiting. It helped more than I would've thought.

A friend gave me a cloth from Karen Wheaton, who had her own prodigal, with God's promises on it.

> *"Your children will come back to you from the distant land of the enemy."*

> *"You will surely recover everything that was taken from you."*

"Soon your descendants will return, and all who are trying to destroy you will go away. Your children will come back to you and be like jewels or bridal ornaments for you to display."

I thought of all the miracles God had worked already: Victoria had left the letter, otherwise, we wouldn't have a clue where to begin. Then she chose to go with the people we sent from our church that night in the Amritsar airport, and not go with Ranjit and Tanvi. She prayed asking God for a sign in our hotel room and cuddled in bed with me that first night. She sat next to me at lunch with Ranjit's family and held her brother's hand at the temple, and ultimately, God took her out of India. He saved her not once, but twice when she went the second time to get married. All eyes were on her because of the investigation and publicity, and Ranjit would surely be careful not to do anything to her now. I had so much to be thankful for.

I learned I could pray for all people in the world collectively and read about Lindsey Doss having a dream about all young people of the world being released from prison, especially prodigals. So I had water fasted and prayed for ten days each month of November and December 2019 and January 2020, not only for my daughter, but for all the prodigals in the world, and all people. I learned that when Martin Luther had fasted and prayed hours a day, the Protestant Reformation happened.

What are You going to do on the world stage, from my fasting and praying? I thought.

Then Covid happened. Several people whose children had been severely estranged from them for years were reunited, including my mom and brother. One of them said it was because of Covid that brought him and several of his friends back into a relationship with their mothers. I knew if God had done it for them, He would do it for me, so I continued to wait for the day my daughter and I would be reunited.

CHAPTER 37

HAND GOD THE PEN

As I lie in bed one night, trying to sleep, I began to think of all the parallels our story had with the Gospel story from the very beginning, when angels left their home in Heaven.

I began to realize, *God knows what it's like to have a broken home.*

Angels left a perfect homethe

They believed lies that God wanted to control them with His rules, and that He didn't really have their best interest at heart.

God could not explain it to them. He had to show them.

So He left everything behind. He left home, his throne, and sacrificed it all, to save us, His children.

And we didn't want to be saved.

Instead, we turned our back on Him.

He sent us messages, love letters, through his Word, but we don't read them, and if we do, we don't believe them, but believe lies instead.

God allowed the enemy to continue in his quest to hurt humanity, for ages. The adversary especially hated mothers, where humanity is birthed, but that humanity would be the jury to judge the foe at the end of the age.

God understands everything we're going through, I thought. *Because He has been through it.*

He was rejected, mocked, crushed, and killed. All the sins of the world were placed upon Him, so He experienced every sin there is, and yet He was *willing.*

He consented to the trial...and the pain.

So that we could be with Him forever.

In October 2022, several years after our daughter left home, I decided to write a book about everything that happened. She still had not contacted us. Not a single word. As I sat down to write, I realized I didn't have a good ending. I ruminated over it for weeks, and one morning while I was on my elliptical thinking about it, I turned on the radio, and heard the announcer say,

"Hand God the pen, and He will write an ending you didn't see coming."

I got busy writing.

Over a year later, in March 2024, I was almost finished. I had stopped months ago to help Sebastion when he broke both his legs jumping out of a tractor, and Mom and I nursed him back to health. Now I was getting ready to go to my special place where there were no distractions, so I could write the conclusion. I was still hoping for a better one, but I had an ending in mind, in case I needed it. I would simply end with the commitment that I would never stop praying for Victoria.

That morning, before I left, the boys came over. They had something they wanted to tell us, as we sat in the living room. They had both grieved in their own ways. Luke had lost his best friend, and Preston, never having been close to Victoria, had mostly grieved from watching us hurt. He loved his family and he hated seeing it crumble.

"Victoria called," Luke spoke first.

It was the first time he heard her voice in over five years.

"She was excited and sounded really good."

She had shared something with him and wanted to share it with Preston, too.

"She invited Preston and me to a gender reveal party."

She was having a baby.

"And there's more," said Preston.

"The invitation states it's for 'Victoria and Finn."

"Finn?" I cried, smiling through tears. "That doesn't sound like Ranjit."

From the very beginning, I always knew she would contact her brothers first. Now I had high hopes we were on our way to becoming reunited.

The party was in two weeks. After living with Sebastion for two years, Victoria had since moved and had been living close to Grant for the last three years… thirteen hours closer to us.

That day, we also found out Brent's mom was getting worse. She had been declining for the last five years with heart and kidney failure, but now also had multiple myeloma. She had had several heart attacks and strokes while the chemotherapy made things worse, causing severe dehydration. Grant had moved his parents in with him. With no notice, he had come and taken everything out of their home of 36 years in one week and sold it the next week. Brent's whole family was now gone, and his childhood home with it.

His mother was now going on hospice with her heart working at ten percent. The doctor said it would be sooner rather than later.

She was dying and I knew what was killing her.

Her family was her pride and joy, and it had been destroyed.

Brent's dad called, asking when he was coming to see his mother. Grant and Kelli had sent Brent and me "no-trespassing" letters when Victoria moved in with them in 2020, forbidding us to come on their property, so Brent needed to be convinced it was okay to see his mother. Grant now informed us that the boys and Brent could come to their home anytime, but I was never allowed on their property. We had been told the same thing the year before. I always told Brent I would never keep him or the kids from his family and told them to go without me. I said I would travel with them, but would stay in the hotel just like last time.

I spent the week prior to us leaving, writing and wondering about the party Grant and Kelli would be hosting in their home for Victoria. I knew I couldn't be there, but I hoped by the time the baby was due, I could be there for the delivery.

My refrigerator still had the sign Mom had put there while we were in India. It read:

"I will not cause pain without allowing something new to be born."

Due to Brent's mother's condition, they canceled the party and decided to find out the baby's gender so they could tell Jeannie before she passed. They popped a balloon and pink confetti came out, flowing over "great grandma." Victoria shared a video of it with Luke. It was as if I had gotten to be a part of it after all.

The baby girl was due in August, five months away. Victoria told the boys that even though the party had been canceled, she wanted them to come hang out with her that weekend, which was also her 27th birthday.

That week I decided I would get the crib out of the shed, the one I had used for all my children. I cleaned it up, put it together, bought a new mattress, and placed it in Victoria's bedroom, the one she had left on that fate-filled day. The room looked just the same as it did then. I hadn't changed a thing. There was a niche in the wall, and it was the perfect spot for the crib, with the beautiful crystal chandelier hanging above it.

I draped lace curtains over the crib and pulled them back on each side with white bows, placing pastel turquoise and white pillows with bows on them in the crib, and added a white dust ruffle. I stood back to take a look. It was a crib for a princess. *I'm going to be a grandmother.* I couldn't believe it, and I was excited for her. I wasn't sure if Victoria's baby would ever be placed in that crib, but it would be ready for any grandchildren that may come.

As Brent visited his mom, we spent the weekend together in the city so I could be there for him during this time, while the boys were seeing Victoria. Since I could not visit my mother-in-law, I sent a bouquet of lavender-colored lilies to Grant's house for her. I had been in the family for over thirty years, and she had been my mother, too.

I've always loved you like a mother. Your family was always my family, my card read. I also sent blue hydrangeas for Grant, as he had just had a birthday. I wanted to show him I still cared, even after all they were doing. I ordered a large dinner for the family and sent that as well.

I purchased two other vases of flowers, yellow roses for Victoria's birthday, and pink dinner-plate-sized lilies to congratulate her on her baby, telling her how excited I was. I made a *Facebook* post for her birthday, as I did every year, adding photos of her with us and all the good times we had.

Her real family is here. They gave her a birthday party and you weren't invited. You should pray harder to be a better mother to the daughter you threw away, Finn had commented under the post.

I had hopes that Finn would be different, that he may help in some way, by wanting to know Victoria's family and wanting his baby to know its family. Now all those hopes had been decimated. Yet, I understood that Finn only knew what he'd been told about me, and I began to pray for him and Victoria every day.

Finn told Preston and Luke this reunion shouldn't have taken five years; and that they weren't there for her. Yet, Luke had crossed oceans going to the other side of the world for her.

"You really don't know what you're talking about," Luke told Finn. "And since you already have a kid with another woman, I don't know what your relationship to my sister is, or how long it will last." Victoria and Finn were living together and he was the father of a little boy.

We found that Ranjit had made it to the U.S., but as soon as he arrived, he went straight to Chicago. He and Victoria were still married, and she didn't have money for a divorce. Under the circumstances, it should be annulled, as it was now evident he was committing marriage fraud, and Victoria had moved on with her life.

Mom and I had visited Sebastion's house in October 2020 when he and Sophie were expecting a baby and they needed to get Victoria out of their house. She had not been paying rent and they needed her bedroom for their baby. Sebastion was having a hard time getting her to leave and asked us to come help or he was going to put her on the street. So, Mom and I went there hoping to help her find an apartment.

When we arrived, Mom and I stayed in a hotel for three weeks deciding how to approach Victoria. It had been two years since I had seen her when she left us that day in the airport as we brought her home from India. While we were in the hotel, a lady called telling me Victoria had applied to rent a room from her and Victoria had put me down as a reference. I was stunned but gave Victoria a good recommendation.

One night, while having dinner out with Sebastion and Sophie, we learned some new things. Sebastion made an admission, "I told Victoria, 'I went against my family for you. I went against my mom and your mom.'" It wasn't an apology, but it was close enough, and Sophie said they felt bad.

Sophie told us Grant called Victoria "ungrateful," and Victoria said Grant was treating her like a two-year-old, telling her what to do, and also said Grant and Ranjit didn't like each other.

"Grant was upset that Victoria went back to India without telling him," Sophie said.

Without telling him? This infuriated me. *So, it was okay for him to be upset she went to India without telling him, but not us? Who was the parent?*

"Victoria doesn't speak to us," Sophie said. "I told her, 'You live ten feet from us, and we have no idea what's going on with you.'" (They were learning what it was like.)

Finally, one day while visiting Sebastion's house, we ended up spending the night upstairs in the guest bedroom because of a blizzard. Sophie told Victoria we were there and Victoria had seen Mom sitting on the couch. The next morning, Victoria was supposed to be at work at 6:00 a.m. and Mom and I stayed in the guest bedroom until 10:00 a.m. waiting for her to leave. She never did.

We were starting to wonder if she was okay, so I knocked on her door, but she wouldn't answer, so I told her I was coming in. As I cracked the door open, I could see her in the corner on the floor, talking on the phone with someone. As I opened the door further, she saw me and leaped over a mattress lying on the floor. Shutting the door on me, she said, "Shut the f*ing door."

After two years of silence, those were her first words to me. Instead of getting better, things had only gotten worse. My daughter didn't speak to me that way. I didn't know her anymore.

Mom and I stood on the other side of her bedroom door.

"I can see your feet and if I had a gun right now this would all be over," she said through the door.

We asked her if she meant she would hurt herself, and she said, "No."

"Is that what Ranjit wants you to do? To kill your parents?" Mom asked.

She didn't respond.

She began to complain about Mom's post that said she had autism and how much it had hurt her.

"I'm sorry. I wasn't thinking about hurting you, I was thinking about saving your life," Mom said.

"Everything I struggle with is because of how you and Mom treat me," she told her grandmother. "Once, when you stayed the night with us, you were sleeping on the couch and I offered you my bed and you laughed and snapped at me. Then you and Mom both laughed about it……"

"I didn't want to take your bed from you, honey…."

"That's abuse!" she shouted.

She was upset that we had taken her from India without her electronics, clothes, or documents.

"Why didn't they send those things to you?" we asked.

"I told them not to. Y'all are so uneducated. If you send a laptop from India, it will break." She didn't say why they hadn't sent the other items.

"That was a very special ticket his dad paid for. I don't know how he found it because that doesn't happen," she said.

"You almost had him killed when you had him arrested. The only reason they didn't kill him is because *the girl*, that's me, told them he didn't do anything to me."

Mom and I looked at each other as if to say, "Is she talking about herself in third-person?" She was distancing herself from her actions.

"You came to India uninvited," she continued.

Then a knock came from downstairs. Leaving Mom standing there, I skipped down the steps. Looking out the kitchen window, I saw two police officers standing on the side of the house. I ran to the front door and opened it to see two more police officers.

"Someone named Evelyn called," they said. "Is everything okay?"

"Evelyn? From Alabama? Twenty hours away?" I asked. Victoria had been on the phone with Ranjit when we arrived, not Evelyn. Apparently, Evelyn was doing his bidding for him in America. All the way from India, he was able to have the cops come try to keep me from talking to my daughter in my brother's house. As the police went upstairs to Victoria's room, I immediately called Evelyn and left a message.

"Evelyn, what is Victoria's last name? Is it Da Cruz or is it Harris? Because I think it's Harris. If you don't stay out of our family, you're going to be dealing with me for quite a while."

The police returned downstairs. "She's not suicidal, but a little depressed. You have a right to be here, but just give her some space," they told us and left.

After the cops were gone, Victoria threw her 64-year-old grandma on the floor, got on top of her, and pulled her elbow back ready to punch her. I began to cry, telling her to stop. Victoria got off her grandma, and before she left the house, we heard her on the phone asking someone if they thought her car was reliable enough to drive. Sophie told us the car was cheap, had a lot of problems, and the purchase of it was sketchy, without a bill of sale. When Sophie arrived home, she wanted Mom to press charges against Victoria. With her being pregnant, she didn't want Victoria coming back into the house and hurting her or the baby.

Reluctantly, Mom filed a report pressing charges because the police told us it would force Victoria to do therapy with us. That's all we wanted out of the charges. "The therapist Sebastion had Victoria go to said she was like a feral cat," we explained to them. She ended up only detained for a night and the next day she was on her way across the country in an unreliable car, a young woman, alone.

She had gone across the world in an airplane and now she was driving across the country. We were sure where she was headed… to Grant's house. Brent said from the beginning he wished she would go there, saying Grant needed a taste of it. "Tell Sebastion I'll pay for her plane ticket there!" he had said.

Luke had seen her location on *Snapchat*, two states away, in the middle of the country, just like he had seen it showing her in India when she married Ranjit, and it had puzzled us, as we didn't think she could go back. Mom and I got on the road as quickly as we could. I just hoped we didn't find her stranded somewhere, or worse.

We caught up with her when she stopped for the night, but didn't allow her to see us, as we didn't want to alarm her. Once we were back on the interstate and made it to the place we needed to turn to go home, we headed south as she continued east, praying she would make it the rest of the way safely. Luke confirmed that she had arrived at Grant's address around midnight, two days after she had left, and we could finally rest.

All we had wanted was to help her move out of Sebastion's house, and I guess we had.

Sebastion and Sophie wanted nothing to do with Victoria anymore, or "your stupid husband," Sebastion had told her, referring to Ranjit, when Victoria arrived a few weeks later with Kelli to get her possessions. They had used Victoria to hurt us, and now they had used *us* to get her out of their house. As Kelli and Victoria arrived, Sophie demanded she pay her rent first before taking any of her possessions.

"Grandma paid my rent for me," she told Sophie. Sophie's mother, who was visiting, looked over Sophie's shoulder and asked Victoria, "Was that *before* or *after* you threw her on the ground?"

Victoria had moved from the town of Royal Hills out west with Sebastion to the subdivision, also called Royal Hills, in the East with Grant. I found it fascinating. It was as if God was saying, "No matter how far she goes, I've got her exactly where I want her!"

As soon as we arrived home from Sebastion's, I wrote a letter to Grant and Kelli, telling them how grateful I was that she had chosen to live with them because it was with family and I knew she was safe. They responded by sending the no-trespassing letters.

The next two days after that were dark. I drove to the grocery store and sat in the parking lot, staring at the woods next to it. I could go inside and get a couple of things, and come back, drive over to those woods, lie down in the midst of them, go to sleep, and never wake up. It sounded so good. I just wanted to rest.

I put the key in the ignition, turned it over.........and drove home.

Every day after that, I considered just being above ground an accomplishment.

All the pressure was off.

I didn't have to do anything. Just be.

I had two amazing sons and a wonderful husband who were such a blessing to me. Joy came the next morning when Victoria texted Luke for the first time. Even though she only wanted help from him with her case with "G-Maw" (as she called her grandmother), her contacting Luke covered all the pain of those dark days. I could see light coming.

Kelli had told Preston, "Your parents ruined that poor kid's life," (speaking of Ranjit). He'll never be able to do anything. Once your reputation is ruined in India, you can't get it back. Do you really think what your mom did is okay? She just won't leave Victoria alone."

I took that to mean Ranjit would surely never get into this country. *We ruined his reputation? He* ruined his reputation when he sent our daughter a one-way ticket to come to his country. I used to send flowers and gifts on Victoria's birthday when she lived at Sebastion's, but since she moved East, I *had* left her alone. I knew she had lived with Grant for seven months, and I had known the day she moved into her apartment, fifteen minutes from his house, but she had not made it known, and I didn't want to disrupt her life, so I gave her, her privacy. Knowing where she lived made me feel like I was still part of her life, in some small way. It made me feel close to her and it gave me comfort to know she was still safe.

So there we were in 2024 visiting Brent's mom. It had been five-and-a-half years without a single word from Victoria, and she still didn't want to see her dad or me, and was upset that we were even in the same town. Our brothers had done a great job "guiding our daughter into adulthood." Under Sebastion's tutelage, she had married Ranjit, a man on the other side of the world who she couldn't have a real relationship with, and now under Grant's mentorship, she was pregnant with another man's baby.

There was a question looming in my mind, *What if I never get to see my grandchild? Would I survive this? And if I did, would I still have my faith? Or would I disown my God?*

Now the stakes were even higher and the pain would be double. I had a daughter I hadn't known for over five years, now I might also have a granddaughter I would not know. What if Grant and Kelli became the grandparents in our place?

I was going to have to face whatever God allowed to happen to me, and then I was going to have to face my relationship with Him.

Would I shout to God, '*You can't do this to me!*'?

'*I've suffered enough!*

'*I've been patient.*

'*I've waited.*

'*I've prayed for my enemies.*

'*But if you allow this,*

'*If you allow my first grandchild to be taken from me,*

'*If you let me be in this much pain,*

'*If you do this,*

'*YOU'RE NOT MY FATHER!*'

Would I say these words to Him?

I felt I was being crushed under the weight of a cold, concrete block, and I couldn't breathe as my heavenly Father stood over me, watching. Was He doing this?

A thought came, *He is close to the brokenhearted and saves those who are crushed in spirit.*

If God allowed this to happen to me, I would be double-brokenhearted. What a closeness, what an intimacy I would feel with Him, just as I had during this whole time, but now the closeness would be even greater, as the pain was greater.

How *even more* intimate it would be ......if I was *willing!* Willing to take on the pain. As Christ had been when He drank from the cup God had given Him and bore the cross laid upon Him, saying, "Not My will, but Yours be done."

Those words, *"You're not my Father!"* resonated with me over and over as I sat in the camper in the woods of the special place, the little town, where I was writing the ending to the story.

The words were familiar.

Where had I heard them?

Then it came to me. They sounded like the words my daughter had spoken to me when we were taking her out of India. I got up and looked through "The India Files" where I kept all the documentation. I found her text to me on that fate-filled night in India, as God had intervened, and we were sitting in the Minister of State's office waiting for them to bring her to us. Yes! Those had been her words to me.

> *If you do this, I'm not your daughter!*

It was painful for her. She thought I was hurting her, but I wasn't trying to hurt her, I was trying to save her! The things we see as God hurting us, are there to save us.

How does pain save? In the same way, when you touch a hot stove, you pull your hand away so that you don't burn your fingers to the bone.

If I had left India without her, I was afraid I would never see her again. She might die, or something terrible might happen to her, and I would have to live with that. This pain she was suffering from us pulling her out of India was to keep something worse from happening to her.

I felt God was causing me great pain, yet He says, "Those who seek the Lord shall lack no good thing."

I reasoned *That would have to mean if having my daughter and granddaughter were good for me, I would have them. I didn't have my daughter right now because it wasn't good for me, and if I didn't have my granddaughter, it would be because it wasn't good for me either. There was still work for God to do in me, and in my daughter, and I was going to have to keep trusting Him.*

God wasn't doing this.

An enemy had done this.

But God was watching,

He was there.

He saw it all,

and He was hurting, too.

He allows people to make choices, and as Pastor Leite said, "Love is to suffer for the decisions of others." Allowing someone to make their choice is the only way to truly love them. One day, those choices will have to be accounted for and things set right with those we've hurt… but today wasn't that day.

This pain, if I had to bear it, would be saving me from more pain. I thought if we had brought her home, we would have been healing, and that may have been the case, however there was another possibility. If God had protected us the night she left, maybe He was still protecting us by our family taking her from us at the airport. If she was under a powerful influence like I believed she was, I could only imagine what she could have done, after being with Ranjit for a whole week and then being upset with us after we took her from India. We might not have fully understood what we were dealing with. This realization made me more grateful for God's love and protection and helped me trust Him more.

So whatever pain was in my life, it was there for my good. I had to see it for that if I was going to survive. My hope was that Victoria would want us to be a part of this baby's life. That she would want it to know her family. She had contacted her brothers; they had heard her voice, and she had visited with them. I could see her making her way on the horizon, my prodigal returning.

And if we didn't reunite, and I had many more years to go down this road, not seeing or even knowing my grandchild, I had decided I would still trust God.

Though He slay me, yet will I trust Him. (Job 13:15)

God and I would be okay.

I was going to survive…

and I would never stop praying for her.

APPENDIX

CHARACTER KEY

Destiny Harris - Main character
Brent Harris - Husband
Preston – Oldest son
Victoria – Daughter, (Tor Tor) and (Tor)
Luke – Younger son
William – Father
Priscilla Reinhardt– Mother
Isabel- William's wife
Sebastion Reinhardt (Seb) – half-brother
Sophie – Seb's wife
Charles – Brent's Father
Jeannie – Brent's Mother
Derrick – Brent's younger brother
Tabby – Derrick's wife
Grant – Brent's youngest brother
Kelli – Grant's wife
Vance- Victoria's ex-boyfriend
Pastor Mark- Destiny's previous pastor
Claudia- Pastor Mark's wife and friend of Evelyn
Evelyn (Silva) da Cruz– Destiny's church friend
Harold – Evelyn's husband
Belinda – Eveyln's stepdaughter
Oliver – Evelyn's best friend
Pastor Leite – Destiny's current pastor
Richard – Church Conference worker in Washington D.C.
Amanda Rodriguez – Human trafficking attorney

Keith Thompson – Brent and Destiny's close friend and spokesperson
Anne Thompson – Keith's wife
Chris and Laura Cotton – Brent and Destiny's church friends
BB – Luke's boss
Fern – Human trafficking agency -*Eye Heart World*
Ranjit Sharma – Victoria's online boyfriend
Tanvi – Ranjit's sister
Pastor Isaiah – Pastor of church in India
Dr. Mustafa Singh–The doctor Victoria stayed with
Sanjay – Dr. Mustafa's son
Felix – Sanjay's friend
Davison – Church youth minister
Esha – Government high official

MEET THE AUTHOR
DESTINY DAWN

Destiny Dawn Harris is a wife and mother to three grown children. She lives in Mobile, Alabama, and graduated from the University of South Alabama with a Bachelor of Science in Business Administration. Alongside her husband, Brent, Destiny owns and runs an automotive detailing business they founded in 1999.

From 8,000 Miles is Destiny's first book, detailing the traumatic events that unfolded in her family's life mid-September 2018. Destiny writes with honesty and vulnerability about all that transpired, with the purpose of bringing strength, healing, and hope to others who are facing difficult circumstances. Destiny's faith in Jesus Christ is the reason she made it through this trauma and she sees everything she writes as a testimony to what she has become and all that God has done for her.

Destiny loves to read and spends time writing, researching, cooking, and baking bread. She also enjoys skiing on both the lakes and slopes with her family. Destiny has a Maltese, Molly, who is always in tow. Her favorite topics to write on are health, spirituality, and business.

Destiny's dream is to one day open a health retreat in the rural area near her home with a focus on serving families who have children with mental health issues. It is her goal to help them have a better quality of life and find respite from the daily adversities that come with mental challenges.

Destiny Dawn is a YouTube channel where Mothers come together to support each other to ease the pain and suffering in the world. It is a space where stories can be shared and wisdom gained because motherhood can be so joyful and, at the same time, break our hearts. Brokenheartedness is a journey and does not have to be a permanent stay. We will get through it together, and you *CAN* come out on the other side… <u>better</u>.

Learn more about Destiny Dawn and follow her YouTube Channel at:

www.DestinyDawnOfficial.com

52202596R00228